ROUTLEDGE LIBRARY EDITIONS: COLD WAR SECURITY STUDIES

Volume 29

NATO ARMS CO-OPERATION

NATO ARMS CO-OPERATION
A Study in Economics and Politics

KEITH HARTLEY

LONDON AND NEW YORK

First published in 1983 by George Allen & Unwin (Publishers) Ltd

This edition first published in 2021
by Routledge
2 Park Square, Milton Park, Abingdon, Oxon OX14 4RN

and by Routledge
605 Third Avenue, New York, NY 10017

Routledge is an imprint of the Taylor & Francis Group, an informa business

© 1983 Keith Hartley

All rights reserved. No part of this book may be reprinted or reproduced or utilised in any form or by any electronic, mechanical, or other means, now known or hereafter invented, including photocopying and recording, or in any information storage or retrieval system, without permission in writing from the publishers.

Trademark notice: Product or corporate names may be trademarks or registered trademarks, and are used only for identification and explanation without intent to infringe.

British Library Cataloguing in Publication Data
A catalogue record for this book is available from the British Library

ISBN: 978-0-367-56630-2 (Set)
ISBN: 978-1-00-312438-2 (Set) (ebk)
ISBN: 978-0-367-61015-9 (Volume 29) (hbk)
ISBN: 978-1-00-310288-5 (Volume 29) (ebk)

Publisher's Note
The publisher has gone to great lengths to ensure the quality of this reprint but points out that some imperfections in the original copies may be apparent.

Disclaimer
The publisher has made every effort to trace copyright holders and would welcome correspondence from those they have been unable to trace.

NATO Arms Co-operation: A Study in Economics and Politics

KEITH HARTLEY
Department of Economics, University of York

London
GEORGE ALLEN & UNWIN
Boston   Sydney

© Keith Hartley 1983

This book is copyright under the Berne Convention. No reproduction without permission. All rights reserved.

George Allen & Unwin (Publishers) Ltd,
40 Museum Street, London WC1A 1LU, UK

George Allen & Unwin (Publishers) Ltd,
Park Lane, Hemel Hempstead, Herts HP2 4TE, UK

Allen & Unwin Inc.,
9 Winchester Terrace, Winchester, Mass 01890, USA

George Allen & Unwin Australia Pty Ltd,
8 Napier Street, North Sydney, NSW 2060, Australia

First published in 1983

British Library Cataloguing in Publication Data

Hartley, Keith
  NATO arms co-operation.
1. North Atlantic Treaty Organization
2. Arms and armor
I. Title
623'.09182'2   UA646.3
ISBN 0-04-341022-7

Library of Congress Cataloging in Publication Data

Hartley, Keith.
  NATO arms co-operation.
Bibliography: p.
Includes index.
1. North Atlantic Treaty Organization. 2. Munitions – Standards. 3. Munitions – Cost control.
4. Disarmament – Economic aspects. I. Title.
II. Title: N.A.T.O. arms co-operation.
JX1393.N67H37   1982   355'.031'091821   82-16285
ISBN 0-04-341022-7

Set in 10 on 11 point Times by Rowland Phototypesetting Ltd
Bury St Edmunds, Suffolk
and printed in Great Britain by Billing & Sons Ltd, London & Worcester

Contents

Preface	*page* ix
List of abbreviations	xi

Part I NATO AND STANDARDISATION — 1

1 The Policy Issues: An Overview — 3
Introduction: what is the policy problem? — 3
The methodology of economic policy — 4
Defence choices and NATO — 5
The political market place — 6
The objectives of standardisation policy — 8
Market failure as a cause of 'too little' standardisation — 12
Standardisation, two-way streets and MOUs — 13
The economics of politics and MOUs — 15
Conclusion — 18

2 The Economics and Politics of NATO — 20
Introduction — 20
NATO as a defence club — 20
The economics of military alliances — 22
The political market and NATO — 24
The threat from the Warsaw Pact — 26
Defence burdens — 28
Weapons costs — 30
NATO standardisation: institutions and achievements — 32
Is there a case for competition and free trade? — 37
Conclusion: the need for evidence — 40

3 Standardisation: Theory and Evidence — 41
Introduction — 41
What are the sources of cost savings? — 42
The model: economies of scale and gains from trade — 43
How reliable is the evidence on scale economies? — 48
Evidence on scale economies — 53
What is the evidence on comparative advantage and gains from trade? — 61
Conclusion — 67

4 Standardisation Policy: A Critique — 69
Introduction: some problems — 69
What are the assumptions of the model? — 69
Weapons standardisation and industrial policy — 74
A framework for choice — 77

vi *Nato Arms Co-operation*

Jobs, technology and balance of payments benefits: the case for nationalism?	82
Conclusion	87

Part II AEROSPACE 89

5 *The Research Design* — 91
Introduction: aims of the research — 91
Why study aerospace? — 91
The costs of alternative policies: a simple model and complications — 93
Research methodology — 96
Conclusion — 100

6 *Free Trade versus Nationalism* — 101
Introduction — 101
The economics of aircraft R & D and manufacture — 101
Market structure and performance — 103
The size of firms — 109
The efficiency of the American and European industries — 110
Learning curves, output and costs — 112
Is competition possible? — 115
Fears of a US monopoly: dependence and the price of spares — 116
Competitive prototyping and a 'fly before you buy' policy — 118
The preferences of producers — 120
Conclusion — 122

7 *Licensed Manufacture and Co-production* — 124
Introduction: sharing production work — 124
Definitions and examples — 124
Why do firms co-produce? — 126
The costs of licensed production and co-production — 126
How valuable are the benefits? — 133
Conclusion — 138

8 *Joint Projects* — 140
Introduction: standardisation and collaboration — 140
The case for a European aerospace industry and examples of collaboration — 141
The central hypothesis — 142
Some methodological problems — 143
Alternative assumptions on joint projects — 146
The case for joint European projects — 148
Departures from the ideal case: some inefficiencies — 153
The case against European collaboration — 154

How can the arguments about joint projects be evaluated? 158
Conclusion 161

9 *How Can Joint Projects Be Evaluated?* 163
Introduction: alternative criteria 163
The views of firms on the benefits and costs of joint projects 164
Performance indicators for joint projects 166
The organisation of joint European projects 173
Collaboration and the political market 176
Conclusion 177

10 *Conclusion: Some Policy Guidelines* 178
Guidelines for competition 178
Guidelines for a limited change (improvement) 179
Closing remarks 180

Part III Appendices 181

Appendix A   Survey of European and US Firms: A Summary of Responses to a questionnaire 183
Appendix B   Joint Projects: Summary of Responses to a questionnaire 212
References 219
Index 226

To

Adam, Lucy and Cecilia

Preface

NATO is a continuing source of controversy. Since its formation, Western Europe has experienced an extended period of peace and security. However, critics point to the dangers of the continuing arms race between the USA and the USSR, particularly in nuclear weapons (e.g. the deployment of cruise missiles). Europeans sometimes feel that they are too dependent on the USA, whilst Americans often believe that Europe is a 'free rider', failing to bear its fair share of the Alliance defence burden. In addition, the success of NATO in contributing to continued peace in Europe has created pressures for reduced defence spending. Rival political parties compete for votes by offering different packages of civil and military goods. In these circumstances, questions arise about the efficiency of NATO as a military organisation. Is it fully exploiting all the potential gains from collective action? Are there opportunities for improving the efficiency of military spending within the Alliance? If so, collective security could be maintained from reduced defence budgets, or security could be increased without extra military spending.

This book examines weapons standardisation as one aspect of NATO's efficiency. Put simply, it has been argued that massive cost savings are available if only members of the Alliance would use the same weapons. This book examines the economic arguments for weapons standardisation, the limitations of the analysis and the available evidence. What is standardisation; why hasn't it occurred; and how large are the likely benefits? In other words, the emphasis is on what we do and do not know in this area. A political economy or public choice approach is used, with its emphasis on policy developments in the political market place of voters, political parties, bureaucracies and interest groups. These agents are central to understanding the current state of weapons procurement policy within the Alliance. The book is divided into two parts. Part I considers the general issues and problems associated with weapons standardisation in NATO. Many of these issues are outlined in Chapter 1, with subsequent chapters considering particular aspects in more detail. Chapter 2 examines NATO as a defence club and the likely benefits from collective action. The sources of cost savings from weapons standardisation and the possible magnitude of the savings are outlined in Chapter 3. Some of the assumptions of the model are critically assessed in Chapter 4, which also presents a choice framework for weapons procurement. The general lack of evidence in this field resulted in a detailed study of aerospace, which tested hypotheses on the effects of alternative procurement policies. The results are reported in Part II. The aims of the research study are described in Chapter 5. The case for competition and free trade is examined in Chapter 6: is competition possible and will it mean a US monopoly? Alternative policies are available such as co-production and joint projects. What are the costs of co-production compared with buying directly 'off the shelf'? Do joint European projects result in cost savings or are they inefficient? These questions and others are answered in Chapters 7–9. Finally, Chapter 10 presents some policy proposals.

The book is designed for students and for general readers interested in defence policy. It should be of interest to second and third year undergraduates, as well as graduates, studying micro-economics – including industry and labour specialists. It can also be used for policy study courses and it provides case study material suitable for industrialists, civil servants and military staffs in all NATO countries. Throughout, the emphasis is on NATO as a whole, with research results embracing America and Europe.

The book was a direct result of a NATO Research Fellowship which provided funds for a study tour of European and US firms and defence agencies. The author is indebted to the many individuals who gave their time willingly and generously. Dr F. Welter, NATO, was an enthusiastic sponsor and supporter; Ollie Heath and Ron Howard were sources of different ideas; Jack Wiseman kindly provided research facilities at the Institute of Social and Economic Research; the Ford Foundation financed a study term and the Social Science Research Council provided funds for continuing research into UK defence policy. Others who have helped, sometimes unknowingly, include Alan Peacock, David Greenwood and Tony Harvey as well as officials in the UK Ministry of Defence. The usual disclaimers apply. Barbara Jacques had the unenviable task of typing, whilst Winifred, Adam, Lucy and Cecilia had to bear the costs of my obsession with those magnificent flying machines and the men who build them!

KEITH HARTLEY
April 1982

List of abbreviations

AWACS	airborne warning and control system
CNAD	Conference of National Armaments Directors
CPRS	Central Policy Review Staff
EEC	European Economic Community
EFTA	European Free Trade Association
GNP	Gross national product
IEPG	Independent European Programme Group
LAC	Long-run average cost
MBFR	mutual balanced force reductions
MES	minimum efficient scale
MOU	memorandum of understanding
MRCA	multi-role combat aircraft
NAMMA	NATO MRCA Management Agency
NAMMO	NATO MRCA Management Organisation
NAMSO	NATO Maintenance and Supply Organisation
NATO	North Atlantic Treaty Organisation
NIAG	NATO Industrial Advisory Group
NIESR	National Institute of Economic and Social Research
OECD	Organisation for Economic Co-operation and Development
R & D	research and development
SALT	Strategic Arms Limitation Treaty
UK	United Kingdom
USA	United States of America
USACADA	United States Arms Control and Disarmament Agency
USSR	Union of Soviet Socialist Republics
VTOL	vertical take-off and landing

Part I
NATO and Standardisation

1
The Policy Issues: An Overview

Introduction: what is the policy problem?

Traditionally, a rise in military spending by the Warsaw Pact has led to demands for similar increases by NATO. A typical response was NATO's 1977 agreement that all member countries would aim to raise real defence expenditure by some 3 per cent per year in an effort to improve the Alliance's defence capabilities. Such a response ignores the efficiency of defence expenditure. How can voters assess the alleged threat from the Warsaw Pact, whether NATO's defences 'need strengthening', whether increased expenditure (on weapons or manpower of which types?) is the only or the most appropriate solution and whether the military sector is giving 'value for money'? Clearly, defence is not a costless activity and it involves considerable sacrifices of public and private sector civil goods and services. Examples include hospitals, roads, schools and care for the elderly, as well as private expenditure on cars, foreign holidays and video recorders. Societies have to ask whether such sacrifices are worthwhile. The answer will depend upon each community's valuation of different goods, including protection and its 'end' product expressed in the valuation of human lives (Jones-Lee, 1976). Not surprisingly, the absence of major wars has led to a greater preference for civil goods and social welfare spending, so that members of the Alliance have been under pressure to *reduce* defence outlays. Moreover, military expenditure has been constrained by economic performance. During the 1970s, NATO nations have had to adjust to rising rates of inflation and unemployment, as well as the major shocks associated with the rise in oil prices. At the same time, weapons are becoming increasingly expensive, which creates further pressures on military budgets and provides nations with an incentive to search for lower-cost methods of obtaining equipment. In the circumstances, and in response to the Warsaw Pact's expenditures, NATO periodically places a new emphasis on methods of improving the efficiency of defence spending: hence the continuing and recurrent concern with standardisation.

Advocates of standardisation start from the proposition that NATO

4   *Nato Arms Co-operation*

is an inefficient organisation for the procurement of weapons and manpower and for the provision of defence services. Critics claim that there is 'too much' duplication of effort within NATO, resulting in an estimated 'waste' of over $10 billion per year (Callaghan, 1975, p. 37). It seems that there are 'too many' different types and models of the same weapons, with adverse effects on the efficiency of the armed forces and of the weapons industries within NATO. 'Too little' standardisation and inter-operability results in a 'wasteful duplication' of research and development (R & D) and production effort. Nor is inefficiency confined to the arrangements for the purchase and supply of *weapons*. Most members of NATO maintain a full and duplicate range of land, sea and air forces, with associated logistic support. There are duplicate organisations for administering defence and the armed forces, as well as for storing and distributing spares and undertaking training. Typically, support costs are some 100–200 per cent of the initial acquisition price of equipment. Moreover, estimates suggest that with standardisation, military effectiveness could be enhanced by 30–50 per cent for most units. In the case of combat aircraft, the ability to divert to other nation's airfields where they could be re-fuelled and re-armed would increase the operability of NATO tactical air units by 200 to 300 per cent (Callaghan, 1975, p. 35). Without standardisation, the belief is that the military effectiveness of NATO's conventional forces is substantially reduced, so increasing the risks of a nuclear conflict. Clearly, these appear to be devastating criticisms of the Alliance: it seems to be an inefficient defence association and questions of efficiency are central to economics. What contribution can economists make to this debate? The rest of the chapter provides an overview of the policy issues and an outline of the general approach which will be used throughout the book.

The methodology of economic policy

When analysing policy issues, economists seek answers to three sets of questions. First, what is the policy problem? In other words, what are the aims or objectives of policy makers? Second, why is there a problem? Such a question concentrates on the causes of the problem confronting governments. Third, what are the solutions to the problem? Each question illustrates the central characteristic of economics as a study of *choice*. NATO, for example, will have various policy objectives, some of which are in conflict, requiring choices to be made between competing aims. Efficiency in weapons production might not be consistent with an 'equitable' distribution of workloads. There might also be competing explanations for the current lack of standardisation, ranging from market failure to an economics of politics model. Similarly, standardisation might be achieved by such policy alternatives as buying an existing weapon 'off the shelf' from an established supplier, or by co-production, or by a group of nations undertaking the joint development and production of a project. In other words, choices cannot be avoided.

Defence choices and NATO

Defence is a classic example of choices. Consider the set of choices which are being made continuously by member states of NATO. They have to decide (choose) (a) how much to spend on defence compared with other things; (b) whether to remain in the Alliance; (c) how to allocate a given defence budget between manpower and weapons, between nuclear and conventional forces, and between land, sea and air forces.

NATO is a voluntary association of independent states and not a supranational organisation. As such, NATO has no dictatorial powers to determine the level and composition of military spending for the group as a whole and for each member state. It cannot determine that member states should specialise in specific forces based on their nation's comparative advantage (i.e. what they do best). It is unable to impose weapons choices which might be desirable from a NATO viewpoint. Nor can it determine the allocation of development and production work on the basis of each member state's comparative advantage in weapons industries. Instead, choices on the level of defence spending, the composition of forces, the purchase of weapons and suppliers are made by each national government. Inevitably, governments differ in their policy aims, each placing different valuations on defence and civil goods and taking different attitudes towards risks and uncertainty. Similarly, within defence each nation will have a different 'willingness to pay' for weapons developed and produced domestically. Indeed, weapons procurement policy tends to embrace objectives other than defence and protection. Consideration is usually given to acquiring advanced technology, maintaining employment and protecting the balance of payments. In the circumstances, national technology, jobs, exports and import saving may be amongst the 'goods' being acquired by weapons procurement policy. Once such wider policy aims are part of the purchased 'product', it becomes correspondingly more difficult to assess the efficiency of procurement choices. After all, choices are inevitably subjective and depend upon the preferences of the purchaser. Here, economists can contribute by attempting to value some of the more intangible elements in choices (e.g. national 'prestige'). They can also seek to identify *who* is maximising *what* for the benefit of *whom*? Answers to such questions cannot ignore the political market place, where information is presented and interpreted and choices are made.

The political market place

Defence policy is formulated and decisions are made in the political market place of voters, politicians, bureaucracies and interest groups of producers and consumers. Their behaviour can have a decisive impact on choices.

Citizens will vote for the political party which they believe will make them 'better off'. But, at an election, individual voters are unable to register a preference for different amounts and types of defence, and there are incentives to 'free ride' under a defence 'umbrella'. Voters also have a limited amount of information on which to make choices, and this is especially characteristic of defence, where considerations of 'national security' restrict public debate. In this situation, vote-conscious governments have discretionary power in interpreting the 'public interest'. Opportunities exist for producers and other interest groups to influence defence policy. Producer groups in the form of weapons firms can use their specialist knowledge to provide persuasive information and lobby for defence contracts. They can show politicians that their activities are in the 'national interest' and make a socially beneficial contribution to domestic jobs, technology, the balance of payments, and ultimately, to votes. Other groups can also attempt to influence defence policy through advocating nuclear disarmament, no cruise missile bases, and withdrawal from NATO.

Policy will be further influenced by bureaucracies in the form of Defence Ministries or Departments, and the Armed Forces. Bureaucrats are likely to prefer larger budgets. They can attempt to raise or protect their budgets by *over-estimating the demand* for defence, *under-estimating the costs* of their preferred weapons projects, and by formulating programmes which are attractive to vote-sensitive governments. For example, they can exaggerate the threat from the Warsaw Pact, and they can point to the apparent, but unsubstantiated, technical 'fall-out' benefits from high technology defence work. Cost escalation provides some evidence of the under-estimation of expenditure. Escalation factors of two or more are typical on weapons projects, which means a final expenditure of twice the original estimate in constant prices. Bureaucrats can also present information to governments in a persuasive form. Projects can be presented as 'vital' to the national interest and 'essential' for the future of a country's advanced technology. And, if a weapons project does not go ahead or is cancelled, it can always be argued that all the previous expenditures will be wasted and valuable research teams will be disbanded and lost

The policy issues: an overview 7

forever! Persuasive though such arguments *appear*, they are usually lacking in economic analysis and empirical support. For example, use of the words 'vital' and 'essential' invites questions of vital to whom, and is it vital and essential regardless of cost? Similarly, social benefits (e.g. jobs, technology) are not costless, and their advocates are obliged to show that the benefits are greater than could be obtained from alternative uses of the resources. Of course, bureaucrats will respond by claiming that defence cannot be subject to 'vulgar notions' of cost–benefit analysis: that certain things cannot be quantified; and that ultimately defence is about the protection and preservation of human lives and 'our civilisation' and that these are 'priceless' assets! However, NATO nations do not allocate the whole of their GNPs to this 'priceless' activity of defence. Politicians also continue to justify their nation's military spending as 'worthwhile'. Such choices show that governments are effectively placing valuations on the apparently intangible activity of defence and deciding that its benefits are at least equal to its costs.

Recognition and understanding of behaviour in the political market place raises the fundamental issue of the methods by which society might constrain the desires of bureaucracies and defence contractors to expand military expenditures. This involves governments using policing and monitoring measures to achieve compliance with their defence policy objectives. Governments can hire, fire or promote staff, they can change bureaucracy organisations to promote competition for budgets, they can bargain about budgets or introduce new information systems, and they can invite foreign firms to bid for weapons contracts. However, the behaviour of bureaucrats and personnel in the Armed Forces and the efficiency with which they provide defence services will ultimately depend upon their *employment contract*. Does the employment contract provide inducements to spend or to save; does it reward personnel for responding to economic incentives and substituting weapons for manpower as labour becomes relatively more expensive? Or, are employment contracts for bureaucrats and military personnel incomplete and costly to police, so allowing individuals and groups at all levels opportunities for satisfying their own preferences, rather than those of voters? The result could be substantial 'organisational slack' or inefficiency within the military sector. Examples could include the desire for a quiet life, the pursuit of 'on the job' leisure and the purchase of high technology weapons which give satisfaction to their immediate users rather than protection for society. In this environment, increasing the level of defence spending is not necessarily the best method of achieving efficiency. These issues are even more complex when the analysis moves from an individual nation-state to NATO as a voluntary, multi-national association

Within NATO, member states have different structures for their

8 Nato Arms Co-operation

political markets. There are differences in constitutions, voting rights, competition between political parties, the use of referenda, and access to information on defence, as well as variations in the size and structure of the military–industrial complex. All these factors are likely to influence policy and choices. NATO acts as a co-ordinating and advisory body for its members. It is an international bureaucratic organisation which is not directly responsive to voters in the members states. As a result, Alliance defence policy is the result of bargaining between Ministers of member states, influenced by NATO and national officials, as well as other interest groups such as weapons contractors and peace movements. On this view, the NATO Council of Ministers might be analysed in terms of small group bargaining behaviour, with individuals acting like trade unions and employers making initially high bids and low offers, respectively. Bargaining is likely over burden-sharing, the levels and composition of military spending in member states, and the possibilities for standardisation. Within the Council, decisions are taken by common consent and not by majority voting. Each member state has one vote so that there are opportunities for 'equitable' solutions, ensuring that small nations share in the benefits of collaborative programmes. Individual Ministers can also make private vote-trading agreements, exchanging their less valued for their more valuable preferences. Such a political environment is unlikely to lead to the formulation of NATO policy measures based on orthodox economic criteria. Consider the implications of this analysis for NATO weapons standardisation policy and the associated controversy between free trade and nationalism. In analysing standardisation, economists are concerned with the aims of policy, the causes of 'too little' standardisation and the possible solutions.

The objectives of standardisation policy

NATO forces operate a diversity of weapons and member states are currently undertaking the duplicate development of new equipment (e.g. combat aircraft, missiles, ships, tanks). Nations such as the USA, the UK, France, West Germany and Italy continue to retain the capacity and the desire for a domestic defence industry, especially in the high technology areas of aerospace and electronics. Each nation's weapons industries are 'protected' from foreign competition: they depend upon preferential purchasing through domestic defence orders, plus any export business. For example, in recent years, the United States, France and the UK–German–Italian consortium have developed and produced eight different types of modern combat aircraft (the F14, F15, F16, F18 in the USA; the Mirage in France; and the Tornado, the Harrier and the Jaguar). The result has been eight separate R & D bills plus relatively short production runs for each project. In the case of the Harrier, the Jaguar and the F14, output has been in the region of 300–500 units of each type, compared with some 2000 units for the F16. Advocates of standardisation claim that there would have been major cost savings if NATO had developed only two combat aircraft rather than eight types. There would have been savings in R & D, lower unit production costs resulting from a greater output of each type, with further reductions in support costs (e.g. spares, maintenance and training). Military effectiveness would also increase if NATO forces used identical weapons and equipment, with a common spares and support system. But any evaluation of NATO weapons standardisation policy has to start with some unambiguous definitions and a clear statement of the policy problem.

Policy initiatives generate a new jargon. During the late 1970s, the NATO objectives of standardisation and inter-operability were to be achieved through rationalisation, collaboration, co-operation, offsets, two-way streets and co-production. Examples included the F16 co-production programme, the work-sharing arrangements on the NATO AWACS and the international collaboration on the development and production of the Tornado aircraft. At its broadest, the policy problem is seen to be the failure of the Allies to agree on common tactics, common training and common weapons, with adverse effects on the military effectiveness of NATO and a waste of resources throughout the Alliance. Thus, NATO in its present form is reputed to be inefficient in its armed forces and in its weapons markets. Equipment is not standardised nor inter-operable, whilst weapons production is 'unco-ordinated' with 'wasteful duplication' in programmes. Standardisation is advocated as the solution and this policy objective embraces 'commonality' in tactics, weapons, training and logistics. Attractive though it might seem, such 'commonality' has major policy implications for each member of the club. To replace 'wasteful duplication' in R & D and production with co-operation, collaboration and international trade based on comparative advantage requires nations with different preferences to agree on which weapons to buy, how and from whom. Weapons procurement policy, or the buying decision, involves a complex choice set. A government has to decide the following:

(a) *What to buy*. A project has to be selected, which means that decisions have to be made on the operational and performance requirements of a new weapon (for aircraft, for example, this means decisions on speed, range, altitude, weapons and landing–take-off capabilities).

(b) *When to buy*. The development of a new weapon embraces R & D and production. In the case of aircraft, there is initial design work, followed by development, the first flight and testing of a prototype, culminating in production and delivery to the Services. Thus, a new aircraft type can be ordered off the drawing board or purchased 'off the shelf' from an established supplier.

(c) *From whom.* A contractor has to be selected and the choice can be based on competition or direct negotiation with a preferred firm. If competition is to be used, further choices are required between the following: (i) the use of price versus non-price competition (e.g. technical proposals); (ii) the stage in a weapon's life cycle when competition ceases and selection occurs (for example, competition might be restricted to paper designs or might continue to the prototype stage with, say, a 'fly before you buy' policy; or there could be competition for the production work); (iii) domestic and foreign firms – this requires a decision on the extent of the market; it involves choosing between such broad policy options as nationalism, buying from abroad, joint projects or some form of licensed or co-production.

(d) *How to buy.* A contract has to be selected. The options range from some form of cost-plus to a fixed price contract, with intermediate cases of target cost and incentive contracts. Generally, cost-based contracts are used for high risk and uncertain R & D work, and fixed price contracts are used where the product can be clearly specified and the risks and uncertainties have been removed (e.g. production work).

Supporters of NATO standardisation policies are often vague on the details of how these weapons procurement choices would be resolved. Nevertheless, it is claimed that there are substantial gains from sacrificing nationalism and independence. One study estimated the Allied 'waste' at considerably in excess of $10 billion* per annum in 1975 prices. This estimate was derived from aggregating annual R & D, procurement and support costs for the USA and European members of NATO. Three 'heroic' assumptions were made. First, that *all* European R & D represented duplication and hence waste ($2.6 billion). Second, that 25 per cent of European procurement expenditure and 10 per cent of US procurement outlays were wasted due to the loss of scale economies through not producing standardised equipment ($2.95 billion). Third, that standardisation would reduce annual support costs by an amount similar to the savings in weapons acquisition costs (Callaghan, 1975, p. 37). Of course, the validity of these estimated savings due to standardisation depends upon the underlying

---

*Note that throughout this volume the word 'billion' is used to mean a thousand million.

The policy issues: an overview 11

model, its assumptions and the reliability of the supporting evidence. Questions arise about the behaviour of firms and industries in competitive and non-competitive situations, whether the assumptions are 'realistic' and the opportunities for further gains from establishing a NATO free trade area in weapons. In particular, is *all* European R & D 'waste', and what is the available evidence on economies of scale in weapons industries?

After the mid-1970s, the policy instruments to achieve the standardisation objective included a US willingness to promote a two-way trans-Atlantic trade in weapons, and proposals for common European defence production to share R & D costs and obtain scale economies not available to an individual nation. America and Britain, for example, entered into a Memorandum of Understanding (1975) designed to reduce the disparity in defence sales between the two countries, and the USA has often indicated a willingness to buy European equipment where this will mean a more efficient use of Allied resources. In addition, the US government and its major defence contractors have increasingly accepted offsets and co-production as a necessary part of any policy of selling American weapons in Europe (e.g. F16s, AWACS). These policy developments in NATO raise a number of fundamental issues requiring critical analysis:

(a) Is NATO an inefficient organisation for the supply of weapons and defence forces?
(b) If NATO is inefficient, what are the sources and causes of such inefficiency, and are standardisation and increased trans-Atlantic trade the only, or the most appropriate, solutions?
(c) Are the policy constraints on standardisation such that it could have major *adverse* efficiency effects, with the USA and other NATO nations buying higher cost and inferior equipment through costlier joint projects and co-production? In other words, are weapons contracts likely to be allocated on equity, rather than efficiency, criteria?
(d) If standardisation is as beneficial as claimed, why has it not occurred? Are there some obvious market failures preventing worthwhile international and mutually advantageous trade and exchange, or are the existing arrangements 'optimal' once it is recognised that all policies and exchange involve costs?

To answer these questions, we need to return to basic principles and ask whether economic theory offers any policy guidelines for NATO: what is the economic logic of two-way streets?

Market failure as a cause of 'too little' standardisation

If societies wish to achieve the 'best' or 'optimum' allocation of resources, then economic theory suggests that properly functioning competitive markets are required. In this way, firms will fully and accurately respond to the demands of individual consumers (consumer sovereignty). Market forces will determine what to produce, how to produce it and who receives the resulting output (Hartley and Tisdell, 1981, Ch. 1). However, theory also shows that, if left to themselves, private markets might 'fail' to work properly, with adverse effects on the welfare of individuals in the community. Market failure can be due to imperfections such as monopolies, restrictive practices and entry barriers, or it can be due to externalities, where private markets might produce 'too much' or 'too little' of a commodity (e.g. pollution, defence). In this context, NATO can be regarded as an international organisation for 'correcting' market failure and improving the operation of markets by obtaining the benefits of collective defence (externalities) and the gains from increased international trade through standardisation and two-way streets.

Barriers to international trade are a major source of failure in NATO weapons markets. Examples include tariffs, quotas, subsidies to domestic firms and preferential government purchasing from home industries, all of which are typical in the weapons business. Such barriers restrict the gains which could otherwise be obtained from specialisation and international trade. Interestingly, in the case of *civil* goods, all NATO nations willingly trade between themselves and with the rest of the world, selling, say, cars and buying wheat, oil and computers. On this basis, each country will export what it does best. Specialisation of production based on each nation's comparative advantage increases the output of all commodities. So, if markets are failing because of barriers to international trade, there are opportunities for state intervention to 'correct' such failures. In this context, two-way streets by reducing trade barriers appear to provide opportunities for worthwhile international exchange in weapons. But appearances can be deceptive. Any analysis of NATO cannot ignore the economics of the political market and the possibility that state solutions can also fail. Furthermore, one of the contradictions in NATO is that nations have joined a defence alliance presumably because of net military benefits; and yet, individual members have maintained a set of domestic policy constraints which adversely affect the economic and the military efficiency of the collective association. It could be that as the defence Alliance is believed to be relatively successful so nations are substituting economic goals for security within a framework which was originally designed as a military association and not a free trade area, nor an organisation for maximising a *nation's (private) economic welfare*. Policy is further complicated by uncertainty amongst Allies *and* rivals. During the development period of a modern weapon, say ten years, governments and their preferences for military goods can change; economies can grow at different rates, whilst technical progress can render obsolescent existing force structures. No one can predict accurately the future: today's threat might be tomorrow's ally! The economist's role is to suggest the most appropriate institutional and policy arrangements for responding to uncertainty.

Standardisation, two-way streets and MOUs

Two-way streets, as reflected in Memoranda of Understanding (MOUs) which aim to reduce trade barriers between nations, can be viewed as methods of improving the operation of the NATO arms market. The 1975 USA–UK Memorandum of Understanding on defence equipment illustrates some of the problems and possibilities of such agreements on two-way trade. This agreement aimed to secure a 'balance' in defence sales between the two countries as well as ' . . . making the most rational use of industrial, economic and technological resources so as to achieve maximum military capability at the lowest possible cost and to achieve greater standardisation and inter-operability of weapon systems' (HC155, 1976, p1 iv). But, the meaning, importance and consistency of the objectives of this MOU are not immediately obvious. Are the main aims standardisation and inter-operability, or an equitable balance of weapons trade? Or, is the MOU designed to eliminate 'wasteful duplication and overlap' in defence R & D and production which goes 'beyond the needs of healthy competition' so securing a 'rational' use of resources amongst the Allies? Alternatively, the MOU might simply be a method of reducing transaction costs between the two nations through eliminating the bargaining associated with individual offset agreements whenever Britain buys American weapons. Confusions also arise about the precise interpretation and economic logic of some of the objectives in particular standardisation, equitable balance of trade and rationalisation of production.

Standardisation and inter-operability are the victims of confused definitions, and often it is not at all obvious whether they are identical or different. Standardisation embraces weapons, tactics, training, support and even language. Inter-operability aims to make different weapons and equipment compatible (e.g. using the same fuel). Significantly, the author's NATO survey discovered a remarkable consensus on standardisation: no one could measure it, nor value it and there was no universally agreed definition! The general belief is that standardisation and inter-operability are good and that more is desirable.

It is, though, recognised that some of the estimates of cost savings result from a *nirvana* approach (an ideal, perfect world) which compares the current NATO situation not with some achievable alternative but with a hypothetical, 'ideal' outcome (unrealisable?), where scarcity and costs are absent! In other instances, there are claims that an international collaborative project, such as the three-nation Tornado aircraft, will lead to savings in procurement and life cycle costs: but there is a lack of published evidence quantifying any savings. It is also accepted that complete standardisation involves a sacrifice of diversity in weapons and force structures, with adverse effects on NATO's ability to meet unforeseen threats and to confront an enemy with varying problems. In the circumstances, discussions of standardisation frequently move into a concern with inter-operability (e.g. using the same ammunition) which is presented as a more realistic short term aim. For our purposes, it is only necessary to emphasise some of the ambiguities which surround a central concept in NATO policy. Such ambiguities are likely to provide vote-maximising governments and budget-maximising bureaucracies with opportunities to exercise discretionary power.

Is an MOU required for standardisation and inter-operability? The usual reply is that nationalism results in political constraints on a free market in weapons and that increased standardisation requires greater opportunities for Allies to buy each other's arms rather than manufacturing their own. Thus, the USA–UK MOU of 1975 aimed to reduce trade barriers such as the Buy American Act, so removing imperfections in the arms market. Desirable though it might be, there is a potential conflict between standardisation and efficiency on the one hand, and the MOU's concern with an 'equitable' balance of weapons trade. For example, the UK could standardise by buying US weapons and, whilst this is likely to lead to gains from trade creation, it will not result in a 'balanced' arms trade (whatever this might mean?). Indeed, why is the MOU concerned with balance in a specific product group, namely weapons? Comparative advantage suggests that gains result from international specialisation and exchange in a free trade, competitive world economy and not necessarily from a *product-specific bilateral agreement:* this suggests a NATO free trade area for all goods and services.

Worries also arise because of the MOU's concern with eliminating 'wasteful duplication' in R & D and securing rationalisation in weapons manufacture. If R & D aims to reduce uncertainty, there are obvious difficulties of determining *ex ante* which projects represent 'wasteful duplication'! Competing R & D projects might also be worthwhile, each providing valuable information and knowledge. An example was the 'fly-before-you-buy' policy which led the USA to select the F16 in preference to the F17. Even if two nations can agree on which R & D projects to select, the elimination of competition and the creation of a temporary monopoly might result in inefficiency in costs, time-scales, and quality. A potential conflict also exists between an apparent desire to create a free market in weapons and a balanced arms trade which rationalises defence industries and maintains 'a highly developed technological, scientific and industrial base in Europe' (Cmnd 5976, 1975, p. 29). European nations are often reluctant to become completely dependent on the USA for weapons and for high technology. They fear an American monopoly, with Europe 'relegated' to metal-bashing. The desire for independence is not confined to Europe. American defence officials and industrialists believe that US governments are also unwilling to become dependent on foreign suppliers for a complete weapons system, especially on advanced technology projects. On this view, the 1975 MOU was seen as a means of enabling UK defence firms to enter the previously restricted American weapons market to supply equipment and sub-systems, such as ejector seats and aircraft 'head-up' displays rather than complete weapons: these are also products where British firms are believed to have a comparative advantage. Where a foreign firm has a cheaper and superior technology weapon, the USA is most likely to prefer licensed production to purchasing 'off the shelf' and direct imports. Once again, national interests and political elements are likely to impede the operation of markets.

The economics of politics and MOUs

If international specialisation and trade in weapons raises economic welfare – makes everyone 'better off' – how do we explain the present market structure and the likely constraints on the creation of a free arms market (even with MOUs)? An obvious explanation is that the majority of NATO members dislike the expected outcome of a free market, so that governments themselves are frequently the source of market failure. Since the USA has a comparative advantage in high technology goods, it is predicted that a free market will result in America specialising in the production and export of R & D intensive weapons, with Europe confined to 'metal-bashing'. For Western Europe, a free market is expected to result in much smaller aerospace, communications, computer, electronics and nuclear power industries, with the resources re-allocated to alternative and more competitive sectors. At least three points have to be borne in mind when assessing this argument. First, even with a free market, European nations will have a continued advantage in some areas of weapons technology. The UK is likely to be competitive in aircraft sub-systems such as ejector seats, electronics, engines and head-up displays, as well as small guided weapons and VTOL technology. Second, it must not be forgotten that the emotive business of 'metal-bashing' can be highly profitable and that the ultimate concern of business is with profitability rather than the technological or skill content of the inputs into the productive process. Third, European governments dislike the expected outcome of a free market in weapons because of its implications for industrial policy. There is a belief that Europe's future comparative advantage lies in high technology goods where it can out-compete low wage countries. The argument is that Europe (i.e. the EEC) is losing its traditional manufacturing markets, such as footwear, textiles, televisions, motor cycles and cars which are increasingly being supplied by Japan and other Far Eastern nations. So, if Europe is to remain a leading trading bloc, it must specialise in advanced technology. The argument is often taken a stage further. It is asserted that the *existing* high technology industries must continue to be supported by governments unless the critics can specify Europe's *future* leading sectors; and we are told that these have to be advanced technology and not boots and shoes or cheese. Clearly, many of these arguments need to be critically assessed. Myths, fallacies and special pleading have to be distinguished and separated from propositions which have some analytical and empirical validity. At the end of such an evaluation, the advocates of an industrial strategy will have to *choose*. And here, the state's record in high technology projects is far from impressive. Examples include the Anglo-French Concorde and the UK's nuclear power programme. Perhaps private markets and their signals of shortages and surpluses can provide valuable information for an industrial policy and strategy (Dosser et al., 1982).

As a potential market-improving policy, the MOU can also be criticised because it is confined to weapons rather than creating a free trade area for all goods and services. Moreover, there are so many constraints in the MOU that it is far from clear what, if anything, is being maximised. And yet, it could be that the general reluctance of NATO nations to accept the superior free market outcome only arises because defence is 'different' from other goods. No one has ever suggested that the UK should, say, grow its own bananas to avoid 'undue dependence' on foreign suppliers and to obtain the employment, strategic, balance of payments and technological fall-out 'benefits' from domestic banana production. Defence is different because individuals cannot express a preference for the commodity in the market place. They can only register their defence preferences in a general form at the ballot box, and these have to be expressed along with a set of attitudes towards such other issues as government expenditure, taxation, income distribution, the role of the state, immigration and foreign policy. In the circumstances, politicians and bureaucrats have discretionary power in interpreting the 'national

The policy issues: an overview 17

interest'. Within a nation, alternative suppliers of defence services are absent and, for security reasons, governments are reluctant to provide information on the costs and effectiveness of alternative force structures and different procurement policies. For example, voters in NATO nations are not supplied with information on the costs of buying weapons off the shelf from the cheapest supplier compared with independence, joint projects and licensed production. Instead, vote-maximising politicians and budget-conscious bureaucracies are likely to be influenced by producer interest groups. Examples include weapons firms and unions with a monetary interest in the allocation of contracts and their continuation. Such groups are likely to be influential in policy formulation if they are large employers located in marginal constituencies. Not surprisingly, to maintain the demand for a domestic weapons industry, there is every incentive for producers, bureaucrats and politicians to create a set of myths on procurement policy. Thus, it is alleged that nations such as the UK and France 'need' a defence industry for 'independence', for advanced technology and for jobs. There is the myth that competition in weapons markets is impossible and that US weapons might be 'cheap but you pay for the spares'. Some of these propositions might be valid; but others are frequently emotional, lacking any economic analysis and evidence. Rarely is attention given to the costs of policies, such as the costs of 'independence', employment preservation and the promotion of national technological prestige.

The economics of politics modifies the standard predictions of comparative advantage and explains the extent and form of NATO standardisation (Downs, 1957; Hartley, 1977). Foreign defence orders are unlikely to attract votes for domestic politicians. In a vote-conscious market, governments have an incentive to ensure that any foreign orders are 'compensated' with domestic work to satisfy producer interest groups (especially where there are state-owned defence industries, as in Europe). Such offsets and work-sharing are likely to be supported by domestic bureaucracies since they lead to higher budgets and opportunities to exercise discretionary power. These political bargains are unlikely to be based on comparative advantage. For US weapons built in Europe, some 25 per cent co-production might raise costs by about 10 per cent. Similarly, with advanced technology weapons, European governments and interest groups will tend to prefer joint projects with other European states rather than with the USA. On the other hand, the American political market is likely to favour domestic projects, with a reluctance to become involved in international collaborative ventures, especially in R & D work. Nationalism and the desire for an independent technical capability is not costless, and it is a major constraint on the extent to which NATO can create a free trade area in weapons. If governments believe that nationalism contributes to votes, they are unlikely to favour market-improving policies. Why should they, when the potential beneficiaries are widely dispersed consumers compared with the more localised producer groups whose income depends on domestic defence orders?

Conclusions

A free market in weapons is consistent with a market-improving policy. But policies will be implemented by governments and bureaucracies, each with their objective functions which can differ from those of consumers in the market place. The political market is unlikely to be concerned with exploiting all the worthwhile gains from specialisation and international trade. Yet it might be that NATO's survival depends on offering arrangements for each nation to pursue its private interests. At a more general level, arms procurement policies cannot be separated from the wider debate about burden-sharing within NATO and the collective defence aspects of the Alliance. In this context, the USA might regard European purchases of its military equipment (e.g. AWACS) as an offset for the contribution of American forces in Europe.

Elsewhere in NATO, potential market failures continue to exist, with information as a possible candidate. Whilst NATO already provides an association for the limited exchange of information, there might be further unexploited opportunities for beneficial collective action. It has been argued that competitive markets might under-invest in information, invention and research. Defence is a market where a concern with national security is likely to restrict the exchange of information and technical knowledge between members of the Alliance. Understandably, private firms will be reluctant to supply advanced technology information at zero price to their potential rivals. There might, though, be possibilities for collective action to improve the operation of the information market in NATO through, say, inter-government licensing and royalty arrangements, especially for state-financed R & D. This might be more efficient than a general, vague agreement to reduce 'wasteful duplication' in R & D. Also, the NATO defence market might be failing to provide weapons suppliers in Europe and North America with information on each members' future demands for equipment. Of course, this can be an indirect method of restricting the entry of foreign firms into a domestic market. Nonetheless, market failure will remain so long as national governments do not act as competitive buyers, shopping around for weapons and allowing domestic and foreign firms to bid for defence contracts.

Further insights into the efficiency of NATO can be obtained by considering why nations combine to form a collective defence association.

2
The Economics and Politics of NATO

Introduction

The economics of international defence associations between a relatively small number of countries has become a growth area in the application of economic analysis, particularly the theory of public goods. The analysis has been useful in explaining the incentives for nations to enter into such arrangements and in providing a framework for discussions of burden-sharing, the organisation of defence production and related issues. But, the approach uses too static a framework and neglects the political market place, the resulting international bargaining process and how this process affects the complexity of interests which emerge as military alliances develop. This chapter shows how the analysis might be extended and also how it can be used to explain some of the recent problems encountered in the continued existence of the NATO Alliance. It also considers the international trade problems which have arisen as a result of attempts to improve the efficiency of defence expenditure. In this way, debates about standardisation and the formulation of NATO policy can be seen as one element in the economics and politics of the Alliance.

NATO as a defence club

NATO is an international organisation in which members have agreed that 'an armed attack against one or more of them in Europe or North America shall be considered as an attack against them all . . .' (NATO, 1980). It is remarkable that fifteen sovereign states with vastly different policy objectives, economic and political structures, growth rates and standards of living should have been able to keep such an organisation in being since 1949. The Alliance of thirteen European countries with the United States and Canada has survived during a period in which there have been major changes in the economic and political conditions within each member state, in international trade conditions, and in relations with and between its

The economics and politics of NATO 21

potential enemies. One example of a major change was the formation of the EEC, which consists of a subset of the European members of NATO and which has radically affected international economic relations and trade between its member states. Technical progress has also had a major impact on NATO strategy. Nuclear weapons have reduced the traditional military advantages of large concentrated land and naval forces; missiles and rockets have replaced aircraft, guns and battleships; jet airliners able to fly out reinforcements quickly have meant home bases replacing overseas garrisons. In other words, technical change has resulted in substitutions between nuclear and conventional forces, between missiles and traditional weapons, and between weapons and manpower.

The continued existence of NATO indicates some of the features which might be required for the long term survival of an international organisation. Presumably, survival reflects the fact that membership of the 'club' is worthwhile, otherwise independent sovereign states would have withdrawn. The membership 'fee' consists of a direct contribution to financing NATO's common infrastructure (airfields, communications, radar warning, pipelines) plus other costs in the form of a collective defence obligation with its general commitments and constraints on the level and composition of defence expenditure. For example, in the mid-1970s, NATO was critical of the UK Labour Government's defence 'cuts' and in response to NATO 'pressure', Britain agreed to increase defence spending in the late 1970s. In return for the 'fee', members benefit from 'collective security' (e.g. the US nuclear umbrella). One US general has claimed that without NATO the USA would have to double its defence expenditure. At the same time, each member in the event of an armed attack directed at it can take whatever action it judges is necessary so that there can be no question of NATO being in any sense a supra-national organisation with wide powers of discretion in the deployment of the defence effort of member states. Indeed, in so far as there is an element of uncertainty in the Alliance response to an armed attack, members are likely to make their own 'insurance arrangements. They have an incentive to maintain a full and balanced range of national forces, to develop an independent strategic nuclear deterrent and to support a domestic defence industry. Retaining control over their own defence effort and independence in the operation of foreign policy, the looseness of organisation leaves members with an incentive to maximise private gains from the NATO Alliance through 'free riding' and adopting weapons more likely to contribute to national welfare than to the military effectiveness of NATO. After all, domestic weapons firms and bureaucracies in the form of Defence Ministries or Departments and national armed forces are likely to pursue *their* preferences and press their own claims rather than consider the wider interests of an amorphous body such as NATO. Each member is therefore faced with a difficult 'trade-off' between national defence coupled with other related domestic policies, and the objectives of combined defence. Views on the nature of the trade-off will not only differ at a point in time and through time between individual members, but also differ as between politically influential interest groups within each member state. In fact, efforts to assess the success or otherwise of the increasing emphasis on the efficiency of NATO as an organisation for the production of weapons and the provision of defence forces cannot ignore the costs to individual members of trying to achieve some 'optimal' economic efficiency criterion. There are no costless policies. It is here that the conventional economic analysis of alliances need to be modified, particularly if it is to be used to make sensible suggestions for improving international trade in weapons.

The economics of military alliances

Defence is usually given as the classic example of a *public good*. These are goods where it is not possible to confine the benefits to those who are willing to pay, and where one person's consumption does not reduce anyone else's consumption. Other examples of public goods include ideas, information, music, street lighting and lighthouses. The central characteristic of a public good is its *non-excludability*: if it is provided to one person, then it is provided to all. A nation provides defence for all its citizens and its provision for one implies its provision for everyone else in the community. In contrast, with private goods, the exclusion principle operates and if, say, I buy a loaf of bread, I exclude you from its consumption.

Given its public good characteristics, a market in defence is difficult, if not impossible, to establish and individuals within a nation state will submit themselves to compulsory exactions (taxation) rather than risk that the service would not be provided. In the absence of compulsion, it might be thought that the costs of defence could be shared between the community on the basis of its benefits to each citizen. But this encounters the problem of *free-riding*. Individuals have an incentive not to reveal their true valuation of defence, so obtaining its benefits without contributing to its costs. Nevertheless, it has always been recognised that the existence of 'publicness' does not necessarily provide a case for public provision and finance of the good, though some form of collective action will be required. Where the advantages of joint action are obvious to all, and the costs of communication between the individuals involved are small, then it may be possible to reach agreement on the amount of provision and on the sharing of costs, without using compulsion. These conditions are best fulfilled

The economics and politics of NATO   23

when small numbers of bargainers are involved. It is for this reason that a contrast is often drawn between national defence, where these conditions do not obtain (e.g. large numbers), and combined defence, where a relatively small number of countries agree on arrangements for mutual protection against a common enemy, without having to submit to a supra-national authority with independent budgetary powers. Thus, a military alliance such as NATO can be viewed as providing a public good in the form of collective defence (an attack on one member is regarded as an attack on all).

Further incentive to a collective agreement lies in the possibility of technical economies of scale, reflecting the relatively high capital intensity of modern methods of weapon production. The smaller the level of defence provision, the higher are likely to be the marginal costs of production. In principle, therefore, combined defence should reduce total costs through, for example, standardisation of equipment and international specialisation, with each member of the Alliance concentrating on the supply of military skills and weapons in which it has a comparative advantage. Thus, the benefits derived from mutual interest in the demand for defence are matched by the resource savings made possible by the combined supply of defence.

Some of the economic benefits of joining an alliance are outlined in Figure 2.1. Before joining, a country is producing and consuming a combination of defence and civil goods (e.g. guns and butter) shown by position X. Entry into the alliance results is an improvement (a gain), with the country now consuming *more* military and civil goods at position Y. However, in this example, the new entrant *reduces* its national defence effort, replacing it with alliance security. This is often taken to be typical when a small country joins an alliance (Kennedy, 1979). Inevitably, the possibilities and opportunities for 'free riding' in an alliance creates controversey over the sharing of defence burdens. An economic theory of alliances predicts that the more defence a nation's allies provide, the less it tends to spend on defence. But, the theory also recognises that larger nations will tend to bear disproportionately large shares of the common burden (Olson and Zeckhauser, 1966; Hartley and McLean, 1981).

Free riding presents a threat to the continued existence of a military alliance. Smaller countries may not reveal their 'true' preferences about the benefits of combined defence if they believe that larger countries' defence efforts will provide them with uncovenanted benefits (Table 2.1, see below). But once we recognise that NATO remains in existence and examine the decision-making structure which will follow from collective defence arrangements covering the creation of combined defence staff with at least some resources at its disposal and of arrangements for the co-ordination of defence effort, we cannot apply the conventional analysis. It cannot be assumed that we are

24 Nato Arms Co-operation

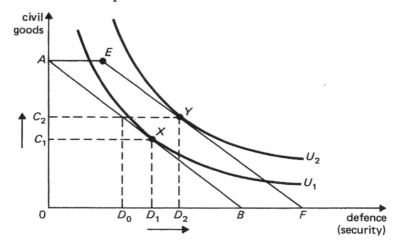

Figure 2.1 The benefits of an alliance. The diagram shows two goods, defence and civil goods. Before entry the nations operates on AB, which shows the maximum combinations of military and civil goods which can be *produced* (the straight lines reflect constant returns to scale). The curves U_1 and U_2 show the satisfaction, utility or welfare which society obtains from *consuming* defence and civil goods. With AB, society's 'best' position is at X. Joining an alliance provides extra security of AE and the country will now prefer position Y, where it has more defence and more civil goods ($U_2 > U_1$). However, the provision of alliance defence, AE, means that the nation can now reduce its own defence effort from D_1 to D_0, enabling it to consume more civil goods, namely C_2 instead of C_1. Complete 'free riding' occurs at position E.

living in a world of a small number of decision makers – 'countries' or their governments – with given preferences (though not necessarily 'true' revealed preferences). In other words, economic theory which assumes that a small group of nations will combine to exploit efficiently the benefits of collective action is limited in that it neglects the political market.

The political market and NATO

Several major actors are involved in the 'public choice' process of the individual members of a military alliance. They include the government in power, the legislature and the opposition parties, bureaucrats, the military command, the diplomatic service, the scientists engaged in R & D and the weapons suppliers. Each group will develop interests of its own, and these need not necessarily coincide.

One source of disagreement arises from the peculiar nature of defence as a source of welfare. Assume that combined defence arrangements are meant simply to minimize the possibility of external attack. Calculating the defence effort necessary to achieve this objective over a span of years is an extremely difficult task. Problems arise because the efficiency of defence output depends on the defence output of potential enemies. As a potential aggressor increases his output, the less efficient will become the existing level of defence provision by defenders. The calculation becomes even more complicated when allowance is made for uncertainty and the enormous influence of technological development on the efficiency of protection. Indeed, improvements have been so rapid that it is no longer possible for even large nations to guarantee complete security from attack, whatever they were prepared to spend. Thus, the efficiency of defence provision cannot depend solely on the technical judgement of military and scientific experts, for protection may be improved from a mutual *reduction* of defence output by opposing military powers (e.g. SALT, MBFR). Efforts to improve protection by such means will involve much wider considerations embracing the whole gamut of international negotiation between 'opponents'. In effect, NATO and the Warsaw Pact can be viewed as 'trapped' into an arms race. Each could be 'better off' if they jointly switched to lower defence spending, but they would need to co-operate and trust one another for the agreement to work (Hartley and Tisdell, 1981, p. 230).

Controversy also arises if an influential member of the alliance suddenly decides that mutual protection would not be harmed if resources were switched out of defence, say, into more intensive diplomatic and trade negotiations with potential enemies, and tax cuts to improve economic incentives. Even within the country concerned, such a view, while the prerogative of the government, will only be arrived at after carefully considering its effects on the government's chances of re-election. The government will receive conflicting advice. Its political advisers will probably agree that voter support is likely to be increased by cutting defence spending, for the gains to voters of lower taxes are probably more immediately apparent than the losses from a cut in military budgets. The military establishment will express horror at the very idea of cutting the defence capability and will focus on attacking the basic proposition – e.g. it will be argued that a cut in defence will 'seriously weaken our defences', leading to a substantial reduction in security and protection. Its scientific advisers seem likely to support the military in arguing that a cut in defence expenditure will reduce 'technological spin-off' which is believed to promote economic growth; or, if they agree with the government view, they will fight hard to preserve that part of the defence budget which finances the development of high technology. Military and scientific interests will have an incentive to muster opposition within the government as well as outside by calling on their professional colleagues to lobby political parties and interest groups. The government's economic advisers are less likely to be personally affected but will point towards the differential employment effects, regional and national, resulting from the budget changes. Their calculations will show the possible effects of job changes on voter support and hence on the government's ultimate objective of re-election. The diplomats will be delighted with the prospect of a more dramatic and important role to play! Therefore, in the circumstances of the national and international political bargaining market, it is not at all obvious that each member of the 'club' will reveal accurately its preferences for defence. For example, if NATO members were certain that in the event of an attack their Allies would respond, each nation would have an incentive to specialise in its force structures rather than create a totally independent capability. Economic efficiency would require each nation to specialise in providing defence forces in which it had a comparative advantage. The USA might specailise in nuclear strategic forces, whilst the UK could provide the Alliance's anti-submarine and VTOL aircraft capability, with other nations specialising in infantry and armoured forces. However, if there is uncertainty about whether the collective defence agreement will be honoured, a member state may prefer to increase its private defensive capability (e.g. France). Furthermore, if a distinction is made between deterrence (i.e. strategic nuclear forces) and protection (e.g. anti-aircraft missiles), then NATO through its emphasis on nuclear and conventional forces does not specialise in providing a pure public good (deterrence). It has been shown that allies might prefer conventional forces which serve their private ends (Sandler, 1977). This means that, from the Alliance viewpoint, agreements whereby all NATO members increase defence spending (e.g. by 3 per cent) are likely to result in the expansion of those weapons and forces which confer national or private benefits rather than Alliance or collective benefits. Once all these factors are considered, achieving an efficient level and composition of NATO defence spending is likely to be an accidental outcome rather than the result of a conscious effort to apply orthodox economic criteria and overcome the difficulties of reaching agreement. Various indicators will be used to influence the defence policies of member states. Emphasis will be placed on the 'threat' from the Warsaw Pact, relative defence burdens and the need to acquire cheaper weapons.

The threat from the Warsaw Pact

During the 1970s, NATO was confronted with two problems which markedly affected members' attitudes to combined defence, both of which have a bearing on defence costs. First, the Warsaw Pact countries made substantial increases in their defence expenditure; second, advanced technology has presented members with an acceleration in weapon costs. The traditional response of NATO to Warsaw Pact countries' actions of this kind has been to try to persuade members to increase their military spending.

One estimate showed that between 1967 and 1976, NATO military expenditure declined from some $171 billion to $147 billion, whilst that of the Warsaw Pact rose from $92 billion to $139 billion (all in 1975 prices). During the same period, NATO military expenditure as a share of GNP declined from 7.1 to 4.6 per cent, compared with a relatively stable 10.7–11 per cent in the Warsaw Pact (USACDA, 1978). A similar NATO study showed that USSR military expenditure as a share of GNP rose from 11–12 per cent in 1970 to 12–13 per cent in 1979 and is forecast to reach 15 per cent by 1985 (Rupp, 1981). Although the evidence appears persuasive, much depends on the meaning and reliability of the data. Expenditure figures are only inputs and any appraisal of efficiency in the defence sector cannot ignore outputs or the combat effectiveness of the armed forces. High levels of expenditure might be a reflection of *inefficiency*, resulting from the lack of competition in weapons markets (e.g. organisational slack), or from 'excessive gold plating' of equipment. Or, the estimates of comparative military spending might be unreliable and suspect. In this context, the official Soviet budget figures suggest that defence expenditure was some 4 per cent of GNP in 1979! International comparisons involve problems of exchange rate adjustments, of ensuring indentical definitions of defence expenditure and GNP, and of valuing items in economies where prices are not an accurate indicator of costs. Usually, comparisons are based on either a dollar costing of Russian defence expenditure, which can then be compared with US spending, or a rouble costing of American military budgets compared with USSR outlays. For example, Russian military expenditure is measured by estimating what it would cost the USA to purchase Soviet armed forces. In effect, this assumes that the Russians would pay US salaries to their conscript troops and US prices for their weapons. But, different nations have different relative prices for manpower and weapons which will also affect the quantities purchased. Compared with the USSR, advanced technology equipment might be relatively cheaper in the USA whilst manpower might be more expensive. As a result, when Russian forces are priced in dollars, they seem more expensive than US forces; but when US forces are rouble costed, they appear to cost more than USSR units! And comparative estimates cannot avoid subjective evaluations. For example, attempts have to be made to calculate how much US defence firms would charge if they had to build Russian weapons. Inevitably, there are considerable opportunities for budget-

nities for budget-sensitive bureaucracies to over-estimate the enemy's defence spending.

Alternative estimates of the threat from the Warsaw Pact concentrate on *numbers*. It seems that the Warsaw Pact outnumbers NATO by 2 : 1 in tactical aircraft, 2.3 : 1 in divisions, 2.5 : 1 in tanks and 3 : 1 in artillery (Rogers, 1981). In addition to their apparent quantitative lead, the Russians have made major advances in the *quality* of their weapons (e.g. SS-20 ballistic missiles; Mig 25 interceptors; Backfire bombers and T-64/T-72 tanks). NATO military commanders respond by advocating further increases in defence budgets, aiming for an annual real increase of 4.5 per cent in the 1980s. But, once again, care is required in interpreting the numbers game. Even if the estimates are accepted, the figures do not indicate the combat effectiveness and efficiency of forces in the rival alliances. Numbers of aircraft, ships and tanks are misleading in the absence of data on the average age of weapons and their operational availability. The numbers of soldiers are similarly misleading if their training and skill levels (productivity) are ignored. Nor do numbers indicate the intangible elements reflected in morale, the quality of leadership, the ability to make decisions and tactics (Smith, 1980, Ch. 4). In other words, published data on numbers fail to provide any indications of final outputs as reflected in deterrence, protection and, ultimately, the probability of survival in different conflict situations.

International comparisons of numbers are not always on the same basis. Nations differ in the extent to which they substitute between nuclear and conventional forces, weapons and manpower, civilians and servicemen, conscripts and volunteers, regulars and reserves and men and women. There are differences in the availability of national forces to each alliance, as well as diversity in each nation's views about its range of potential enemies and in the extent to which armed forces are used for internal policing. Sometimes, stress is placed on NATO's inferiority in one region of Europe or the Atlantic to the neglect of its superiority elsewhere. Moreover, if nations have varying comparative advantages, this is likely to be reflected in different force structures and in the extent to which technology (quality) might be substituted for manpower and weapons. In other words, there are opportunites for critically assessing the numbers game, particularly when budget-maximising bureaucracies are monopoly suppliers of information and defence services.

Defence burdens

NATO agreement to increase military spending raises the question of how the defence burden is to be shared, particularly between the USA and Europe. Possible criteria are payments in proportion to benefits, equality, or the ability to pay with financing arrangements similar to a progressive income tax system (Kennedy, 1979). Interestingly, the economic theory of alliances predicts that the large members will bear a disproportionately large share of the common burden, whilst smaller nations will free-ride. A frequent indicator used to express relative burdens is the percentage of GNP devoted to defence spending. Table 2.1 gives the data for NATO member countries between 1950 and 1980 (see also Table 2.3).

As Table 2.1 shows, differential burdens exist between the USA and Europe, as well as amongst the European members of the Alliance. The relative burden on the USA has been much greater than that on its Allies. Britain is also amongst the pact leaders, whilst Canada and Luxembourg are examples of free-riders. On the basis of relative burdens, the UK has often claimed that its military contribution should be brought more into line with that of its major European Allies (Hartley, 1981a; Peacock, 1972). However, the optimal level and composition of defence expenditure for members of the Alliance must be controversial and there are obvious criticisms of selecting some arbitrary share figure as the appropriate target for a member nation. There are international differences in the definitions of defence expenditure and GNP and not all inputs are valued at market prices.

Table 2.1 *Defence burdens in NATO*

Country	Defence expenditure as a percentage of GNP (%)			
	1950	1960	1970	1980
Belgium	2.8	3.9	3.3	3.3
Canada	2.9	4.9	2.8	1.8
Denmark	1.8	3.1	2.8	2.4
France	8.3	7.4	4.6	4.1
Federal Republic of Germany	n.a.	4.6	3.7	3.3
Greece	6.6	5.4	5.6	5.6
Italy	4.2	3.7	3.0	2.4
Luxembourg	1.5	1.2	0.9	1.2
Netherlands	5.4	4.5	3.8	3.1
Norway	2.6	3.7	4.1	2.9
Portugal	4.1	4.5	7.9	3.6
Turkey	6.9	5.7	4.7	4.3
UK	7.3	7.3	5.6	5.1
USA	5.5	9.9	8.7	5.6
NATO Europe	5.8	5.7	4.2	3.7
Total NATO	5.4	8.2	6.7	4.4

Source: NATO Information Service, Brussels; also NATO (1976).

Many nations use 'cheap' conscripts whilst the USA and the UK rely on an all-volunteer force. There are difficulties associated with using official exchange rates, whilst the composition and location of forces and their availability to NATO might not be shown accurately by aggregate defence expenditure. Such figures also exclude each nation's expenditure on non-defence substitutes which contribute to 'security and protection'. Examples include the diplomatic service, overseas aid, the formation of the EEC and EFTA, and even Concorde has been presented as a contribution towards European integration. Moreover, if the share of GNP is being used to determine the amount and distribution of defence expenditure, should we not be making comparisons not only with our Allies but also with out potential enemies? Finally, ratios are misleading because they measure inputs and not the output of defence effort and therefore throw no light on the efficiency of military effort.

Defence burdens, standardisation policy and rising weapons costs can be viewed as inter-related, rather than independent, issues. The USA as the pact leader has often argued that European members should 'offset' some of its large burden by purchasing their weapons from American industry. Such purchases would result in greater standardisation of weapons within the Alliance. Also, rising weapons costs and limited defence budgets have meant that NATO cannot ignore worthwhile opportunities to increase the efficiency of existing levels of military spending. Standardisation could contribute to this end if it results in lower weapons costs, but it is not the only policy option. The increasing costs, complexity and skilled labour requirements of modern weapons means that conscription is a relatively costly method of training military manpower. The more efficient solution requires highly skilled, experienced and hence long-service regulars (i.e. a volunteer force), able to use effectively and to maintain modern weapons, so providing the armed forces with a worthwhile return on their substantial and rising training investments.

Weapons costs

The armed forces are continuously searching for weapons of improved performance, almost regardless of cost. This demand for technical progress means that each new generation of weapons is costlier, resulting in higher bills for R & D and production. Table 2.2 shows some examples of the level and the trend in the costs of successive generations of weapons in the UK and the USA.

Typically, in real terms, new equipment can be 2.5 times as costly as its predecessors, and the sums involved are substantial. In the UK, acquisition of a new torpedo will cost about £1,000 million, whilst a

Table 2.2 Weapon Costs

		£m
1.	*Programme costs of UK weapons* (estimated R & D and production costs, 1979 prices)	
	Stingray lightweight torpedo	920
	Sea Eagle air-to-surface anti-ship missile	350
	New sonars for surface ships and submarines	170
2.	*Unit production costs of UK weapons* (1980 prices)	
	Nuclear powered fleet submarine	175
	Type 22 frigate	120
	Tornado strike aircraft	11.4
	Chinook helicopter	3.5
	Lynx helicopter	2.1
	Challenger main battle tank	1.5

		Cost trends
3.	*Production costs of successive generations of new equipment* (constant prices)	
	(a) *UK weapons*	
	Strike aircraft (Hunter, Harrier)	4.0×
	Guided missile	3.5×
	Armoured vehicle (FV432, MCV80)	3.5×
	Frigate (Leander, Type 22)	3.0×
	Helicopter (Wasp, Lynx)	2.5×
	Trainer aircraft (Gnat, Hawk)	1.5×
	(b) *US weapons*	
	Tanks (M60, XM1)	3.0×
	Fighter aircraft (F4E, F15)	2.5×
	Aircraft carriers (*USS Forrestal*, *Nimitz*)	1.8×
	Attack submarines	1.5×

Sources: Cmnd 8212 (1981); also Cmnd 7826–I (1980) and Gansler (1980, p. 16).

nuclear powered submarine costs £175 million (1979–80 prices). There are at least three implications of these cost figures:

(a) Throughout NATO, increases in real costs and limited defence budgets have resulted in the purchase of fewer new weapons. In the USA, purchases of tactical aircraft have declined from some 3000 per year in the 1950s to about 300 per annum in the 1970s. The result is rising real R & D costs *per unit* and fewer opportunities for economies of scale in production: hence the increasing

32   *Nato Arms Co-operation*

emphasis on NATO standardisation policies to offset some of these trends.
(b) They indicate the possible opportunities for cost savings from weapons standardisation measures. For example, standardisation policies which result in only modest cost savings of, say, 10 per cent could lead to substantial reductions in expenditure on ships and aircraft (e.g. consider the savings on a buy of 400 aircraft).
(c) Questions arise as to whether there are alternative opportunities for controlling the trend towards more expensive weapons. Throughout NATO, procurement policies are administered by bureaucrats and, especially in Europe, are characterised by an absence of competition for weapons contracts and by cost-based pricing. Bureaucracies also have every incentive to *spend* rather than save. How many military staff and civil servants have received a pay increase or been promoted on the basis of savings (i.e. for not spending)? This financial environment seems conducive to 'excessive gold plating' – i.e. a concern with the technical sophistication of weapons which gives satisfaction to the operators, but where costs are ignored.

NATO standardisation: institutions and achievements

Given the apparent attractiveness of weapons standardisation, what has NATO achieved? An indication of the opportunities for savings can be seen in Table 2.3 which shows each member state's expenditure on defence *equipment*.

In 1980, total NATO spending on defence equipment was some $43 billion. A modest saving of 10 per cent would reduce this expenditure by over $4 billion per annum, with additional savings possible on R & D bills and on support costs. But NATO is only an advisory and co-ordinating body. It differs from a national government in that it does not determine weapons requirements for the Alliance and then allocate contracts for development and production. Nonetheless, NATO has continuously attempted to 'improve' the arrangements for the purchase and supply of weapons in member states. Specialist institutions were established and policy has developed through four broad stages.

In the first stage, a Military Production and Supply Board was established (1949) to promote co-ordinated production, standardisation and technical research in the field of armaments. After various modifications, this body developed into the Defence Production Committee (1954) which was responsible for supervising joint *production* programmes and work on standardisation. In the meantime, a Military Agency for Standardisation had been created (1951) to promote

Table 2.3 NATO expenditures on equipment

Country	Equipment expenditure as a percentage of total defence expenditure (%) Average 1970–4	1976–7	1980–1	Total defence expenditure (US$ million) 1980–1
Belgium	10.6	11.0	14.4	4 000
Canada	7.3	8.0	15.4	4 400
Denmark	16.8	19.4	18.3	1 600
Germany	11.9	13.2	14.8	26 700
Italy	15.4	13.1	17.5	8 700
Luxembourg	1.6	3.4	1.8	n.a.
Netherlands	12.8	15.5	18.0	5 200
Norway	13.5	11.4	19.3	1 700
Portugal	7.5	1.9	6.1	800
Turkey	4.0	28.5	4.7	2 100
UK	17.0	20.6	25.2	26 300
USA	21.1	17.4	20.3	140 500

Sources: NATO Press Service; also Cmnd 8212 (1981, p. 67).

military standardisation, thereby enabling NATO forces to operate together more effectively. Early standardisation agreements emerged for such items as ammunition and vehicle components. Subsequently, in the second stage, emphasis was placed on developing collaboration on individual projects and the results are shown in Table 2.4. It can be seen that the majority of co-operative projects involved the European manufacture of weapons designed and developed in the USA. Only the two aircraft projects (G91 and Atlantic) were designed, developed and produced in Europe in response to a *NATO* requirement. Recognition that collaboration is not restricted to production led to a change in the terms of reference of the Defence Production Committee which became the Armaments Committee (1958) with an extended remit to include R & D (Vandervanter, 1964).

Stage three started in 1966, when the mandatory and unanimity aspects of the earlier system were ended. NATO-wide agreement on requirements was no longer needed and NATO Basic Military Requirements were abolished. The aim was 'to make co-operation as easy and as advantageous as possible', the philosophy being that 'if only two countries co-operated to produce a weapon for their forces, this was better than nothing . . .' (NATO, 1976, pp. 140–1). The Armaments Committee was disbanded and a new body, the Conference of National Armaments Directors (CNAD), was created to implement the policy changes. CNAD has the task of promoting international collaborative projects and exchanging information on operational requirements and national equipment plans. CNAD also established the

Table 2.4 *NATO collaborative ventures, 1954–63*

Project	Date of start or agreement	Quantity purchased	Buyers
Aircraft			
Fiat G91 – NATO requirement	1954	640+	Italy, West Germany, Portugal
Atlantic maritime patrol aircraft – NATO requirement	1957	87	France, West Germany, Italy, Netherlands
Starfighter – European manufacture of US aircraft	1960	c. 1 000	Belgium, West Germany, Italy, Netherlands, Canada
Missiles			
Hawk – European manufacture of US missile (Phase I)	1958	4 000+	Belgium, France, West Germany, Italy, Netherlands
Sidewinder – European manufacture of US missile	1959	10 000	Belgium, Denmark, France, West Germany, Greece, Netherlands, Norway, Portugal, Turkey
Bullpup – European manufacture of US missile	1962	5 000+	Denmark, Norway, Turkey, UK
AS-30 – European manufacture of French missile	1962	c. 2 000	France, West Germany, UK
M-72 anti-tank weapon – US weapon	1963	n.a	Canada, Netherlands, Norway
Mk-44 naval torpedo – European manufacture of US design	1960	n.a	Canada, France, Italy, UK

Source: NATO (1976).

NATO Industrial Advisory Group (NIAG, 1968) composed of senior industrialists who provide advice, and assistance, as well as representing the views of their national defence industries on Alliance armaments policy. The result of these policy changes was reflected in fourteen NATO projects by 1976, including the Jaguar and Tornado aircraft, the Milan and Seasparrow missiles, together with howitzers and communications systems. In the meantime, a new association was formed, namely, the Eurogroup (1968). This consists of the European Defence Ministers of NATO (except France). It represents European interests in NATO by providing a forum for exchanging views on common defence questions and for improving European co-ordination and collaboration in the production and procurement of defence equipment, as well as in training and logistic support.

The fourth stage emerged by the mid-1970s, when there was a renewed interest in NATO weapons standardisation policies. This reflected the growing 'threat' from the Warsaw Pact, the economic constraints limiting NATO military spending, a developing US–European interest in a two-way street for weapons, and estimates of substantial savings from standardisation (e.g. Callaghan, 1975). America recognised that European opposition to greater weapons standardisation reflected their belief that it would lead to US domination of high technology defence equipment. And Europe was especially concerned about the alleged technology 'gap' with the USA and the opportunities for using defence procurement and arms collaboration as a means of protecting European high technology industries (Hartley, 1982, Ch. 10). Thus, in 1977, a new US policy initiative (under President Carter) offered to

(a) Promote a 'genuine two-way street' with the USA willing to buy European defence equipment where this would mean more efficient use of Allied resources.
(b) Encourage the development of a Common European defence production effort. It was recognised that the Independent European Programme Group (IEPG, 1975) – consisting of the Eurogroup and France – was the principle forum for promoting equipment collaboration and co-operation among European Allies, and for 'strengthening' the European defence industrial base.
(c) Join the European states in examining methods of improving co-operation in weapons development, production and procurement on a trans-Atlantic basis (Kirby, 1980).

Weapons supply is only one aspect of standardisation policy. Elsewhere, some commonality has been achieved in infrastructure and in support. NATO's Common Infrastructure Programme involves the collective finance and provision of fixed installations available to all members of the Alliance. Examples include airfields, pipelines, communications networks and radar early warning systems. There is also a NATO Maintenance and Supply Organisation (NAMSO) which supplies spares and logistic support for a number of jointly used weapon systems, particularly missiles and electronic systems (e.g. Bullpup, Hawk, Sidewinder, F104). However, this is by no means a complete and comprehensive description of the development of NATO institutions and standardisation policy. The account is deliberately superficial. Description is not explanation. The aim is to explain the extent and form of NATO standardisation policy. Explanation can then be used to guide governments and NATO in formulating an appropriate policy and institutional framework. After all, various NATO institutions exist and others have been tried: why has not there been more standardisation? Obvious difficulties arise in devising some criteria for assessing the success or otherwise of NATO standardisation policy. For those who advocate complete standardisation *à la* Warsaw Pact, then NATO might be judged a relative failure. On the other hand, once it is accepted that there are no costless solutions, it has to be recognised that complete standardisation might be too costly (i.e. it might not be worthwhile to eliminate completely diversity in weapons). Indeed, the present amount of standardisation might be regarded as highly successful and 'optimal' for a voluntary international club consisting of independent sovereign states, each with different preferences and each creating a set of extensive and diverse constraints on common action. An independent and self-interested nation might have little incentive to participate in weapons standardisation policies if it can 'free ride', leaving collaboration to other member states. In other words, it is possible to envisage a set of weapons standardisation 'clubs' *within* the Alliance. The situation resembles that of trade union membership. Higher wages negotiated by a trade union are available to everyone, including non-members. If so, self-interested individuals will not voluntarily contribute to the costs of a union since they will receive the benefits regardless of membership! On this basis, it has been claimed that unions remain in existence mainly through compulsion and coercion (e.g. closed shops, picketing, violence; see Olson, 1965). However, a sovereign state within NATO will *voluntarily* support weapons standardisation where it is worthwhile. This arises under two related conditions. First, weapons standardisation might be associated with a collaborative industrial programme. In this situation, some of the major economic benefits in the form of jobs, technology and the balance of payments are 'tied' to participation in the joint industrial project. In other words, many of the benefits accrue to, and are captured by, the partner nations in the collaborative venture (i.e. they are not NATO-wide public goods). Second, a nation will support standardisation when nationalism is too costly. But identifying the *general* conditions favourable to weapons standardisation is only the start of a continuing debate about the appropriate policy solutions. For example, following the 1977 US initiative, some American industrialists advocated European co-production based on the F16 'model' as the preferred solution. Predictably, Europeans favoured the 'family of weapons' approach in which Europe and the USA would each specialise in *developing* different types of weapons with commitments to cross-purchase or co-produce. Conflicts are inevitable. Choices have to be made between competition or monopoly, between efficiency or equity and between international trade or nationalism. In this context, economic theory provides 'guidelines' for NATO standardisation policy.

Is there a case for competition and free trade?

If nations with private enterprise economies wish to achieve the greatest satisfaction or economic welfare for their citizens, then economic theory establishes a presumption in favour of competition and free trade. Applied to weapons standardisation policy in NATO, this would mean that member governments should act as competitive buyers, with competitive bidding for contracts and no barriers to new enterprises and foreign firms competing for orders. Governments would purchase from the least-cost supplier using fixed price contracts (Hartley, 1974). A standard objection to this solution is that the economies of member states in NATO are not generally characterised by competition and free trade. If so, efforts to apply competitive and free trade solutions in weapons markets *only* might not raise economic welfare; they could leave welfare or efficiency unchanged or even lower it! In other words, limited or partial competitive free trade solutions might be inappropriate. On this view, current NATO standardisation policy might be defended in terms of a search for the 'next best' alternative. However, since the conditions required for such a 'second best' solution are often complex and require more information than is normally available, existing NATO policy is only likely to achieve this result by accident! Moreover, if competitive free trade policies are 'socially desirable', why haven't they been adopted by NATO members? Frequently, the continuation of monopoly and international trade barriers are the *result* of government policy. Policy can always be changed: hence the current imperfect and apparently inefficient NATO arrangements for standardisation have to be viewed as a preferred outcome for the member states. Once again, this is less surprising when it is remembered that economic principles are applied not in a vacuum, but in political markets. Consider how political

38 Nato Arms Co-operation

elements and institutions might influence proposals to introduce competition and free trade into NATO weapons markets.

To give effect to the doctrine of comparative advantage so as to reduce combined defence costs, members of the Alliance would have to agree to allow free trade in arms and equipment among themselves. This is clearly a tall order but the USA has attempted to improve the operation of the NATO arms market by offering bilateral agreements with its NATO partners in the form of Memoranda of Understanding (MOUs). The agreement with the UK, for example, aimed to secure a 'balance' in defence sales between the two countries as well as 'making the most rational use of industrial, economic and technological resources so as to achieve maximum military capability at the lowest possible cost and to achieve greater standardisation and inter-operability of weapon systems' (see HC155, 1976). Note that the process by which this desired result is to be reached is not that generally assumed in instituting 'freer' international trade – more competition in arms production. Instead, the MOU with the UK was designed to eliminate 'wasteful duplication and overlap' in R & D and defence production which goes 'beyond the needs of healthy competition'. It follows that the benefits from standardisation and inter-operability of weapons are to be achieved by the normal political bargaining process and not by the forces of competition.

It is easy to guess why governments will prefer to give substance to MOUs, by clear specification, if that is possible, of what defence products are to be standardised, who is to produce the standardised product and in what areas inter-operability will occur. The first reason is that the creation of free trade in weapons, or even a NATO free trade area, would mean major shifts in the existing distribution of production between countries, with large potential gains to the USA. The standard prediction is that the USA, with a comparative advantage in advanced technology goods, would become the main producer and exporter of weapons embodying research and development and Europe would be left only with 'metal-bashing'. Given the present distribution of defence production, with major R & D and aerospace projects based in European countries, the costs of adjustment to these countries in terms of redeployment of resources would be considerable. By itself, free trade in weaponry provides no mechanism by which the 'losers' would be automatically compensated.

There is a second reason why free trade in weapons, even with compensatory arrangements, is unlikely even to be approximated. Apart from the fact that such arrangements would not obviate the necessity for shifting resources in high cost countries out of defence, with all the attendant social costs, there appear to be powerful arguments which prevent governments from denying resources to industries which have a large technological input (e.g. aerospace, electronics). It is part of the conventional wisdom of industrial policy in several NATO countries that *future* comparative advantage lies in advanced technology goods in which they can out-compete low wage countries who are increasingly successful in traditional manufacturing markets such as textiles, footwear, and even television sets and motor cycles. It is further argued that the private capital market 'underprovides' for high technology because it takes 'too short' a view and consequently charges 'too high' a price for investible funds. Moreover, private firms may be prevented from reaping the gains from technological investment because of the difficulties in obtaining and conserving their property rights in new discoveries and their applications. Producer groups in defence industries with a high technology input also point to the technological 'fall-out' which is obtained. They even claim that continued state support will have to be given unless and until other 'leading' sectors can be identified which will offer greater technological benefits. This drift of argument has been hotly contested by economists (Hartley, 1974). Even those among them who concede that there is something in it would agree that it tells us nothing about the amount of resources which ought to be devoted to high technology, other than what the market would provide, and how it should be distributed. We are concerned not with the quality of the argument, but with explaining its prevalence.

Here again, the answer lies in the opportunities for discretionary behaviour on the part of those with a strong interest in preserving the *status quo*, namely our old friends, vote-maximising politicians and producer interest groups, including the military establishment and their bureaucratic and scientific advisers. They clearly have a major stake in large-scale domestic government involvement in defence production, for reasons given above. Voters are powerless to control their actions for defence cannot be made a function of their individual demands expressed through the market but only their general preferences as expressed through the ballot-box. Governments have a perfect excuse for not making voters better informed on defence economics, namely that presentation of information on alternative defence systems and their relative costs would offer vital information to potential enemies which, it will be claimed, will reduce the efficiency of defence itself. They clearly have an interest, too, in supporting the conventional wisdom of high technology as the clue to prosperity. What worries us is that the propositions used to support this view are long on emotive appeal and short on economic analysis and empirical evidence.

Conclusion: the need for evidence

Conventional economic analysis, while providing a rationale for combined defence arrangements in respect of burden-sharing and also of greater efficiency, ignores important aspects of the process by which international defence agreements are reached and of the problems associated with keeping them in being. NATO experience can only be understood – with an eye, it is hoped, to seeking improvements in its operation – by employing the broader framework of analysis provided by the economics of politics and public choice. There is a further dimension to the debate about NATO weapons standardisation. It is reputed to offer major cost savings and yet there are few published studies providing reliable estimates of the likely magnitudes. Prior to the Callaghan estimates, only guesses existed. 'One can only guess how much on the average European NATO Allies pay for major equipment as compared with US prices – 10 to 20 percent might be a reasonable guess' (Marshall, 1967). Moreover, proposals for standardisation are often vague and ill-defined. Clearly, an analytical framework is required to identify the sources of potential savings from standardisation, the assumptions of the model, the available evidence on the likely magnitudes involved and the implications of departures from the 'ideal' case. All too often, these issues have been ignored and standardisation has resembled a hazardous voyage of exploration into the unknown!

3
Standardisation: Theory and Evidence

Introduction

The official case for standardisation has been summarised:

> The primary goal of co-operation in armaments is increased military effectiveness within probable NATO budget constraints. The more that equipment, munitions, and their logistic supports are interoperable, if not fully standardized, the more effectively Allied forces can operate together against the common foe. In addition, to the degree that we can rationalize research and development as well as procurement on an Alliance or multilateral basis, there can be a reduction in overlapping programs, increased economies of scale and production, and more effective equipment for the same price. However, these payoffs will take time and will demand far-reaching changes in national practices. The obstacles are enormous and have severely constrained such payoffs in the past (Komer, 1977, p. 207).

Indeed, it has been recognised that ' . . . co-operation in arms procurement can only work successfully through the establishment of a co-ordinated programme within which offsets and compensation can be viewed across a broad spectrum' (North Atlantic Assembly, 1977, p. 345).

Although standardisation is frequently advocated for NATO as a whole, it is noticeable that diversity of weapons is also a national characteristic. Within each member state, the armed forces are far from standardised in terms of administration, equipment, support, training, uniforms and tactics. Consider the apparent duplication of training and of combat aircraft between a nation's air force and its naval air arm. Similarly, the UK air force operates a variety of combat aircraft (e.g. Buccaneer, Canberra, Harrier, Jaguar, Lightning, Phantom, Vulcan), although it plans to replace five different types with the multi-role Tornado. Indeed, at one time, the UK acquired three types of V-bomber, each involving duplicate R & D expenditure, unexploited scale economies due to relatively short production runs

(Valiant 108, Victor 84, Vulcan 124: total 316), and extra support costs. Imagine the savings if the UK had selected only one V-bomber, i.e. produced and operated over 300 of one type. This is the simple case for standardisation at the national level. It is claimed that the savings must be correspondingly greater for NATO-wide standardisation.

It is not the aim of this chapter to comment on the desirability of standardisation, although the continued diversity of weapons within national forces raises interesting questions about the behaviour of independent services (bureaucracies) and the generation of requirements for new equipment. Instead, this chapter presents a model or an analytical framework which identifies the conditions under which standardisation might be expected to result in cost savings. Consideration is also given to the empirical validity of the model. In this context, it has to be remembered that during the 1970s a major policy initiative on standardisation was adopted, despite a surprising lack of analytical and empirical support. Whilst standardisation embraces all aspects of the military production function (i.e. the numbers and productivity of weapons, manpower and the efficiency with which these inputs are combined to produce security and protection), this chapter concentrates on the opportunities for savings within *weapons* procurement.

What are the sources of cost savings?

Standardisation is believed to offer reductions in the unit costs of weapons through a more efficient utilisation of NATO's resources currently allocated to defence R & D and production. Three types of costs saving are claimed:

(a) Savings in development resources are expected if 'duplication and overlap' in R & D work is reduced or even abolished (*ceteris paribus*).
(b) Economies of scale will reduce production costs. Compared with a variety of small scale outputs, the pooling of orders leading to one large production run will result in scale economies and lower unit production costs. At the same time, larger orders for a given type of weapon will enable 'fixed' R & D costs to be spread over a greater output, so further reducing total unit costs (i.e. R & D and production).
(c) Gains from trade will arise if standardisation results in the creation of a free trade area in weapons. On this basis, each NATO member would specialise in those parts of the weapons development and production process in which it has a comparative advantage (i.e. what it does best). In this way, it would reap

the gains from international specialisation and mutually advantageous trade and exchange.

This outline of the sources of cost saving from standardisation suggests a two-stage approach to constructing a model. First, for each nation, it is necessary to identify the shape of production cost curves and the minimum efficient size of firm for each major weapon. What are the absolute cost savings associated with a greater scale of output *within* each nation; and where are American and European firms in relation to minimum efficient size? But answers to this question will not identify which nation within NATO is the lowest cost source of supply for any one weapon. At this second stage, it is necessary to determine the relative position of cost curves *between* nations. Which NATO countries have a comparative advantage for which weapons and what are the possible magnitudes of such cost differences?

The model: economies of scale and gains from trade

Economies of scale are one of the major sources of cost savings from standardisation. Scale economies show the reductions in unit production costs when a firm is able to increase in size by varying all its factor inputs (e.g. machinery, men). Such economies are available at the plant and firm level. They arise from technical factors associated with larger scale *plants* (e.g. division of labour and specialisation; indivisibility or lumpiness of plant and machinery), or from economies in management, R & D, marketing and finance associated with operating a larger *firm* which may be a single or multi-plant enterprise (Silberston, 1972). Once scale economies are exhausted, unit costs cease to fall and this point defines the *optimum* size of firm. Standard economic theory predicts that further expansion of firm size beyond the optimum will encounter dis-economies of scale and rising unit costs. Apparently, management becomes more difficult and the managerial task of co-ordination is reputed to become increasingly more complex and costlier (i.e. there is control loss). The result of these economies and dis-economies of scale is reflected in the economists' traditional U-shaped long-run average cost curve which represents the cost factors determining the size of a firm (Hartley and Tisdell, 1981, Ch. 6). This cost or scale curve assumes given prices for factors of production (e.g. wages, price of machinery) and given technical knowledge. It also assumes that firms aim to operate as efficiently as possible by trying to minimise their costs of operation. As a result, scale curves show the unit costs of producing a product at different scales of output during a specified time period, usually a year. An example of a U-shaped long-run average cost (LAC) curve is shown in Figure 3.1.

44   Nato Arms Co-operation

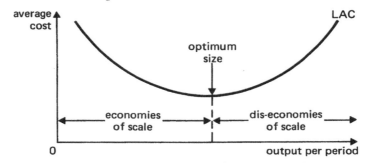

Figure 3.1   U-shaped scale curve. The declining portion of the long-run average cost (LAC) curve shows economies of scale; the rising portion reflects dis-economies.

The relationship between firm size and unit costs is a determinant of an industry's structure. Where scale economies are substantial, a national market might only be able to support one or a small number of firms, resulting in a conflict between efficient scale and competition. The price of efficient scale might be monopoly or oligopoly, with possible adverse effects on prices (including spares), outputs, technical efficiency, choice and innovation.

The evidence on scale curves in the UK, Western Europe and the USA shows that typically they are L-shaped, sloping downwards at first and then tending to become horizontal. The point at which the curve becomes horizontal defines the minimum optimum or efficient scale (MES). Beyond the MES there are relatively few further cost savings. There appears to be little support for dis-economies of scale: this may reflect their complete absence or the fact that in general firms have chosen to avoid such sizes. These conclusions apply to a wide variety of industries. There are, however, few studies of costs in defence industries. In the circumstances, it is necessary to use evidence from related industries as possible proxies for scale curves in weapons. An example of a typical L-shaped scale curve is shown in Figure 3.2, which provides the basis of a simple model of the cost savings from standardisation.

Advocates of standardisation maintain that NATO weapons firms are operating below the MES and as a result are incurring *substantial cost penalties*. Consider various nations operating at different points on the scale curve in Figure 3.2. For example, in the case of aerospace, output Q_1 approximates the requirements of such European states as Belgium, Italy and Norway (say 100 units each), whilst Q_2 could be Britain, France and Germany (say 200–400 units each), with Q_3 representing the USA (say 1000+ units) and Q_4 might be the USSR and the Warsaw Pact (with numbers in the region of 5000+ units). Operating in the range Q_1 to Q_2 results in considerably higher costs

Standardisation: theory and evidence 45

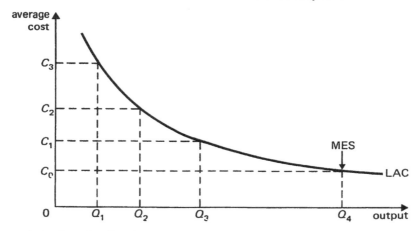

Figure 3.2 Standardisation and scale economies. The figure shows a typical L-shaped scale curve which has been estimated in a variety of American and European industries. This simple case assumes a given and identical cost curve for all nations. However, if, say, the USSR is less efficient than NATO states, it will be operating on a higher scale curve (and vice versa).

compared with producing at Q_4: hence the attraction of pooling orders, as in the F16 European consortium (348+ units) and joint projects such as the three-nation Tornado (809 units; see Part II). Clearly, evidence is required on the unit cost implications of operating below the MES and where different NATO nations are in relation to the MES. Usually, published studies show the cost effects of operating at between one-third and one-half of the MES. In addition to production economies, there are potential savings in R & D. These result from the abolition of 'duplication' and the spreading of fixed development outlays over a larger output, as well as from possible scale economies in R & D work. Figure 3.3 illustrates the effect of a larger output on unit R & D costs. For example, if the R & D bill is £1000 million, then a doubling of output from 100 to 200 will reduce unit development costs from £10 million to £5 million. Estimates of the savings from standardisation need to indicate the reductions in unit costs in development and in production (plus the savings from eliminating something called 'wasteful duplication' in R & D).

Further savings are possible if there are cost differences *between* nations. Consider two countries, with A represented by scale curve LAC_2 and B by LAC_1, as shown in Figure 3.4. At output Q_1 in Figure 3.4, nation B is the lower cost supplier and can produce the output at unit cost C_1 compared with C_2 for country A: the difference between the production cost curves is an indicator of comparative advantage and shows the opportunities for gains from international trade. Na-

46 *Nato Arms Co-operation*

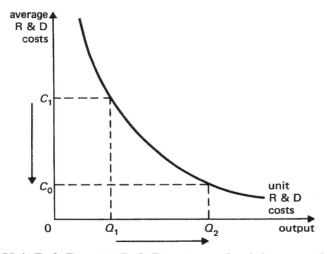

Figure 3.3 Unit R & D costs. R & D costs are fixed; hence an increase in output means that such costs are spread over a greater volume, so reducing *unit* R & D costs. This assume a *given* R & D cost curve, which remains unchanged after 'wasteful duplication' (competition?) has been eliminated. The expected reductions in unit R & D costs might not occur if monopoly is associated with inefficiency (i.e. a shift to a higher cost curve).

tions are also likely to have different comparative advantages in development work, so resulting in different R & D cost curves.

This framework can now be used to analyse the sources of cost savings from standardisation. The possibilities are summarised in

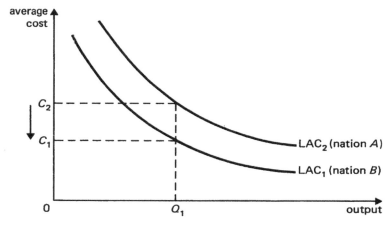

Figure 3.4 Gains from trade. Nation *B* is the lowest cost supplier and could produce Q_1 at C_1.

Figure 3.5. There are two nations, with A represented by LAC_2 and B by LAC_1. Initially, nation A (the USA?) is at the cost–output position (C_2, Q_2), whilst country B (UK or France?) is at (C_3, Q_1) on LAC_1: country B is the lower cost supplier and can produce Q_2 at C_1. If B specialises and produces both Q_1 and Q_2, equal to Q_3, its unit costs will be C_0. There are potential unit cost savings for B of $C_3 - C_0$, and for A of $C_2 - C_0$. Figure 3.5 also shows that under 'independence', nation B can achieve the same unit costs as A at output levels lower than Q_2 – i.e. Q_1' gives unit costs of C_2 for country B. International differences in productivity and wage rates will determine a nation's competitiveness. If A's productivity is twice B's but its wage rates are three times as great, then unit costs will be lower in B (i.e. B's unit labour costs will be two-thirds of A's). But which nations in NATO have a comparative

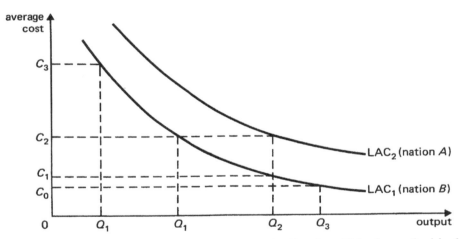

Figure 3.5 The maximum savings from standardisation. This shows the ideal case in which standardisation results in the exploitation of scale economies and of gains from free trade.

advantage for which weapons? And would there be gains from international specialisation and separation of R & D and production work? In other words, the model in Figure 3.5 shows that in estimating the likely savings from standardisation, evidence is required on the cost advantages of operating at a larger scale *within* a nation and the relative position of cost curves *between* nations. Unfortunately, published evidence on cost curves in weapons industries in America and Europe is conspicuous by its absence. But published industrial and international trade studies offer broad generalisations and 'educated guesses' about the potential range of cost savings, so providing some empirical content for the model. However, informed guesses are not perfect substitutes for research studies directed at specific defence industries throughout NATO. Indeed, a major contribution of this chapter will be the identification of data deficiencies. In other words, it will provide insights into what is *not* known and what should be known to answer questions about the likely magnitude of cost savings from standardisation.

How reliable is the evidence on scale economies?

Before reviewing the evidence on economies of scale, some attention has to be given to the problems of empirical work. Is the evidence reliable or suspect? Presumably, the supporters of standardisation have no doubts! Estimating scale-curves requires that variations in factor prices, efficiency and technical knowledge be isolated and held constant. Difficult though this might be *within* a country, the estimation problems are much greater *between* nations. A scale curve for, say, tank manufacture in France with a given set of factor prices may differ from that for another economy with different relative factor prices. In other words, estimates of economies of scale in France or the UK might not apply to other countries. Having recognised the point, one UK study found industries where there were technical limits on the scope for factor substitution (between men and machinery) and cases where the costs of operating capital equipment were a small proportion of costs. So, it was suggested that ' . . . our conclusions would probably apply to many other countries even if relative factor prices were appreciably different' (Pratten and Dean, 1965, p. 13). Indeed, a number of international studies of industries treat the UK and Western Europe as a reasonably homogeneous unit with similar scale curves, but these can differ from US experience (Burn and Epstein, 1972). Problems also arise because of international differences in the definition of an industry and changes in census classifications over time. Estimates of scale have to focus on similar products, on comparable stages of production and on common technologies. Understandably, some economists have their reservations: ' . . . it is important to recognise that the widespread faith in the "economies of scale" has not gained much support from the relevant theoretical and empirical literature' (Gold, 1981, p. 5).

Various techniques are used to estimate scale curves. Since these estimating methods form the basis of the industry studies reported in this chapter, some general understanding of their limitations is required before applying uncritically the estimated scale factors to indicate the possible 'savings' from weapons standardisation. Three estimating techniques are available, namely, statistical cost analysis, engineering estimates and the survivor technique:

(a) *Statistical cost analysis* uses available and actual cost data from firms producing different levels of output. With this method, problems arise because of differences between economists' and accountants' concepts of cost (i.e. opportunity costs and money outlays); variations in products or product 'mixes'; and the difficulties of valuing fixed capital assets based on old, antiquated technology (e.g. different firms use different depreciation methods). Confusions are likely between short-run and long-run curves and, unless all firms are efficient, statistical 'best fits' might not be least-cost. Moreover, there are the standard difficulties of holding constant all causes of cost variations other than scale (e.g. factor prices, technology) and of allocating costs for a single product in a multi-product firm (Smith, 1955). In the circumstances, it has been asserted that cross-section contemporaneous accounting data for different firms give little, if any, information on scale economies: ' . . . accounting cost data tell us nothing about *ex ante* costs of outputs of different sizes, but only about the efficiency of the capital market in revaluing assets' (Friedman, 1955). Further confusions are likely once it is recognised that the existing distribution of firms in any industry reflects 'mistakes' in addition to planned differences designed to exploit any comparative ability.

(b) *Engineering estimates* use experts such as managers and engineers to estimate the cost of production for hypothetical plants of different scale (Pratten, 1971a). This approach is reputed to allow other influences to be held constant, especially technical knowledge and relative factor prices. However, the method usually concentrates on plant economies in production, neglecting firm level economies. It is also subject to the limitations of interview – questionnaire techniques, with a possible bias towards finding large scale economies. For example, the 'best' managers are likely to be interviewed and they might be optimistic about their abilities to exploit scale economies at output levels which are considerably beyond their experience. Nor is it always obvious that 'other influences' (e.g. technology) are being held constant in interview situations.

(c) *The survivor technique* assumes that firms and plants which are increasing their share of industry output over time are of optimal size. It reflects the view that an efficient size of firm is one that meets any and all problems (i.e. it survives). The technique avoids the difficult problem of valuing resources properly. For estimates of the potential gains from standardisation, it is perhaps significant that one US study using the survivor method found a wide variation of optimum firm sizes in each industry (Stigler, 1958). In other words, it might be misleading to focus attention on single-point estimates of optimum size if actual industry structure reveals a diversity of experience consistent with efficiency and survival. But a critic of the survivor technique has claimed that it is an '. . . art, not a purely objective scientific process', and that it cannot safely be used on its own (Shepherd, 1967). For example, in a study of 117 American industries, the survivor test failed to give clear, unambiguous results for over 60 per cent of the sample (Shepherd, 1967). Nor does the technique provide evidence on the slope and shape of scale curves. Moreover, a comparison of the evidence from survivor and engineering methods can give completely different orders of magnitude of minimum efficient scale. For example, in the case of cement the minimum efficient plant size as a percentage of the UK industry's output was estimated to be 1.4 per cent using the survivor method and 10 per cent using engineering estimates (Rees, 1973). But are such conflicting and ambiguous results a reflection of the limitations of the empirical work? Or, do they reflect massive inefficiencies in industry structure in any set of market conditions? The proponents of the latter view are required to explain why such apparently inefficient firms continue to survive, when markets are competitive and there are alternative suppliers. 'If we ask what size firm has minimum costs, and define minimum costs in a sense in which it is in the firm's own interest to achieve it, surely the obvious answer is: firms of existing size . . .: foolish questions deserve foolish answers' (Friedman, 1955). Of course, some national weapons industries in NATO (e.g. aerospace) are subject to government protection and limitations on competition. In which case, the economic arguments for standardisation can be presented convincingly in terms of the mis-allocation of resources associated with government-created imperfections and restrictions on the operation of a competitive market (e.g. monopoly, entry barriers, tariffs and preferential purchasing).

Standard economic theory distinguishes plant- and firm-level economies as the major sources of cost reductions associated with larger firms. Most of the empirical work is on *plant* economies. However, in countries such as the UK, increased concentration has resulted more from a rise in the number of plants owned by firms than through increasing plant size (Prais, 1976, p. 46). Such developments could be consistent with firm-level economies. Alternatively, they could reflect the desire for monopoly power and the managerial pursuit of nonprofit objectives (e.g. a quiet life, size). A British study concluded that over 70 per cent of the variation in the level of concentration can be explained by scale economies (i.e. plant- and firm-level economies) (Sawyer, 1971). But, what little direct evidence there is on *firm*-level economies suggests that they are generally small. *One US study estimated that the economies to a multi-plant firm compared with an efficient single plant enterprise averaged under 2 per cent of unit costs.*

The standard analysis of scale economies is static and it neglects the possible relationship between size of firm and cost-reducing dynamic factors. Technical progress and learning economies are the dynamic sources of lower costs. Supporters of large firms maintain that they promote technical progress. The hypothesis is that only large firms in oligopoly industries can afford the costly research and development necessary for technical progressiveness. However, a survey of empirical work has concluded:

> The hypothesis that sheer size and a monopolistic-type market structure are sufficient prerequisites of a greater volume of research rests on shaky empirical foundations. It is true that R & D effort is concentrated in large firms, but research intensity appears not to increase significantly with size or the degree of concentration of the market (Kennedy and Thirlwall, 1972, p. 49).

There is more convincing empirical support for learning economies as a source of lower costs. Indeed, some of the cost estimates of (static) scale economies include learning effects.

Learning curves, also called experience or progress functions, show the extent to which unit costs decline with increases in cumulative output. The basic idea is that the more frequently labour and management perform a specific task, the more efficient they will become at that task (i.e. they learn by doing). For example, an 80 per cent labour learning curve is typical for the UK aircraft industry (Hartley, 1969). This means that man-hours per aircraft or per unit of weight (pound, kilogram) will decline by 20 per cent for each *doubling* in cumulative output. Thus, the second unit requires 80 per cent of the man-hours for the first unit and the 400th takes 80 per cent of the man-hours for the 200th unit. An example of an 80 per cent labour learning curve is shown in Figure 3.6.

For a number of industrial manufactures, such as aircraft, machine tools, turbo-generators, marine diesels, ships, steel and refrigerators, labour learning curves with slopes of between 60 and 97 per cent have been observed. Tank manufacture approximates a 90 per cent curve. Learning varies between industries and, within an industry, between firms and between different stages of the production process within the firm. A US study of machine tool production estimated labour learning curves of between 75 and 83 per cent with a mean slope of 80 per cent. Learning economies were found to be much greater in assembly than in machining operations: assembly gave an average 74 per cent curve

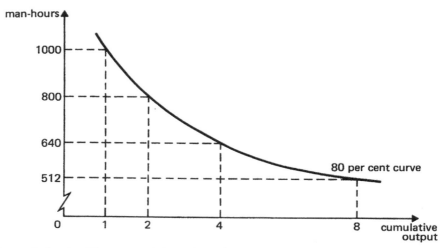

Figure 3.6 An 80 per cent labour learning curve. In production work, labour learning curves of about 80 per cent (79.5–81 per cent) are typical in the UK aircraft industry. In this example, if the first unit requires 1000 man-hours, the second will take 800 man-hours (80 per cent of the first).

compared with 86 per cent for machining (Hirsch, 1956). For shipbuilding, learning curves of between 78 and 84 per cent have been estimated. Similarly, in the 1960s, a major British airframe firm found that a 77 per cent learning curve applied to three of its projects. This 'composite' curve consisted of a 70 per cent curve for assembly, a 76 per cent curve for detail manufacture and a 92 per cent curve for 'other' activities (Hartley, 1969). For the US aircraft industry a 75 per cent labour learning curve is typical for airframes whilst curves of 87 and 89–90 per cent have been estimated for missiles and jet engines, respectively. In other words, there is a diversity of experience and, on *a priori* grounds very little can be said about the magnitude and uniformity of the learning curve. Nevertheless, learning curves for some fifty industries have been identified. On this basis, a general 'rule of thumb' has been proposed namely that, 'the characteristic decline in the unit cost of value added is consistently 20–30% each time accumulated production is doubled. This decline goes on in time without limit . . .' (Cmnd 7198, 1978, p. 82). *Not surprisingly, learning is highly significant in labour-intensive operations.* In addition to learning in production work, there is evidence of similar economies from experience in R & D. A study of British and American airliners found that firms with previous experience from related military and/or civil work might complete a project in about 80 per cent of the time required by a manufacturer without such experience (Hartley and Corcoran, 1978). The extent to which learning or previous experience in R & D

Standardisation: theory and evidence 53

determines a nation's competitiveness depends on whether technical progress is evolutionary or revolutionary. The possibility of revolutionary developments will tend to reduce the benefits of previous experience. But, for decision makers, revolutionary advances are more readily identified *ex post* than *ex ante*. Technical progress is another example of the uncertainties which confront decision makers in weapons procurement policies, including standardisation.

Evidence on scale economies

Industry studies provide evidence on cost–quantity relationships and the minimum efficient scale (MES). The UK is especially well documented and can be taken as typical of the European members of NATO. Ideally, estimates of the cost savings from standardisation require data on actual output in relation to the MES for each type of weapon, and the cost implications of departing from the MES. However, published data are often not available for individual weapons, so cost–quantity information has to be based on broad groups, such as aerospace, electronics, shipbuilding, motor vehicles and 'others' (e.g. clothing, footwear). Obviously, such estimates can be criticised because of massive aggregation. For example, cars and heavy commercial vehicles are taken as typical of the military vehicles group (e.g. tanks, armoured fighting vehicles, self-propelled artillery).

Most of the available British evidence on scale economies, embracing about one-third of manufacturing industry, is summarised in Tables 3.1 and 3.2. This evidence relates to plant or technical economies. Once firm-level economies are considered, it is most likely that the estimates in Tables 3.1 and 3.2 will under-estimate rather than over-estimate the importance of scale economies. For example, a study of the UK machine tool industry found that large firms might gain buying economies of scale equivalent to 2.5–5 per cent savings in unit costs (Pratten, 1971b).

Table 3.1 distinguishes four groups of industries, namely engineering, process, textile and clothing and 'others'. Except for aircraft and electronics, few of the industries are wholly in the defence sector. In the circumstances, five alternative 'guidelines' can be used for estimating the potential cost savings of standardisation policies:

(a) All manufacturing industries could be considered as typical of the UK defence industries as a group. Table 3.2 shows that by operating at the minimum efficient scale (MES) compared with 50 per cent of the MES, unit costs can be reduced by about 10 per cent, a figure which is consistent with other international studies of scale curves (Scherer, 1973).

Table 3.1 *Estimates of the minimum efficient plant scale, UK*

Industry	Minimum efficient plant scale (MES): total output per annum	MES as a percentage of UK output (%)
Engineering		
1. Aircraft	BAC 1-11 type airliner; >50 aircraft	100+
2. Bicycles	160 000 units	8
3. Domestic electrical appliances		
(a) range of ten appliances	500 000 units	20
(b) Electric cookers	300 000 units	30
(c) Electric refrigerators	250 000–800 000 units	22–69
(d) TV tubes	750 000–1.5 million units	100
4. Electronic capital goods		
(a) range of products	Output of £200m (1969 prices)	100
(b) One product (e.g. radar)	1000 units	100
(c) Electronic calculators	3–4 million units	100+
(d) Computers	1000 units or 10 per cent of world market	100
5. Machine tools	300 employees	100+
6. Motor vehicles		
(a) cars	500 000–1 million units	29–57
(b) Heavy commercial vehicles	20 000–30 000 units	5–7
(c) Tractors	90 000 units	76
(d) Clutch mechanisms	300 000 units	12
(e) Automobile storage batteries	1 million units	14
(f) Rubber tyres	5000 tyres per day	6
(g) Anti-friction bearings	800 employees	2
7. Motors		
(a) Electric motors	£10 million (1969 prices)	60
(b) Industrial diesel engines	100 000 units	56
(c) Large marine diesel engines	100 000 horsepower (75 MW) per annum	10
8. Turbo-generators	4 per annum; 8 GW per annum	100+
9. Transformers	10 000 MA per annum	n.a.

Table 3.1 *continued*

Industry	Minimum efficient plant scale (MES): total output per annum	MES as a percentage of UK output (%)
Process industries		
1. Bread	12–30 sacks per hour	0.5–1
2. Brewing	1–4.5 million barrels per annum	3–13
3. Bricks	25 million	0.5
4. Cement	1.2–2 million tons	7–11
5. Chemicals:		
(a) Ethylene plant	300 000 tons	34
(b) Sulphuric acid	1 million tons	30
(c) Ammonium nitrate	300 000–350 000 tons	27–31
6. Synthetic rubber	100 000 tons	25 (?)
7. Detergents	70 000 tons	20
8. Iron and steel		
(a) Steel	2–9 million tons	8–37
(b) Pig iron	2–3 million tons	13–20
(c) Iron castings	50 000 tons (cylinder blocks)	1
(d) Aluminium semi-manufactures	200 000 tons	36
9. Oil refining	10 million tons	10
Textiles and clothing		
1. Cotton and synthetic textiles	37.5 million square yards (31.4 million m^2)	6
2. Synthetic fibres	80 000 tons (polymer)	18
3. Footwear	1200 pairs per day	0.2
4. Wool textiles	20 per cent reduction in the number of mills	n.a.
Other Industries		
1. Books	100 000 (paperback)	n.a.
2. Cigarettes	36 billion	2.1
3. Glass beer bottles	133 000 tons	n.a.
4. Plasterboard	18–20 million m^2	17–19

Sources: Pratten (1971a); Cmnd 7198 (1978).
Notes: (i) The data were collected between the mid-1960s and early 1970s; most refer to the second half of the 1960s. Thus, the estimates are dated and in some cases the MES may now be higher. (ii) Data based on engineering estimates. (iii) GW = gigawatts; MW = megawatts; MA = megavolt-amperes. (iv) n.a. = data not available. (v) UK output figures are based on 1973. (vi) In 1968, R & D as a percentage of net output for some of the industries was: aircraft 33 per cent; electronics 17 per cent; machine tools 4 per cent; cars 4 per cent; diesel engines 6 per cent; turbo-generators 5 per cent; chemicals 4 per cent; oil refining 8 per cent.

Table 3.2 *The slope of scale curves, UK*

Industry	Percentage increase in costs per unit at 50% MES compared with costs at MES (%) Unit costs	Value added per unit	Type of industry	MES as a percentage of UK output (%)
Unit cost increases of 20% or more				
1. Books (hardback)	36	50	O	100
2. Bricks	25	30	P	0.5
3. Dyes	22	44	P	100
4. Newspapers	20	40	O	30
5. Aircraft (airliner of BAC 1-11 type)	>20	>25	E	100+
Mean (1–5)	(25)			
Unit cost increases of 10–19%				
1. Bread	15	30	P	1
2. Electric motors	15	20	E	60
3. Iron castings (cylinder blocks)	10	15	P	1
Mean (1–3)	(12)			
Unit cost increases of 5–9%				
1. Beer	9	55	P	3
2. Chemicals	9	30	P	27–31
3. Cement	9	17	P	10
4. Marine diesel engines	8	15	E	10
5. Electronic capital goods (e.g. radar, computers)	8	13	E	100
6. Domestic electrical appliances	8	12	E	20
7. Motor cars	6	10	E	29–57
8. Steel	5–10	12–17	P	8–37
9. Oil refining	5	27	P	10
10. Synthetic fibres	5	23	O	18
11. Iron foundry (small castings)	5	10	P	0.2
12. Turbo-generators	5	10	E	100+
13. Machine tools	5	10	E	100+
Mean (1–13)	(7)			

Table 3.2 continued

Industry	Percentage increase in costs per unit at 50% MES compared with costs at MES (%) Unit costs	Value added per unit	Type of industry	MES as a percentage of UK output (%)
Unit cost increases of under 5%				
1. Diesel engines	>4	>10	E	56
2. Detergents	2.5	20	P	20
3. Footwear	2	5	T	0.2
4. Sulphuric acid	1	19	P	30
5. Plastic products (range)	Small increase in costs			
Mean (1–5)	(2.4)			
All industries				
Mean	10.48			
Median	8.0			

Source: Pratten (1971a).
Note: E = engineering; P = process; T = textile and clothing; O = other industries.

(b) The engineering sector only could be taken as typical of the defence industries. Table 3.2 indicates that the unit cost savings of doubling output to the MES approach 8–9 per cent.
(c) The few industries shown in Table 3.2 which are *directly* involved in defence could be taken as typical of the defence industries (see also Part II). For aircraft and electronics, the unit cost savings of doubling output to the MES might average some 14 per cent.
(d) The industries where the MES is 100 per cent or more of the UK market could be typical of the defence sector. On this basis, the unit cost savings of doubling output to the MES are in the region of 8–12 per cent. This group includes industries with a high ratio of development to production costs, where a firm with a small total market is at a competitive disadvantage.
(e) The cost data in Table 3.2 could be applied to broad groups of defence-related products. On this basis, the unit cost effects of operating at 50 per cent of the MES for the following items are [1]

	Percentage (%)
Aerospace and guided weapons	<20
Shipbuilding	10
Vehicles (cars)	6
Ordnance and arms	10
Electronics	8
Engineering (average for group)	9
Others	
Turbo-generators	5
Synthetic clothing fibres	5
Footwear	2
Median	8

These estimates suggest that if defence industries are operating at 50 per cent of the MES, there are potential cost savings of between 8 and 14 per cent from operating at the MES. *From this evidence, unit cost reductions in the region of 10 per cent seems a reasonable 'rule of thumb' when output is doubled from 50 per cent of the MES.* Four qualifications are important. First, data are not published on the output of defence industries in relation to *their MES*. If defence firms are operating at less than 50 per cent of the MES, the potential reductions in unit costs from operating at the MES are likely to be much greater due to the steepness of the scale curve at low outputs. This is most likely for highly specialised weapons, such as tracked vehicles. British data on heavy commercial vehicles suggests a 25 per cent unit cost reduction as annual output rises from 3000 to over 30 000 units (Rhys, 1972). But such cost penalties can be exaggerated where there are military versions of civil products or where highly specialised weapons use standard components which are manufactured on a much larger scale (e.g. vehicle engines). Second, the MES is not the minimum cost point. A doubling in scale for firms already at the MES might further reduce unit costs by up to 5 per cent (technical economies only). Third, scale economies are a static concept which neglect the cost reductions from learning by experience. In some cases, labour learning curves have been converted into unit production cost curves by assuming that unit cost reductions are about one-half of the reduction in direct labour costs. An 80 per cent labour learning curve results in a 90 per cent unit production cost curve showing that unit costs decline by about 10 per cent for each doubling in cumulative output. And it has been suggested that learning is typical of a large number of industries (Cmnd 7198, 1978). *If so, advocates of standardisation might claim an additional 10 per cent saving in unit costs from doubling cumulative output.* This assumes that learning economies have not been included in estimates of scale curves (Gold, 1981, p. 7). Fourth, an average saving of 10 per cent from scale economies does not allow for the relative weightings of different defence expenditures. It is simply an average of percentage savings. However, once the various percentage unit cost savings are applied to each category of defence expenditure, the results are changed considerably. Table 3.3 gives a simple example. The effect of assuming that aircraft and clothing have the same cost savings can be compared with a situation where they have different cost savings, even though the average remains 10 per cent.

Table 3.3 *Expenditures and percentage savings*

Item	Expenditure	10% cost saving	15% cost saving	5% cost saving
Aircraft	100	10	15	–
Clothing	10	1	–	0.5
Total amount	110	11	15	0.5
Cost saving		10%		14%

For simplicity, it will be assumed that the UK evidence on scale curves and the MES is generally typical of other NATO nations. There is support for such an assumption. A study of scale economies in France, West Germany, Sweden, the UK, the USA and Canada concluded that there is

> ... little divergence among the views of producers in the six nations with respect to basic process optima, nor did perceived limits on the size of plants which could be managed successfully vary much between nations for a given product mix. *Interviewees who had thought about the problem exhibited remarkable unanimity in their estimates of the minimum cost plant size* ...

(Scherer, 1975, p. 81; see also Weiss, 1976, p. 126; emphasis added). Admittedly, wide variations exist in the size of plants actually chosen, but these are generally explained by identifiable market characteristics. Moreover, this same international study found that in many instances, the cost penalty of operating below the MES was quite small. At one-third of optimal scale, a cost penalty of under 5 per cent was found in nearly half of the products studied and of less than 10 per cent for three-quarters of the products. In other words, the evidence from individual industry studies can give a misleading impression that scale economies for a country's manufacturing sector are more important than is the case on average. Such evidence suggests caution in accepting some of the higher estimates of savings from scale economies. Nevertheless, it has to be remembered that defence industries are often 'different' in that they are frequently protected from domestic and foreign competition, supported by governments and, in some countries, are publicly owned (e.g. aerospace in Britain and France; shipbuilding, steel and tanks in the UK). A study of tank manufacture estimated the costs of the USA, West Germany and the UK each building a different model for their national requirements compared with producing one type for the whole of NATO (Smith, 1979). A total NATO requirement of 21 000 tanks over ten years was assumed. The output of three different types (XM1, Leopard II and Challenger), with at least 7000 of each in the USA and Germany and 1000 in the UK, was calculated to cost almost $23 billion (1979 prices). Minimum efficient scale was estimated at an annual output of 720 units (sixty per month), with the USA and West Germany each operating at this scale, and the UK at around 50 per cent of the MES. If the three nations purchased the West German Leopard tank, each producing 7000 units and each operating at the MES, there would be a possible production saving of almost $2 billion compared with the independent national programmes. This suggests savings in production costs of about 10 per cent from standardisation and scale effects, *plus* a saving of UK development outlays estimated at some $2 billion (1979 prices).

Whilst estimates of the MES appear similar for given industries in NATO, it is possible that nations will be at different points on their scale curves, so displaying varying opportunities for cost reductions from larger outputs. An indication of the extent to which the UK and European nations are actually exploiting available scale economies can be obtained from the evidence on average firm and plant sizes and concentration ratios (de Jong, 1981). Larger plants and bigger firms indicate scale economies and such economies also explain higher concentration ratios. Compared with several European countries, Britain has relatively more large enterprises (i.e. employing over 40 000). In France and West Germany, giant enterprises occur only about half as frequently as in Britain or the USA (Prais, 1976, p. 156). Typically, the largest firms are in industries such as cars, chemicals, electrical equipment and electronics. The largest US firm is twice the size of the largest European unit. As for *plants*, the average sizes are about the same in West Germany and the USA, slightly smaller in the UK, and considerably smaller in France and Italy (Scherer, 1975, p. 65). Elsewhere, most comparative studies of industrial concentration show that the pattern of concentration is similar in industrial nations, with high concentration industries in one country tending to be the high concentration industries in another (Cmnd 7198, 1978, p. 61). Where comparative data are available, it seems that concentration ratios based on the four largest firms are higher in the UK than in Europe (Cmnd 7198, 1978, p. 62). And evidence shows a positive relationship between a firm's market share for a product and its unit cost *advantage* over smaller rivals. Firms with over 40 per cent of the market might have a 10 per cent unit cost advantage relative to firms with less than a 10 per cent market share (Cmnd 7198, 1978, p. 90). Thus, it seems reasonable to conclude that the opportunities for exploiting scale economies are likely to be similar between the UK and Europe. If anything, most European nations appear to operate at a smaller scale than the UK, so that in these countries greater cost savings might be available from larger outputs. Further gains are possible if there are international differences in the relative positions of scale curves. Nations can gain from international specialisation and trade based on comparative advantage. Such gains are likely if standardisation policies create a competitive market and a NATO free trade area in weapons.

What is the evidence on comparative advantage and gains from trade?

There is an extensive theoretical and empirical literature on this subject, so that our treatment must necessarily be superficial. Three questions arise. First, how can a nation's competitiveness be measured? Second, what is the general evidence on competitiveness, including international differences in productivity? Third, what are the likely gains from a free trade area in weapons?

Efforts to measure comparative advantage encounter a series of difficulties. For international comparisons, are we comparing identical products? Consider, for example, the type of cars produced (e.g. size and engine capacity; Maxcy, 1981) in Europe and the USA, as well as the 'mix' of car output by size ranges and price, and also the proportion of commercial vehicles in the total output. Such problems cannot be avoided in international studies of differences in labour productivity by industry (United Nations, 1971). Difficulties also arise when price data are used to measure international competitiveness. Prices can be 'distorted' in relation to costs by tariffs and freight charges, by any price discrimination between home and export markets and by the fact that the current exchange rate might not be in equilibrium. In view of these problems of assessing comparative advantage, only large differences in indicators of international competitiveness for a given product, together with persistent differences in trends between competitor countries, should be used as reliable, but not precise, guides to comparative performance.

One feature of the exchange rate problem is of major importance to weapons standardisation policies. When making international comparisons of expenditure on R & D, official exchange rates are inappropriate – i.e. official exchange rates reflect *traded* goods, but R & D is remote from trade. Thus, international comparisons of national R & D expenditures require the construction of special exchange rates for R & D. The results are dramatic. A study of sixteen nations found that, in all but two cases, official exchange rates appear to be inaccurate proxies for R & D exchange rates (Macdonald, 1973). The British–American R & D exchange rate was estimated to be £1 = $4.76 at a time when the official rate was £1 = $2.8 (1963–4)! From the UK viewpoint, the official rate *understated* the cost of American R & D or, from a US point of view, *overstated* the cost of British R & D. The UK will believe that a project costing, say, £100 for R & D will cost $280 in the USA when, in fact, the true cost is $476. Similarly, the USA will expect R & D work costing $280 to cost £100 in the UK – in reality the UK cost will be £59! Other studies have shown similar results (OECD, 1970, p. 116). For British and American military aircraft, the R & D exchange rate was estimated at £1 = $5.5 in the 1960s. A comparison of the F111 and TSR-2 using this R & D exchange rate concluded that if the TSR-2 had been developed in the USA, the 'effort' would have been similar to the UK effort but, at the official exchange rate (£1 = $2.8), the actual cost would have been twice as great (Royal Aeronautical Society, 1969, p. 36). There are two implications for weapons standardisation policies. First, when official exchange rates are used for international comparisons of R & D, it is claimed that they will distort and misrepresent the value of the real resources employed in R & D in the various countries. Second, for weapons manufacture, international specialisation based on comparative advantage might require that R & D and production work be allocated to different nations. For example, the UK or France might have a comparative advantage in aircraft R & D (or parts of R & D), and the USA a relative advantage in production and in flight-testing. However, such an international division between development and production work is not costless: there are the direct costs and delays in transferring technology from developer to producer nations.

Once these issues are recognised, how can we measure comparative advantage? Various indicators are used to measure a nation's comparative advantage and hence its competitiveness. There are at least five possibilities:

(a) A nation's export performance by product groups measured in terms of levels, trends and relative shares. A popular indicator is whether a nation's share in world manufacturing exports is rising or falling. The economic logic of such an index is simple. Nations with higher efficiency levels in a given industry, relative to industry in general, will register higher export sales for that industry than their relatively less efficient competitors. In other

Standardisation: theory and evidence 63

words, the hypothesis is that costs determine prices and prices determine international competitiveness.
(b) The trend of imports into a nation's domestic markets.
(c) The level of tariff protection. High tariff rates indicates a lack of competitiveness and are a crude indicator of the gains from free trade in weapons.
(d) A balance of trade index, of which there are a number of variants. One measure for each commodity group is $(X-M)/(X+M)$, where X = exports and M = imports. The closer is the ratio to +1, the greater is a country's competitive advantage (Aaranovitch and Sawyer, 1975, p. 249).
(e) Labour costs and international differences in productivity determine unit costs and competitiveness.

Evidence from international studies of comparative advantage, tariff rates, productivity and the effects of forming the EEC provide broad insights into the possible benefits of a NATO free trade area in weapons. Between 1953 and 1971, the USA had a strong and increasing comparative advantage in research-intensive products (e.g. aircraft, chemicals, electrical machinery, office machinery and pharmaceuticals). Aircraft continued to occupy first place on the American comparative advantage scale (Balassa, 1977). By contrast, research-intensive industries did not rank among the first ten on the comparative advantage scale of the other major industrial nations. Instead, the 'revealed' comparative advantage of the EEC mirrors the US *disadvantage* in non-durable consumer goods, such as clothing and textiles. Also, the USA is at a relative disadvantage in the labour-intensive shipbuilding industry (Balassa, 1977). However, these are no more than broad generalisations and do not imply that Europe has no comparative advantage in any areas of high technology. A US study of relative price advantages within NATO concluded that 'There does not appear to be any distinct pattern with respect to the "high technology-low technology" distinction' (Wolf, 1978, p. 143). Europe is, for example, price competitive in some relatively high technology weapons (e.g. the Harrier VTOL aircraft and the Roland II missile). Nor should too much emphasis be placed on *past* performance. The whole point about technical progress is that it does not follow precedents: it creates them!

The level of tariff protection also provides an indication of the gains from free trade in weapons. For example, in the 1950s, for a sample of weapons, average EEC tariff rates varied between 5 and 15 per cent; UK rates varied up to 30 per cent, whilst the USA imposed tariffs of up to 46 per cent. Similarly, in the 1960s, British military aircraft were protected by a tariff rate of between 30 and 50 per cent: the decision to buy TSR-2 rather than the F111 was equivalent to imposing a notional tariff of 100 per cent or more on the US aircraft (Cmnd 2853, 1965). But one of the classic examples of protection was the Buy American Act, which prevented the US Defense Department from purchasing foreign-produced equipment unless the price was 50 per cent lower than the price of similar US products. Policy changes occurred after 1975 with the US willingness to waive the Buy American Act in the interests of standardisation, its negotiation of MOUs to promote freer competition in weapons markets, and its acceptance of two-way streets.

International trade advantage – at least for EEC nations – appears to be *positively* related to relative plant size (i.e. plant-level economies of scale seem more important than firm-level economies; Owen, 1976). However, relative plant size is only a crude indicator of international differences in productivity. For example, in 1968, median plant size in British manufacturing (480 persons) was larger than in the USA (420 persons); but output per head was so much greater in the USA that the median American plant's net output was just over double that of the median British plant (Prais, 1976, pp. 144–62).[2] Indeed, the evidence generally shows that US productivity is higher than in the UK, France, Germany and Sweden (Scherer, 1975, p. 73). In the case of France, it has been estimated that over nineteen manufacturing industries, the average US–French labour productivity ratio was 2.06, with the American 'advantage' in the capital-intensive industries (e.g. cars, chemicals, machinery; Chandraseker, 1973). Differences in rates of output and length of production runs are a major explanation (but not the only one) of the productivity differentials between the USA and Europe, including the UK. Typically, an American manufacturer's output is three to four times that of his UK equivalent. And, on average, a doubling of output increases labour productivity by some 14 per cent (Pratten, 1976, pp. 29–31; Pavitt, 1980). However, since 1955, the gap between US and European productivity levels has narrowed considerably, as shown by the broad magnitudes and general trends in Table 3.4. In 1960, US labour productivity was about twice that in Europe; by 1977, American productivity was only one-third higher and in some cases the gap is now quite small (Maddison, 1979). But, during the 1970s, Europe's traditional advantage of lower wage rates compared with the USA was substantially reduced by relative inflation and exchange rate variations. Table 3.4 shows that by 1976 the price and exchange rate index for Europe was 148 compared with 113 for the USA (1970 = 100).

Estimates suggest that the benefits from the creation of the European Common Market were quite small, as little as 1 per cent of Community GNP (Swann, 1970, p. 36). The reasons for such small benefits are significant for weapons standardisation policies. First, only a small part of total output enters international trade. Second,

Table 3.4 Productivity and costs

Country	Labour productivity: GDP per man-hour (US$ 1970 prices) 1950	1960	1970	1977	Average labour costs per employee in 1976 (EUR)	Gross product per person employed in 1976 (EUR)	Index of domestic prices in 1976 (1970 = 100)	Variations in prices and exchange rates in 1976 (1970 = 100)
Belgium	2.19	2.98	4.84	7.19	9394	13794	164	168
Denmark	1.82	2.45	4.04	5.02	9215	12841	172	169
France	1.67	2.56	4.28	6.05	8393	12764	165	151
West Germany	1.43	2.75	4.64	6.39	9164	13987	143	163
Italy	1.28	1.97	3.68	5.17	5308	6718	207	123
Netherlands	2.09	2.88	4.68	6.41	10577	15192	167	180
UK	2.25	2.83	3.91	4.63	4883	6976	214	126
USA	4.11	5.22	6.67	7.65	9491	14253	146	113
EEC(9)					7259	10576	167	148

Sources: Maddison (1979); Cavallari and Faustini (1978).
Notes: (i) EUR = European common units of account at current prices and exchange rates. (ii) EEC(9) = European Economic Community consisting of the seven European states in the table plus Eire and Luxembourg.

examples of really costly protection are rare. In other words, most of the gains from international trade based on comparative advantage are already being obtained, since no nation can afford *not* to reap them. Applied to weapons standardisation policies, such conclusions imply that the likely gains from a free trade area in weapons might be quite small (i.e. most of the gains are already being reaped)! However, the advocates of standardisation policies might claim that weapons are one of the few instances of really costly protection, in which case the potential benefits are likely to be significant. In this context, one study of Britain's entry into the EEC suggested that the gains from free trade might be equal to the additional benefits of increased scale economies. In other words, the total gains could be twice the gains from scale economies only (Williamson, 1971, p. 45).

For the prophets of doom who claim that the abolition of protection will mean the end of their beloved industry, it is relevant to stress that industrial studies of the effects of free trade frequently show a diversity of experience even within one product group. For example, with chemicals, a free trade area between the USA and the UK would result in each nation having a comparative advantage in different sectors of the chemicals industry (Burn and Epstein, 1972, p. 252). Similarly, a study of the EEC concluded that ' . . . the position of Britain's manufacturing industries relative to the EEC's is not a matter of right-across-the-board strength of some sectors accompanied by marked weakness of others, but rather of each sector having its more promising and its relatively vulnerable parts' (Han and Liesner, 1971, p. 99).

To summarise, various pieces of evidence suggest that there are potential and substantial gains from free trade in weapons. First, there are differences in relative prices. For example, *some* British weapons are not price-competitive with US equipment (e.g. fork lift trucks); whilst for turbo-generators in North America, UK prices have been 10–20 per cent *below* the prices quoted by US suppliers (CPRS, 1976, p. 56). In the mid-1970s, UK cars were at a 10 per cent cost disadvantage compared with their EEC rivals (CPRS, 1975, p. 93). Similarly, even if British and US steel makers produced at the MES, they would still incur a cost penalty of almost 20 per cent compared with Italy (Cockerill, 1974). Second, the evidence on tariffs. Nominal tariffs are misleading indicators of protection. In 1971 *effective* rates of protection were higher than nominal rates by a factor of about 33 per cent for the UK and some 60 per cent for the EEC (NIESR, 1971, p. 41; Maddison, 1979, p. 28). For the UK, some of the highest effective rates of protection applied to the engineering sector (e.g. 38.5 per cent for electrical machinery). European countries also seem to protect their R & D intensive industries (Constantapoulus 1974). Third, defence industries are likely to be heavily protected, especially when it is remembered that domestic governments use preferential purchasing policies (e.g. TSR-2 and F111; Buy American Act). In the circumstances, a free trade area in weapons is likely to produce additional cost savings of some 10 per cent across the board; and this is likely to be a lower bound estimate. The estimate is based on the following propositions:

(a) A nominal tariff rate of some 10 per cent is taken as typical for NATO nations (full forward shifting is assumed). The Buy American Act suggests a much higher rate for weapons!
(b) The gains from free trade might be similar to the savings from scale economies; and a figure of 10 per cent was plausible for scale effects.
(c) The estimate can be made with some confidence. Once allowances are made for effective tariff rates and government preferential purchasing, the unit cost savings from a NATO free trade area could be as high as 20–30 per cent and over, at least for some weapons.

Conclusion

A model has been presented for identifying the sources of cost savings from weapons standardisation under the 'ideal' situation where scale economies and gains from trade are fully exploited. A survey of the published literature has provided some empirical content for the model. *Standardisation in weapons procurement could result in unit cost savings of 20–30 per cent comprising the following:*

(a) Scale effects, following a doubling of *output per period*, might reduce unit costs by 10 per cent.
(b) Learning economies from a doubling in *cumulative output* could also reduce unit costs by some 10 per cent. However, it has to be recognised that learning economies are sometimes included in scale effects, so that there is a danger of double-counting (hence the 20–30 per cent estimate).
(c) Free trade effects, via competitive markets and comparative advantage, could result in further savings of 10 per cent. Not only is this figure derived from international trade studies (e.g. on tariffs and effects of EEC) but it is further supported by evidence on the effects of introducing competition into defence markets. Increased competition in the US defence market reduced production costs by 8–9 per cent: the figure is likely to be higher in the non-competitive European markets where some major weapons firms are state-owned (Ashcroft, 1969).

A figure of 20 per cent should be regarded as a lower bound estimate of the unit cost saving opportunities from NATO standardisation in weapons acquisition. Further savings are available in support or life cycle costs, as well as from any abolition of 'duplicate' R & D (development expenditure of £1000 million per project is typical of modern weapons). The evidence suggests that NATO policy makers should direct their standardisation efforts towards the industries with the greatest scale factors, namely those where there are substantial cost penalties from operating below the MES (Tables 3.1 and 3.2). But, of course, these are often the sectors where nations 'value' independence. Moreover, the model used to estimate the likely gains is based on a number of assumptions. These have to be specified in order to appreciate the limitations of any estimates of cost savings. Finally, the estimates are based on the 'ideal or best case' situation: they will be reduced where higher cost policies are adopted (e.g. constraints on competition and free trade; Tucker, 1976).

Notes

1 Shipbuilding is not shown in Table 3.2, but the estimate is based on an 80 per cent learning curve converted to a 90 per cent unit production cost curve (for each doubling in output). Ordnance and arms data are not available, so it was assumed that the sector is typical of the whole group shown in Table 3.2 (average).
2 In making the USA–UK comparisons, Prais (1976, p. 284) uses a purchasing power parity exchange rate of £1 = $3.1 in 1968 (official rate was £1 = $2.4). With international differences in wages, high labour cost nations, such as the USA, are likely to operate larger plants to be cost competitive (i.e. to reduce man-hours). For turbine generators, the MES in Western Europe is 8000–10 000 MW, compared with 15 000 MW in the USA (Burn and Epstein, 1972, p. 74).

4
Standardisation Policy: A Critique

Introduction: some problems

Any critical appraisal of weapons standardisation policy has to start from the assumptions of the model used to estimate the maximum cost savings (Chapter 3). Then, it has to be recognised that policy will be formulated in political markets of governments, bureaucracies and interest groups, with the inevitable tendency to depart from simple economic models aimed at efficiency and least-cost solutions. The implications for industrial policy and the compensation of potential losers cannot be ignored. Nor can choices be avoided. Choices require information on the costs and benefits of alternative weapons procurement policies and these will be presented in a programme budget framework. Here, it has to be recognised that choices are subjective and will depend on the preferences of the choosers. The range of items included in any cost–benefit assessment and their valuations will obviously differ between nations which, in turn, will differ from the viewpoint of NATO as a whole. NATO as a collective body is likely to value highly the standardisation aspects of alternative procurement policies, whereas a European member of the Alliance might be more concerned with promoting high technology. This chapter aims to develop a *general* information framework for assessing alternative procurement policies, which can be adapted and used in a variety of perspectives.

What are the assumptions of the model?

The model outlined in Chapter 3 is based on a number of assumptions. Their specification provides an indication of the limitations of the model and its associated estimates of cost savings from weapons standardisation. The major assumptions of the model (Figure 3.5) are given under the next six subheadings.

The pricing policy for weapons

A full cost or average cost pricing model is assumed, with weapons prices based on unit costs plus a profit mark-up (Hartley, 1969; Hartley and Tisdell, 1981, Chs 7 and 15). In other words, it is assumed that reductions in unit costs will be reflected in lower prices. Otherwise, the cost savings of larger scale will not benefit consumer nations through lower prices, with implications for the distribution of gains between producers and consumers. Clearly, the prices of weapons will depend on a firm's objectives, the presence or absence of actual or potential competition, and the form and extent of government regulation of defence contractors. If standardisation policies restrict competition, there are potential *adverse* effects through monopoly pricing, especially for spares. For example, consider the European belief that US aircraft are 'cheap', but you 'pay' for the spares: this argument is sometimes used to support an independent UK aerospace industry. The worry about monopoly pricing is reinforced when it is remembered that the estimated gains (to whom?) from standardisation also depend upon a nation's pricing policy for recovering its R & D costs on major weapons.

The internal efficiency of firms

Firms are assumed to be technically efficient, with the scale curves representing cost-minimising behaviour. However, in non-competitive markets, such as defence, enterprises are likely to be characterised by organisational slack or X-inefficiency. Competition acts as a possible self-policing mechanism, inducing firms to minimise costs. If standardisation is associated with greater competition in NATO weapons markets, the resulting 'shock effect' leading to cost-minimising behaviour, will be a further additional source of cost savings. US evidence shows that, with scale economies taken into account, competition within a national market can reduce average costs by about 10 per cent (Leibenstein, 1978, p. 209). In the case of weapons, one American study has estimated savings of at least 25 per cent on average from a competitive procurement policy (Hall and Johnson, 1968). But the outcome depends on a competitive 'shock effect'. If standardisation creates monopoly, it could cause inefficiency! Consider the possibility that standardisation will eliminate 'wasteful duplication' in R & D. Immediately, there are problems of choice under uncertainty. The 'correct' development programme is usually apparent with hindsight: it is more difficult to select the winner *ex ante*, in a state of relative ignorance. 'Experts very often are wrong not only in what they predict will happen but also in what they predict won't happen' (Nelson, 1981, p. 1047). Moreover, once a development programme has been chosen, the winner secures a monopoly, thereby losing the stimulus and incentive to efficiency provided by rivals. Standardisation proposals need to be much clearer on the extent to which competition is to be used, or avoided, in the various stages of a weapon's life cycle (Chapter 1; Tisdell, 1981).

No dis-economies of scale

However, a major expansion of firm size beyond existing experience levels might encounter managerial dis-economies and hence rising unit costs. Also, if production is concentrated in a few localised plants, there could be dis-economies in transport and distribution. Any such dis-economies will *reduce* the estimated cost savings from standardisation. This could be a particular problem for European nations, such as country B (UK, France?) in Figure 3.5 (Chapter 3): will country B follow LAC_1 if output levels of Q_2 and Q_3 were to be feasible? For example, the UK aircraft industry has no experience of US production runs and there might be learning costs for a new entrant into the large scale league. Indeed, in the UK and some European aircraft industries, evidence shows that learning curves tend to 'flatten out' and become horizontal at a relatively early stage (e.g. 100–200 units) whilst in the USA learning seems to continue indefinitely. The resulting cost curves are shown in Figure 4.1, which suggests that nation B only has a comparative advantage for weapons involving short production runs.

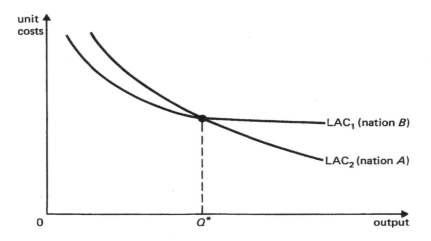

Figure 4.1 Cost curves. Possible shapes of cost curves based on evidence from the European and US aircraft industries. Nation B is the least-cost producer up to output Q^*, after which A becomes the least-cost supplier (see Figure 3.5). Dis-economies of scale would cause both cost curves to rise.

The adjustment period and associated requirement for a re-allocation of resources

The maximum cost savings from standardisation are only possible when all NATO nations are in a position to change their stock of weapons. To achieve the maximum cost savings will require a re-allocation of resources to reflect each nation's comparative advantage in weapons development and production. Such a re-allocation will take time and might require the introduction of public policies to 'improve' the allocative process, especially in labour markets (Hartley, 1974, p. 66). Similarly, if standardisation concentrates output in a smaller number of firms, an expansion of capacity will be required, with inevitable delays in the delivery of weapons during the adjustment process. The appropriate time-scale for the adjustment period is clearly a matter for public debate. Even with complete agreement and harmony between governments on the most desirable form of standardisation(!) some five to ten years is likely to be the *minimum* adjustment period.

Ceteris paribus

The model assumes given technology and relative factor prices. But markets are dynamic and not static, especially for weapons. Whilst the future is uncertain, it can be predicted that technology and relative factor prices will change, and that these changes will occur within as well as between countries. With technical progress and changes in productivity and factor prices, a nation's comparative advantage will change; and these trends will be reflected in market exchange rates. What are the likely trends in technology and the major exchange rates over the next ten or twenty years? Within a standardisation framework, such questions cannot be ignored, since the answers (forecasts) will clearly affect the 'optimal' procurement policies. Standardisation policies cannot assume a static world in which today's (or yesterday's) pattern of international comparative advantage and trade flows will necessarily apply in the future. No one can predict the future accurately. The task for policy makers is to create an institutional and market environment which allows firms to adapt and adjust to change (e.g. permits new entrants to weapons markets). In this context, it is not at all obvious that governments and bureaucrats guided by interest groups have a comparative advantage in predicting the future accurately.

Other policy targets

Economic theory shows that a 'best' or optimum allocation of resources, as reflected in a competitive free trade system, represents the maximum savings and benefits which can be obtained from standardisation in weapons procurement. Policies leading to a departure from the competitive solution (e.g. work-sharing; co-production; collaboration based on political criteria) are likely to result in smaller savings than the maximum available. Departures from the best case are usually explained in terms of a government's concern with wider policy objectives, such as the balance of payments, domestic jobs, national security and high technology. Often, worries are expressed about the employment effects of NATO standardisation, particularly in defence industries and in regions dependent on weapons contracts. For example, it has been estimated that if the UK adopted a competitive procurement policy, employment in its aircraft industry could fall by 50 000–100 000 (Hartley, 1974, p. 66). But such estimates have to be considered in terms of developments in the economy as a whole and the determinants of aggregate employment. Here, general evidence on the employment effects of increased imports is relevant. Whilst increased imports might have serious local or industry-specific effects, the evidence shows that, in general, their impact on employment in developed nations is small in relation to total employment (or to job quits). American studies found that in 1969 some 77 000 jobs were lost for every $1 billion of imports (1969 prices): this was 0.1 per cent of civilian employment and 3 per cent of imports (Hsich, 1973; also Hartley, 1982). Much depends on the other determinants of total employment in an economy, namely the level and composition of aggregate demand (e.g. government spending and taxation), productivity, export performance, wage levels and the operation of the labour market. Even the local employment effects of increased imports can be exaggerated. For example, between 1951 and 1966, with import competition, employment in the UK Lancashire cotton textile industry fell by 60 per cent, or 215 000 workers. The labour force re-adjusted through outward migration and greater diversification of industry in Lancashire (regional policy): between 1955 and 1964 unemployment in the textile areas was close to the national average (Hsich, 1973). In other words, labour markets can, and do, adapt and adjust to change. Nevertheless, the fear of unemployment from NATO weapons standardisation and the concern of national governments with wider policy targets cannot be ignored in policy formulation. The result is likely to be a substantial departure from the 'best' case model, as nations attempt to 'protect' their national interests and bargain over a 'fair' share of NATO defence business. On this basis, NATO weapons standardisation is inextricably associated with industrial policy in the member states.

Weapons standardisation and industrial policy

To its advocates, standardisation and co-ordination of weapons procurement from development to production aims to create 'healthy and controlled competition', which would eliminate 'needless' duplication whilst achieving ' . . . rationalization, specialization, fairness and equity in all procurements, including trade liberalization, offsets . . ., and removal of restraints of any kind' (Cornell, 1980, p. 19). Even where these aims can be specified clearly and unambiguously, there are potential conflicts between some of them (e.g. specialisation and equity). Often, the impression is created that all standardisation is good and more is desirable, regardless of costs. Less attention is given to the implications for industrial structure, market performance and public policy. References are made to the need to create 'healthy and controlled competition', and to avoid 'needless duplication', the aim being to emulate the long production runs of the Warsaw Pact. But to provide the basis for a NATO industrial policy such concepts as 'controlled competition' and 'needless duplication' have to be defined. For example, does 'controlled competition' mean free or restricted entry of firms to all NATO weapons markets; and does it require competition at the design, prototype and production stages in the life cycle of new weapons? What type of centralised decision-making and co-ordinating framework is required to 'create, regulate and control' the 'optimal' industrial structure for NATO weapons standardisation? Would such a centralised unit have the technical competence and the political ability to select the 'winners' *ex ante*, so avoiding 'wasteful duplication'? As stressed above, choices made without competition from alternative developments (duplication?) are more likely to be wrong. Nor is it obvious that an efficient industrial structure can be reconciled with an allocation of work which is 'fair and equitable', providing all NATO members with opportunities for participation.

Frequently, the alleged industrial benefits of standardisation are based on the Warsaw Pact model which avoids duplication and obtains economies of long runs. But this does not necessarily mean that the Pact's industrial structure is more efficient. In the absence of competition, inefficiencies can emerge in development and in production compared with, say, the USA and other NATO arms industries. The danger is to assume that all industries operate on a single and unique least-cost curve and that the USSR is way down such a curve, whilst NATO is not: cost curves can have different positions and slopes. Clearly, evidence, is required on the comparative efficiency of weapons industries in NATO and the Warsaw Pact.

There are examples where incentives to efficiency in R & D and production seem to be greater under competitive private enterprise than under nationalisation and collective ownership. The US aerospace industry believes that competition in R & D is a major factor in the industry's competitive advantage. Also, the existence of rival US suppliers for airframes, engines and components ensures competitive bids for production and sub-contract work, so that major contractors can exploit the gains from specialisation. Admittedly, there are other weapons industries in NATO which operate in highly protected, non-competitive and regulated markets where there are substantial opportunities for inefficiency. In these circumstances, economic theory would favour a free trade area in weapons with competitive bidding for fixed price contracts where firms would be at risk, with every incentive to be efficient. Government profit controls on defence contracts would be abolished, with competition acting as a 'policing and monitoring' device. Critics of competitive solutions are required to explain how their alternative market arrangements would operate and how firms would behave.

The alternatives to a competitive solution are government-regulated, imperfect markets with non-competitive cost-plus type contracts. Is this what is meant by 'healthy and controlled competition'? Such arrangements are inefficient. Government regulation often benefits the regulated industry rather than society. Managers in regulated firms also have incentives to pursue objectives other than profits. They might prefer a quiet life, on-the-job leisure, luxury offices, pretty secretaries, generous expense accounts and company cars. Cost-plus type contracts provide the financial framework for inefficiency as reflected in organisational 'slack', labour hoarding, cost escalation, time slippages and 'excessive gold-plating'. In non-competitive weapons markets with cost-based contracts, firms have every incentive to 'buy into' an attractive new programme by submitting optimistic cost, time and performance estimates (see Table 4.1). The successful contractor acquires a temporary monopoly and its optimism will be financed by the government so that the penalties for under-estimation are likely to be absent. In fact, cost-plus contracts in which the firm recovers all its costs regardless of their level, plus a state-determined profit margin, are believed to offer little or no efficiency incentives: they have been called 'blank cheque' contracts (Hartley and Tisdell, 1981, Ch. 14).

Bureaucratic solutions also have potential for failure. Budget-conscious bureaucrats in Defence Ministries, the armed forces and state-owned or nationalised weapons industries are likely to over-estimate the demand for a preferred weapon and to under-estimate its costs. Examples of cost escalation on American and British weapons projects are shown in Table 4.1. It can be seen that cost escalation factors of 2.0 or more are typical on advanced technology weapons. Decision-making governments have to determine the reliability of the cost estimates, as well as time and performance estimates, which are

Table 4.1 Cost escalation on weapons

Project	Cost escalation factor
1. *UK 1958 sample*	
100 projects	2.8
Airframes	2.3
Guided weapons	17.4
Munitions	1.9
2. *UK 1965 sample*	
Aircraft and missiles ($n = 16$)	2.7
3. *UK military aerospace projects, 1953–70* ($n = 13$)	2.7
4. *UK Army sample*	
25 projects	1.7
Pre-1964	2.7
1964–65	1.6
Post-1965	1.4
5. *Individual UK weapons*	
Mk 31 Torpedo	5.3
Type 41 Frigate	1.7
Major refits	1.4
6. *US aircraft and missiles*	
1962 sample ($n = 12$)	3.2
1965 sample ($n = 15$)	2.9
7. *Individual US aircraft*	
F100	1.2
B47 (median)	1.25
B52 (median)	1.4
C133	1.55
F111 (median)	1.98
B58 (median)	3.8
C5A (median)	1.36

Sources: Harman (1970, Hartley and Cubitt (1978), Knutton (1972), Peck and Scherer (1962).

Notes: (i) Cost escalation is actual development costs divided by original estimate. (ii) Examples of time escalation or slippages: UK 1965 sample = 1.3; UK Army ($n = 25$) = 1.3; US 1962 sample = 1.36; US 1965 sample = 1.3.

presented as a basis for weapons procurement choices. Otherwise, cost estimates which are 'too low' can lead a government to buy 'too much' of a project which appears to be relatively cheap. Once started, projects are difficult to stop. Bureaucracies can also arrange and present information to support their case. It will be claimed that a new project is 'vital' to a nation's defences and will prevent the country sliding down the international league table. Comparisons will be made with other nations which subsidise high technology defence industries. Emphasis will be given to the valuable (but difficult to quantify) technological fall-out for the rest of the economy, to the possibility of a new industrial revolution and the provision of the next generation of jobs, and the need to avoid being dependent on foreign ideas. Governments seeking re-election might be attracted by these alleged benefits, especially if state support for high technology seems to offer a solution to a country's economic problems. International collaboration is particularly appealing since bureaucrats and politicians further benefit from opportunities for foreign travel, bargaining for a 'fair' share of the work, allocating contracts and ensuring that the national interest is protected. In contrast, bureaucrats can always oppose a competitive free trade solution for weapons as 'impracticable', as well as involving imports with associated 'losses' of jobs and valuable foreign exchange. The result is a set of myths about weapons procurement policy: analysis and evidence are conspicuous by their absence. And yet, sensible public choices require information on the costs and benefits of alternative weapons procurement policies. An information framework is required which identifies the consequences of alternative decisions and the magnitudes of likely 'trade-offs' involved in different courses of action.

A framework for choice

In purchasing weapons, nations are faced with four broad policy alternatives, ranging between the extremes of complete independence and purchasing everything from abroad. The alternative policies are as follows:

(a) *Complete independence*. This is extreme nationalism where a country purchases all its weapons from domestic firms only. For European members of NATO in particular, complete independence is costly, involving the sacrifice of the potential gains from international specialisation and trade. Within Europe, independence means that a nation has to bear all the R & D costs of modern weapons and, unless it is a successful exporter, its production runs will be relatively small. And yet, NATO nations continue to favour some independence in weapons procurement. What are the benefits of independence and how much are nations willing to pay for these benefits? Case studies provide insights and some examples are given in Part II. For instance, if the UK had purchased its Phantoms 'off the shelf' directly from the USA, their unit prices might have been some 23–43 per cent *lower*. Such estimates are also an indication of the possible gains from standardisation in combat aircraft; alternatively, they show the cost penalties of work-sharing arrangements which depart from the assumptions of the 'best case' model of standardisation (Chapter 3).

(b) *Behave as a competitive buyer and shop around.* Search for the 'best buy' and purchase from the lowest cost supplier in NATO or other markets, where the manufacturer offering the lowest cost could be a domestic or foreign firm. Competitive bidding would be organised, with firms invited to submit clearly defined proposals with legally binding contractual commitments on price, performance and delivery dates. This option can range from the purchase of a completely new weapon 'off the drawing board', or an agreement to buy a weapon still in its development stage, or an 'off the shelf' purchase of existing equipment.

(c) *International collaboration* involving joint development and production. Here, a distinction might be made between international projects involving two or more nations, with the partner firms selected by governments, and international collaboration where firms are left to select their partners on commercial criteria. Joint projects appear to be ideal for weapons standardisation. A typical case might be two nations each producing an aircraft with R & D costs of £1000 million (duplication), each with domestic requirements for 200 units. *Ceteris paribus*, a joint venture with equal sharing would save £1000 million on R & D (i.e. £500 million per nation) and result in learning economies which would reduce unit costs by 10 per cent as output is doubled from 200 to 400 units. There are other benefits of joint projects. Each partner retains a domestic defence industry; it continues to be involved in high technology; and compared with a national venture, it obtains a product which is more competitive in export markets. But 'other things' are not held constant on actual joint ventures. Each partner might require modifications which will increase R & D costs and reduce some of the economies from long runs. Each nation will also demand a 'fair share' in each sector of advanced technology (e.g. airframe, engines and avionics), and might insist upon duplicate final assembly lines. Thus, joint work is frequently allocated on equity rather than efficiency criteria. As a result, joint weapons projects are unlikely to lead to the cost savings of the 'ideal' case, although there might be savings to each partner compared with a single national programme.

(d) *Licensed production, co-production or work-sharing* (e.g. F104, F16, AWACS for NATO). These involve the domestic manufacture of another nation's weapons, either wholly or in part. It is believed that this option results in higher costs than if the output had been purchased directly 'off the shelf' from the original manufacturer. Higher costs for licensed production might result from shorter production runs and the loss of learning economies, duplicate tooling and the costs of transferring technology. There are also licence fees, which could be some 10 per cent of sales. In return, manufacturing under licence saves substantial R & D resources which would have been required for an independent national venture. American officials have estimated that despite cost escalation due to modifications, the licensed manufacture of the French–German Roland missile saved the USA between $400 million and $600 million of development expenditure compared with a national venture (1977 prices; North Atlantic Assembly, 1977, p. 147). Balance of payments problems can also be avoided, work is provided for skilled labour, domestic defence capacity is maintained and there are possible benefits from access to new production technology. The valuations placed on these social benefits can be estimated by comparing the extra costs of licensed manufacture with an 'off the shelf' purchase. Once again, case studies such as the European co-production of the F16 and industrial collaboration on the AWACS for NATO can provide evidence on the likely magnitude of costs and benefits associated with this policy option.

In choosing between these four broad policy alternatives, or selecting a 'mix', a government has to know the costs of the options and their effects on its policy objectives. Table 4.2 outlines an information matrix or programme budget which would show policy makers the consequences of alternative choices and the magnitude of the 'trade-offs'. The table is only designed to illustrate the approach. The four broad policies described above are shown, although the list could be extended to include further variants. Possibilities include a foreign purchase with offsets or work-sharing on the same project or involving a family of weapons; alternatively, at the NATO level, there could be competing development projects between, say, an American firm and a European firm or consortium, with the 'winner' manufactured on a co-production basis throughout the member states of the Alliance. Indeed, whilst the framework in Table 4.2 is presented in terms of a national government, it can be adapted to provide a collective NATO view of the costs and benefits to the Alliance of alternative policies. In which case, NATO would presumably place a high valuation on the standardisation implications of weapons procurement and this would enter the list of benefits.

Ideally, the options in Table 4.2 should be for a given weapon with specified performance, delivery dates and quantity. It might be a requirement for 300 combat aircraft capable of a speed of 3000 m.p.h. (4800 km h), a range of 3000 miles (4800 km) in all weathers, with first delivery in 1990 and completion by 1995. This approach assumes a given contribution of the weapon to a nation's defence output. Atten-

Table 4.2 *Choices and a programme budget*

Policy	Total price		Features of weapon (assume a given quantity)		Contribution to NATO			National economic benefits			
	Acquisition	Life cycle	Performance	Delivery schedule	National defence	Standardisation	Collective defence	Jobs	Technology	Balance of payments	Others (specify)
1. *Complete independence* (i.e. independent R & D and production)											
2. *International collaboration involving R & D and production*											
(a) Firms selected by governments											
(b) Firms selected on commercial criteria											
3. (a) *Licensed production*											
(b) Co-production											
(c) Work-sharing											
4. *Competitive buying*											
(a) At the design stage											
(b) During development											
(c) 'Off the shelf'											

Standardisation policy: a critique 81

tion can then be focused on the costs of the alternative policies and their implications for other policy targets – e.g. how much extra would it cost the USA, or the UK, etc., to undertake a given (identical) project, holding constant its quality, quantity and time-scale? Of course, other things are rarely held constant and the usual situation is one where choices are required between weapons differing in performance and time-scale, as well as costs. Typically, the choice framework in Table 4.2 might be for different types of aircraft, ships or tanks (e.g. US XM1, German Leopard and UK Challenger tanks; Metcalf and Edmonds, 1981). For each class of weapon and for each policy option, information is required on the following:

(a) *The expected life-cycle costs of the weapon.* The costs of acquiring and operating a weapon throughout its expected life might be one and a half to two times the initial capital expenditure. The extra costs of each policy, compared with not purchasing from the least-cost supplier, need to be expressed in terms of the sacrifice of numbers, possible delays in delivery, and quality implications – all of which will affect defence output (e.g. probability of survival, number of targets destroyed). For example, a modern combat aircraft might require R & D expenditures exceeding £1500 million (1982 prices), without resulting in one aircraft in operational service. How many F14s, F15s, F16s, Mirages or Tornadoes could be obtained for such an outlay and what would be the effect on defence output?

(b) *The expected life-time benefits of the alternatives.* Ideally, Defence Departments are concerned with defence objectives and other government departments should be responsible for job, technology, and balance of payments targets. But states with an established weapons industry usually wish to retain their capacity. The USA is no exception. Its substantial weapons industry and world power status means that politicians, bureaucrats and producer groups (firms and unions) are generally reluctant to purchase a foreign weapon directly 'off the shelf': there is a preference for licensed manufacture of *complete* systems, with foreign companies restricted to competing for sub-systems. Similarly, European nations fear 'undue' dependence on the USA for supplies and spares, with a possible loss of independence in foreign policy, monopoly pricing and technological domination. A domestic defence industry seems to contribute to the security of supply, responds to national defence requirements, provides jobs and promotes high technology, as well as saving and earning foreign exchange.

Whilst the list of benefits appears impressive and persuasive, there remain considerable opportunities for critical evaluation. The exact nature of the benefits has to be specified; the alternative use value of resources cannot be ignored; and evidence is required. For instance, are the employment benefits of a policy defined in terms of the total number of jobs, or by type of skill, or by location (e.g. in a high unemployment area), and what are the magnitudes involved? Similarly, any balance of payments target has to specify the expected value and time-scale, always assuming this to be a legitimate policy aim in an era of floating exchange rates. Here, it has to be remembered that some weapons projects involve a time-horizon of 20 years or more, which requires reliable long term forecasts of trends in a nation's balance of payments! As for advanced technology benefits, these require estimates of numbers, type and their value to a nation's economy. Difficulties of measurement should not discourage attempts at quantification. Often measurement problems indicate that there is nothing to measure! In this situation, budget-conscious bureaucrats have every inducement to claim that their output is 'priceless', cannot be quantified and is incapable of being accurately assessed using vulgar notions of cost–benefit analysis. Rarely is it asked whether the resources used in domestic weapons projects would make a greater contribution to jobs, balance of payments and technology objectives and, ultimately, to human satisfaction, if they were used elsewhere in the economy.

In view of the frequency with which some of these arguments about jobs, technology and the balance of payments are used to support the *status quo* in weapons procurement policy, a more detailed appraisal is required. The arguments are best seen in terms of the standard case against buying weapons from abroad. After all, if NATO weapons standardisation is to achieve the maximum cost savings, all member states will have to be more willing to buy from abroad.

Jobs, technology and balance of payments benefits: the case for nationalism?

The case against importing weapons provides the basic arguments in favour of a domestic defence industry. Generally, advocates of a national source of supply claim that defence is 'unique and different' (all interest groups believe that their industry or occupation is unique – e.g. coal miners, deep-sea fishermen; teachers). The precise case for a domestic weapons industry (its uniqueness) can be summarised as follows:

(a) Defence industries are characterised by high technology (e.g. aerospace, electronics, nuclear power, shipbuilding, vehicles). They are reputed to be the technological leaders contributing to innovation which, it is then asserted, determines a nation's rate of economic growth. It is further maintained that defence high technology is much less likely to be copied by rival nations.

(b) High technology is a continuous process. Buying abroad disrupts the accumulation of knowledge and creates a technology gap which is costly to remove if ever the nation wishes to re-enter the field.

(c) A domestic defence industry will contribute to the balance of payments through import-saving and export earnings. Indeed, the case for supporting weapons manufacture is sometimes expressed in terms of similar state support given to other domestic industries (e.g. agriculture, coal-mining, shipbuilding); as well as the protection given in foreign nations.

(d) A domestic defence industry provides a national source of supply which contributes to increased security and some independence in foreign policy. Dependence on a foreign monopoly can be avoided, which otherwise might lead to higher prices of equipment and spares, as well as weapons not designed for national requirements. Further benefits from a domestic industry include greater control over a project and its continuation, as well as freedom to export to the rest of the world.

(e) Overseas purchases of weapons will require a re-allocation of resources out of domestic defence industries and into other sectors of the economy. It is claimed that such a re-allocation will result in unemployment, a waste of highly specialised skills and emigration. There will be losses of tax revenue to the national Treasury and increased expenditure on unemployment pay. Such budgetary effects are then used to argue for applying a premium (protection) to overseas purchases of weapons. In the UK during the early 1970s, estimates suggested that home prices could exceed overseas prices by *at least* 10–15 per cent before a foreign purchase of weapons could be justified.

Each of the above arguments for a domestic defence industry is subject to an alternative and contrary view. In the case of high technology, evidence shows that since 1945 inter-country differences in productivity growth rates are *not* correlated with inter-country differences in R & D spending (Nelson, 1981, p. 1035). A critic of UK R & D policy has stated that,

> The mistakes of the past were to place too much emphasis and to commit too much of the available money to too many big projects,

aircraft, rockets, etc. . . . . The argument is that more of Britain's top scientists should be applying themselves to the real problems of the country rather than to fields most exciting to the scientists themselves (Maddock, 1977; see also Henderson, 1977; Pavitt, 1982).

As for the need for continuity and the problem of technical gaps, much depends on the nature of technical progress and evidence on the relative costs of continuity versus breaks. Previous experience is less relevant where technical progress is revolutionary rather than evolutionary. Similarly, with the balance of payments argument, it is not sufficient to argue that purchasing overseas tends to increase the disequilibrium in the balance of payments. Presumably all imports have this effect! Nor is it obvious that weapons procurement policy is the most appropriate instrument for improving a nation's balance of payments: other measures include a general deflation of public and/or private expenditure, import controls or variations in the exchange rate. Moreover, the fact that some other domestic industries are protected might be an argument for changing policy towards these sectors rather than extending protection to weapons manufacture. And the 'foreign rivals are subsidising' argument is also dubious since, if foreigners wish to offer free gifts, a nation could respond by willingly accepting them and specialising elsewhere. At this point, advocates of a domestic defence industry argue that once the national industry has contracted or disappeared, there are dangers of being dependent on a foreign monopoly which will charge higher prices. But, if this is an argument against buying American, it fails to recognise that the US weapons market contains rival suppliers. Paradoxically, the alternative is for each European nation to become dependent upon a protected, small scale and inefficient domestic monopoly! Here, critics of overseas purchases often modify their argument and claim that some minimum domestic weapons capacity is required, although rarely do they define and justify the appropriate minimum size (is it the *status quo*?) What, for example, would be the costs and benefits of a slightly smaller domestic capability than the required minimum? There remains the employment argument.

Given that the Western economies are likely to be confronted with major unemployment problems during the 1980s, it is likely that the jobs argument will dominate economic policy, including weapons procurement. Consider the argument used in the UK, which might be taken as typical of other European members of NATO. *If* the purchase of weapons from a British supplier had the effect of reducing the level of UK unemployment, the net cost to the Treasury of buying domestic equipment (i.e. the price of the equipment − additional tax payments− social benefits saved) could well be less than the net cost associated with the purchase of cheaper foreign equipment. It is then suggested that, in these circumstances, the government should, when comparing the cost of domestic and foreign weapons, *add* to the price of the foreign equipment a premium (cf. a tariff) whose size would depend on assessments of the UK labour market. Once this approach is accepted, the next question concerns the appropriate size of the premium and whether any general guidelines can be formulated. A starting point would be to assume that if overseas purchases of weapons result in unemployment and unused capacity in UK defence industries, then a 'buy British' policy would be costless, since the resources have no alternative use value – i.e. they would be otherwise unemployed and society would not sacrifice anything else by using the resources for producing weapons. A modified version of this approach concentrates on labour only and would require the government to estimate the *numbers* and duration of unemployment resulting from a decision to acquire a foreign weapon (do you assume no offsets, co-production or work-sharing?). This would give an estimate of the jobs saved by buying British, so providing a basis for devising an operational formula for the premium:

$$\text{Premium} = N \times M \times D \times C$$

where N is the total *direct* employment per annum – i.e. jobs saved, M is the employment multiplier to allow for direct and indirect employment effects (Greenwood, 1979, p. 342), D is the number of years or duration of the project, and C is the annual Exchequer costs of unemployment.

As an example, assume that a UK buy 'saves' 10 000 jobs per annum; that the employment multiplier is about 2; that project duration is ten years; and that the Exchequer costs of unemployment are £3800 per person per year (1981–2 prices). The estimate of unemployment costs includes lost tax receipts and National Insurance contributions, the payment of unemployment and social security benefits, rent and rates rebates and administration costs (HM Treasury, 1981). As a result, the estimated premium to be applied by the UK is £760 million (i.e. the amount to be added to the foreign price, or deducted from the UK expenditure). However, this only provides a broad indication of the 'upper bound' of the premium. Ideally, the estimate needs to be expressed in present value terms. Nor is it possible to ignore the specific assumptions being made about the operation of the UK labour market.

The case for applying a premium or using a shadow price for labour cannot be separated from a government's judgements about the expected duration of unemployment, wage rates and labour mobility, all of which will affect the extent to which the labour market will 'clear' (i.e. remove surpluses and shortages). Obviously, in the UK in the early 1980s, the shadow price of *some* labour in *some* regions will be substantially below the ruling wage rate. But shadow pricing is only relevant to labour which would be otherwise unemployed. Not *all* British defence workers are likely to be unemployed if the UK acted as a competitive buyer and purchased more weapons from overseas. Skilled workers would probably obtain jobs quite quickly whilst, over the life cycle of a new weapon project, today's unemployed might be a 1990s shortage. Also, British defence industries have a comparative advantage in some products, so that they would not be eliminated completely. And, in advocating a UK buy, it is not sufficient to argue that large scale unemployment means that the labour employed has no alternative uses: this is equally valid for any UK policies which provide jobs for the unemployed (e.g. building roads, painting old people's homes). Thus, some criterion other than shadow pricing is required to justify state support for the domestic defence industry.

The major deficiency of the employment as well as the technology and balance of payments arguments for supporting a domestic defence industry is their general neglect of costs and the alternative-use value of resources. Using the choice framework in Table 4.2, buying from abroad appears unattractive in terms of its jobs, technology, etc., benefits. But this is deceptive and misleading since it ignores the alternative use value of the resources released from UK defence industries – i.e. their contribution to employment, technology and ultimately, human satisfaction, when used in other industries in the economy. Take the case where a US weapon is the cheapest buy for a nation such as the UK. There will be three effects. First, there will be increased UK spending on other weapons, or higher public expenditure on civil goods, or lower taxes will lead to more private spending; and, to Keynesians, increased spending will lead to more output and hence more jobs in Britain. Second, higher US exports will raise the level of internal spending, which will eventually result in more imports into America, some of which might be supplied by the UK. Third, the resources released in the UK will be re-absorbed elsewhere in the economy (Kaldor *et al*, 1979). Here, consideration has to be given to *net* benefits: would the resources used in the UK defence industry make a *greater* contribution to employment, technology, the balance of payments and human satisfaction if they were used elsewhere in the economy? Consumers in properly functioning markets would determine where the resources would be re-employed. Critics dismiss this approach for its failure to specify which industries would attract the released resources and whether these would be high technology. However, the future is uncertain and no one can predict it accurately. Who in the UK in the 1950s forecast the discovery of North Sea oil and the demise of the British car industry? At the time of the Industrial

Revolution in the UK, when the textile industry was the leading sector, who forecast the development of the aviation, car, chemicals and electricity industries? Should the fact that no one could forecast these developments have led to government support for the textile industry? In the last resort, the issue is whether properly functioning private markets with large numbers of rival firms, risking their funds and seeking profitable opportunities, are the 'appropriate' solution to choices under uncertainty; or whether state solutions relying upon vote-sensitive politicians and budget-conscious bureaucracies are likely to be 'superior' (Hartley, 1979). This is not to deny that if NATO regards a free trade area in weapons as desirable, it will require appropriate adjustment policies, particularly towards labour markets. Re-training, mobility, information and regional policies will provide a mechanism by which the gains from free trade can *compensate* the losers. Otherwise, groups likely to bear the adjustment costs of increased foreign competition will seek to persuade election-conscious governments to protect existing defence industries.

Conclusion

The pursuit of NATO weapons standardisation encounters numerous paradoxes. There are claimed to be 'vast' cost savings from standardisation, and yet NATO nations have seemingly 'failed' to exploit the apparently worthwhile opportunities for international specialisation, trade and exchange. Is this because the savings have been exaggerated, or are nations adjusting to the situation by adopting various sharing arrangements to reduce the cost penalties of independence? Could it be that a degree of independence is regarded as worthwhile (i.e. its benefits are believed to be at least equal to the costs), so that the imperfections in NATO weapons markets have to be seen as *government-created* and hence preferred? It is also fascinating to observe the USA as a major example of capitalism and competition advocating socialist solutions as reflected in the Warsaw Pact 'model'. Furthermore, the governments of the major trading nations accept the benefits of specialisation and international exchange for the majority of goods, but continue to present defence as 'different'. But weapons standardisation policies are also advocated in the political market place. The case for NATO standardisation is presented as 'overwhelming', but there is little critical appraisal. Perhaps this is not surprising when the proposed policy solutions remain vague and ill-defined. For example, is it envisaged that there will continue to be competition (i.e. duplication?) in R & D and in production? What criteria will be used for selecting the winners, and who will select them? Selection will involve group choices, with all the problems of predicting the likely behaviour of individuals in a committee. Any NATO procurement choices will be made by coalitions of self-interested, rather than selfless, individuals which need to be given specific rules for choices, with rewards and penalties based on performance. Ultimately, the worry is that all the gains from 'ideal' NATO standardisation will be appropriated in inefficiencies as each nation, responding to its political market, demands its 'fair' share of defence work. At this point, case studies can make a contribution to the debate by providing evidence on the magnitude of the costs and benefits of actual policy choices. Such studies can contribute to policy formulation by showing what was expected and what was actually achieved, bearing in mind that governments and politicians change and that the valuations of policy targets are subjective. Certainly this chapter and the choice framework of Table 4.2 has posed a set of questions: Part II of this book aims to provide some answers.

Part II
Aerospace

5
The Research Design

Introduction: aims of the research

It has been shown that NATO weapons standardisation policy is an area which is dominated by vague ideals, numerous but unsuccessful policy initiatives and a general lack of serious independent analysis, critical appraisal and empirical evidence. Part II aims to remedy some of these deficiencies, especially the lack of evidence. It reports the results of a detailed study of military aerospace projects, using a general cost–benefit approach to appraise alternative weapons procurement policies (see Table 4.2). This chapter explains the choice of aerospace, the research methodology, and the sample of firms included in the study.

Why study aerospace?

Various procurement policies have been advocated as a means of improving weapons standardisation and reducing unit costs. Each option has different cost–benefit implications for a nation and for NATO as a whole, and the preferred solution will depend upon the policy objectives and constraints facing decision makers. In this study, the choice framework was represented by the alternative policies outlined in Table 4.2, namely complete independence, acting as a competitive buyer, licensed manufacture or co-production, and collaborative or joint ventures. Questions have already been raised about the *magnitude* of the costs and benefits of these alternatives, and the possible contribution of each policy to greater NATO weapons standardisation. The research study concentrated on the implications of alternative procurement policies for *aerospace projects*, thereby embracing the American and European industries and markets. Aerospace was chosen for a number of reasons:

(a) It illustrates the classic conflict between nationalism and free trade. It shows all the economic and political pressures favouring domestic suppliers for costly, advanced technology weapons. Examples include the UK purchase of the Nimrod AEW rather than involvement in the NATO AWACS scheme, and the American and French preference for domestically supplied combat aircraft (e.g. French Mirage series). Aircraft appear to be 'ideal' candidates for standardisation policy because they have high unit values and relatively short production runs, particularly in Europe. Indeed, the classic 'trade off' emerges between the real income gains from specialisation and international trade in a NATO common weapons market or free trade area, and the alleged sacrifices of jobs, technology (and the related human capital) and the balance of payments associated with a completely independent domestic defence industry. An indication of the gains from free trade can be obtained by considering the price implications of a nation acting as a competitive buyer and 'shopping around'. Examples of foreign purchases directly 'off the shelf' include the US purchase of British Harriers, and the UK acquisition of American transport aircraft and helicopters (e.g. Hercules and Chinook).

(b) It provides evidence on work-sharing, licensed manufacture and co-production. Examples include the UK work-sharing on its purchase of American Phantoms; European industrial collaboration on the NATO AWACS programme; the European licensed production of US aircraft and missiles (e.g. F104, Hawk and Sidewinder missiles); the American co-production of the French–German Roland missile and British Harrier, as well as the European F16 consortium. These options are likely to be costlier than buying 'off the shelf' from the established supplier. But what is the evidence on the cost penalties? One study has estimated that the F16 co-production programme will cost the European nations 18 per cent more than if they had purchased the aircraft directly from the USA. It has also been estimated that, as a result of co-production, the USAF will pay some 3–8 per cent more for their F16s (North Atlantic Assembly, 1977, p. 134). These are some of the prices which have to be paid for standardisation through co-production.

(c) It provides evidence on joint projects where two or more nations agree to share the development and production costs of a new project. Collaboration is undertaken where independence is regarded as 'too costly', usually because of the scale of R & D required (or 'too risky' in the case of civil projects). Consideration of the range of collaborative European ventures provides an indication of the scale and type of project which some NATO nations can no longer afford to undertake alone. Examples include complex strike aircraft such as the British–German–Italian Tornado; the Anglo-French supersonic airliner and the European Space Agency's involvement in space satellites. Other examples of European collaborative ventures include the Anglo-French helicopter package, the French–German Alpha Jet Trainer and the Euromissile Dynamics Group. Such joint projects enable a nation to retain its domestic defence industry and reap the 'benefits' of continued involvement in high technology work. In this form, collaboration resembles a *club*, with a small group of nations combining to purchase a set of benefits (e.g. technology, weapons, jobs) which each would be unwilling to finance independently. Joint arrangements are believed to be an appropriate solution to 'greater rationalisation, less wasteful duplication and increased weapons standardisation' within NATO, and particularly for the traditionally 'small, fragmented and inefficient' defence industries in Western Europe (Hartley, 1981b).

(d) It illustrates the tensions within the Alliance between the USA and Europe. No analysis of NATO weapons policies can ignore the USA because it is a major buyer as well as a competitive supplier of aerospace equipment. Explanations are required of the American industry's competitive position, its likely impact on the pricing of weapons and spares, and its effects on the transfer of technology. Such explanations might also provide 'guidelines' for government policy towards the European aerospace industries.

Thus, a study of American and European aerospace projects, their industries and markets provides evidence on the costs and benefits of alternative weapons procurement policies viewed from a national perspective. The diversity of benefits and differences in their valuation between nations means that this aspect of any public choice is more difficult to analyse and assess. In contrast, the cost implications of alternative policies are more readily quantifiable and this provides a solution to the problems of valuing any benefits. *If a departure from the least-cost method of acquiring weapons involves extra costs of $X million, does society believe that such expenditures are worthwhile* (i.e. would they be better spent on other things)? In other words, are the benefits of the higher cost policy valued at $X million or more? Empirical economists have the task of measuring X. A starting point is a model which outlines the cost implications of the alternative policies.

The costs of alternative policies: a simple model and complications

Start with the simplest case, assuming that all NATO nations have a given and identical cost curve, with unit cost differences reflecting variations in the scale of output. An example is shown in Figure 5.1,

94 Nato Arms Co-operation

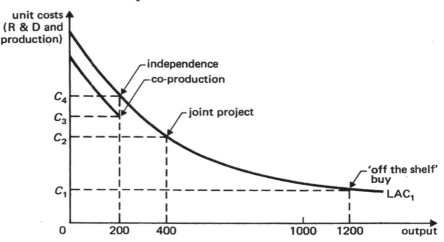

Figure 5.1 The costs of alternative policies: a simplified example. This simple example is based on a single cost curve, with unit cost differences reflecting variations in the scale of output – i.e. spreading of R & D costs and scale economies, plus learning.

where R & D and production costs are represented by the long-run average cost curve, LAC_1. A nation requires 200 units of an aircraft. A preference for independence will result in unit costs of C_4 per copy. Licensed manufacture or co-production is cheaper at C_3 per unit, since the buyer is assumed to save on R & D costs compared with independence. Collaboration with equal sharing and a total output of 400 units would involve unit costs of C_2. In contrast, a purchase of 200 units from an existing production run of 1000 (e.g. an 'off the shelf' buy from the USA) will result in unit costs of C_1. An estimate of the magnitude of the savings in *production costs* can be obtained by using a simplified 90 per cent unit cost curve showing that unit costs decline by about 10 per cent for each doubling in cumulative output. For example, an increase in output from 200 to 400 units will reduce unit production costs by some 10 per cent (e.g. independence versus collaboration). Additional savings in unit costs will result from the spreading of fixed R & D outlays over a larger output.

The analysis can be modified to incorporate more realistic assumptions. It can be assumed that nations have different relative costs (i.e. comparative advantages) and that joint projects can be inefficient (often termed technical or X-inefficiency). Consider Figure 5.2, which for simplicity is confined to *production* costs only. Three cost curves are shown for nations A and B, together with a collaborative venture.

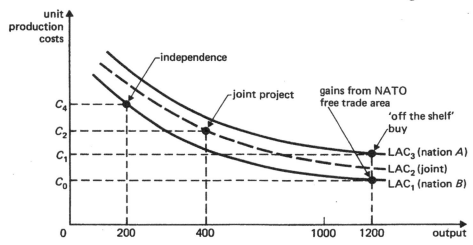

Figure 5.2 The costs of alternative policies: some complications. Nations are likely to have different relative costs and international collaboration may be inefficient.

For nation B, operating on LAC_1 and requiring 200 units of a combat aircraft, an independent solution would involve unit production costs of C_4. Licensed or co-production for the same nation is assumed to require identical unit *manufacturing* costs (a nation without a domestic aircraft industry might incur higher unit costs for licensed work). A joint venture for 400 units is assumed to involve some inefficiency, operating on LAC_2, and resulting in unit costs of C_2, which are still less than under independence. An 'off the shelf' purchase of 200 units from nation A, already producing 1000 units and operating on LAC_3, would result in unit costs of C_1. For comparison, the creation of a NATO free trade area in weapons, with specialisation by comparative advantage, would exploit the maximum gains from trade. Nation B is the least-cost supplier and could produce 1200 units at C_0 per copy. As a result, there are potential cost savings of C_4-C_0 for nation B and C_1-C_0 for country A. A similar analysis can be applied to R & D, showing that a larger output will reduce unit R & D costs and that nations might have different comparative advantages in R & D work. But Figure 5.2 only establishes *qualitative* relationships which form the basis of testable hypotheses. The relative position of the cost schedules is an empirical matter: what are the quantitative magnitudes? For example, evidence might show that the cost curves intersect, with nation B a low-cost supplier for a small output and country A being the least-cost source for larger outputs (see Figure 4.1).

Research methodology

Evidence on the costs of alternative policies and an indication of the associated benefits was obtained from an interview questionnaire study. Copies of the questionnaires used in the research, together with a summary of the responses are shown in the Appendices. To economists, weapons procurement is a particularly attractive research area since it embraces a range of methodological, analytical, empirical and policy issues, all of which were relevant in formulating the questionnaires and interpreting the results. Methodological problems arise in determining how economists can and should analyse co-production and joint projects. Extensive opportunities exist for applying economic theory, including models of market structure and performance, and firm behaviour in state-regulated markets, international trade theory, and the appropriate form of organisation for international collaboration, as well as the economics of public choice. Analysis also suggests a variety of testable hypotheses, ranging from propositions about the competitiveness of the American aerospace industry to the possible magnitude of inefficiency on joint projects. The resulting policy issues embrace a search for performance indicators and evidence on the implications of different choices and the impact of the political market.

The research project used two questionnaires designed for firms and joint projects. The *firm* questionnaire was used as the basis for a structured interview and all firms in the sample were asked a standard set of questions. Major aerospace firms in the USA, the UK, France and West Germany formed the sample, and interviews were conducted with senior company executives. Whilst the sample embraced all the major airframe units in NATO, it was inevitably restricted by limitations of time, finance and geography. American firms were included because the USA is a major buyer as well as a competitive supplier of aircraft, with considerable experience of licensed manufacture and co-production, but no previous involvement in joint projects. The questionnaire for firms was divided into six sections, each designed to test specific hypotheses on the following:

(a) *The efficiency of the US, British and European aircraft industries.* Does efficiency differ and, if so, why? Questions embraced efficiency, time-scales, and the major features of the US industry, as well as a set of hypothetical questions about how American firms would have performed if they had undertaken such projects as Tornado, Jaguar and Harrier. In view of the European 'fear' of a US monopoly, this section also included questions about monopoly pricing and spares pricing. Europeans often maintain that 'US equipment is cheap, but you pay for the

spares'. In this context, evidence is provided on spares pricing policy by US companies.
(b) *The economics of aircraft manufacture in Europe and the USA.* This section asked questions on the length and rates of production, learning curves, the sources of lower unit costs and the ideal or optimum size of firm. It explored the extent of competition (number of rivals) and the likely results (on size, structure and prices) of a free market in weapons. Questions were also asked about the effects of introducing competition into procurement. For example, what are the likely effects on costs, time and escalation of a 'fly before you buy' policy? The responses to all the questions in this section were useful not only in testing hypotheses, but also in predicting the likely effects of alternative weapons procurement policies – e.g. a NATO free trade area, and the cost savings through buying directly from the USA (see evidence on US learning curves compared with the UK).
(c) *Alternative weapons policies.* Five options were considered, namely to buy at home, to buy abroad, joint collaborative products, international consortia (with the partners selected on commercial criteria, without government interference) and licensed manufacture or co-production, including industrial collaboration (e.g. work-sharing). Questions were designed to identify some of the costs of alternative policies (e.g. effects on R & D and production costs), as well as the preferences of firms.[1]
(d) *The benefits and costs of joint collaborative projects, including co-production.* Various benefits were considered, such as the effects on cancellation, standardisation, jobs and technology. Possible costs included compromises in operational requirements, administration, escalation and profitability.
(e) *Licensed manufacture and co-production.* Why do firms become involved in licensing or co-production; how do they determine fees and work-sharing arrangements and how profitable is the work? In considering alternative procurement policies, evidence is required on the effects of licensed production on unit costs, jobs and technology transfers.
(f) *Exports.* Questions were asked about export pricing and profitability. Such questions provide further evidence on firm behaviour and their possible response to a NATO free trade area in weapons (e.g. is there any inducement to sell abroad; it is profitable?).

Appendix A shows a copy of the firm questionnaire, together with a summary of the responses of the US and European companies included in the sample. Further supporting interviews were conducted with NATO officials, the US Department of Defense, the UK Ministry of Defence and the F16 Program Office in Brussels. Since joint ventures raised a different set of questions, they were the subject of a separate questionnaire.

The *joint* projects questionnaire (Appendix B) was used to test specific hypotheses about such ventures (e.g. collaborative premia). Interviews were conducted with all the major UK, French and West German airframe firms involved in joint projects, together with a sample of engine and equipment companies, as well as senior officials in the UK Ministry of Defence and NAMMA in Munich. The questionnaire for joint projects was also divided into six sections, some of which were identical to those in the firms' questionnaire:

(a) *The organisation of procurement for joint ventures.* Efforts were made to assess the efficiency and performance of procurement staffs of different sizes and varying forms of organisation.

(b) *Industrial organisation.* What criteria are used to allocate work between different national companies and what are the implications for employment and the transfer of technology?

(c) *Operational requirements.* What is the extent and form of any compromises in operational requirements on collaborative projects?

(d) *The economics of joint projects.* Do joint ventures involve higher costs and longer time-scales than if the work had been undertaken in one nation? If so, why and how much higher? Alternative estimates of collaboration premia can be incorporated into any assessment of the cost savings from joint ventures.

(e) *Standardisation and support costs.* What is the effect of standardisation on unit support costs? In view of NATO standardisation policy, do we have any evidence on the magnitude of cost savings over a weapon's life cycle? The answers are revealing. There was general agreement that there would be cost savings, but there was little knowledge of the likely magnitudes!

(f) *The benefits and costs of joint projects.* The answers provide a European perspective from firms involved in joint ventures and they can be compared with the views of US companies in the firm questionnaire (Appendix A). Similar comparative questions were asked about the efficiency of the US and European aircraft industries. Once again, the answers can be compared with the views of US companies.

Appendix B shows the joint projects questionnaire together with a summary of responses from the European companies and officials with actual experience of such ventures. The firm and the joint projects questionnaires present original material which the reader can use as a general data bank for undertaking his own calculations of the implications of alternative policies. However, the questionnaire results are subject to a variety of limitations:

(a) Not all the questions were answered by all the respondents, nor were they always answered in the desired form (e.g. rankings proved difficult to obtain). Frequently, time constraints prevented a comprehensive coverage of all the questions.

(b) Questions containing a section for 'other' responses provide additional information, as well as insights into the extent to which the original questionnaire design contained a comprehensive set of predictions (e.g. some aspects of behaviour, etc., might only be revealed through answers to the 'others' section).

(c) The greater the number of identical or similar responses, the more reliable the generalisation.

(d) Care has to be taken to minimise or avoid biases on the part of the interviewer and of the respondent. For example, should the interviewer 'prompt' the respondent and suggest possible answers? Bias amongst respondents can be reduced by including different questions on the same theme, thereby providing some check on the consistency of replies. Additional checks were provided by pairwise comparisons (e.g. F111 and Tornado) and the examination of specific procurement choices (e.g. UK worksharing on Phantoms and its decision to buy the Nimrod AEW).

(e) Questionnaires only test *beliefs*, although these may be the basis for choices and decisions. However, further difficulties can arise in identifying the 'real' decision makers.

(f) The sample may be limited and small, so doubts arise as to whether it is 'representative'. However, in the area of weapons procurement, questionnaires are often the only method of obtaining information and testing hypotheses.

(g) There are difficulties of holding constant 'other relevant influences' and assessing the *quantitative* importance of any one variable. Here, one possibility is to ask which is the most important amongst a set of influences. Then, its quantitative importance can be assessed by asking whether it accounts for most of any changes (e.g. over 75 per cent of the change), or very little (e.g. under 25 per cent of the change). It is also recognised that some questions are extremely simplified. For example, most nations adopt a 'mix' of procurement policies, rather than relying upon one solution. Nonetheless, responses to simplified questions provide evidence on the limiting cases, and qualifications could always be made during the interview–discussion.

Conclusion

Why has there been so little NATO standardisation? The aerospace industry provides the classic answer: there are national industries in the USA, the UK, France, West Germany, Italy, Canada, the Netherlands and Belgium. As a result, high R & D costs have to be spread over smaller outputs and there are fewer opportunities for economies of scale and learning. The remainder of Part II presents the results of a research study using interview–questionnaire techniques in which firms were asked for their views. Ultimately, it is firms which provide one of the basic foundations for the operation of any market, responding and adapting to government-imposed constraints. Officials from government defence agencies were also interviewed. In addition, pairwise comparisons of similar aircraft provided an alternative method of assessing the efficiency of joint projects compared with a domestic 'buy'. Further insights into the valuations which governments have placed upon such policy targets as jobs and technology were obtained from specific procurement choices (e.g. project histories). Throughout, efforts have been made to test hypotheses about the effects of alternative procurement policies and to identify 'rules of thumb'. At the outset, an understanding of the aerospace market is required and the relative competitive positions of the American and European industries.

Note

1   Critics of the classification of alternative policies have suggested an alternative taxonomy which can be used to analyse various procurement policies. They suggest a classification based on seeking answers to two questions: (a) who does the design work? and (b) who does the production work? For example, one firm, either domestic and/or international can be involved in either or both design and/or production. It is also worth mentioning that at the start of the research project, the Lockheed–Rolls Royce Tristar was believed to be an example of an international consortium. However, this view was revised. It is an *international* supplier relationship with Rolls as a foreign supplier of engines for a US-designed airliner. Nonetheless, the principles involved continue to be relevant, namely allowing firms to select their partners and the appropriate form of organisation on commercial criteria (i.e. risks, profits), without state interference.

6
Free Trade versus Nationalism

Introduction

Weapons procurement policies will be influenced by the views of producer groups and budget-conscious procurement agencies. Every effort will be made to erect a set of myths favouring domestic weapons contractors. Economic theory provides a basis for assessing these myths by considering their meaning, logic and consistency, and by seeking to quantify some of the magnitudes involved in the policy debates. Is competition possible; what are its likely effects on NATO aerospace industries; and can European firms compete with US producers? This chapter uses the interview results to answer these questions. Initially, the basic economics of the aerospace industry are outlined, after which an assessment is made of the market structure and its performance. The size of American and European firms is reviewed and incorporated into an analysis of the relative efficiencies of the various industries. There follows an appraisal of the views of aerospace firms on competition, independence and collaboration. The detailed evidence is presented in Appendix A, Sections A–D and F.

The economics of aircraft R & D and manufacture

An understanding of the aerospace industry requires a knowledge of the relationships and 'rules of thumb' which dominate its economics:

(a) In R & D work, costs are positively associated with the weight of an aircraft, as shown in Figure 6.1(a). Also, the long term trend in R & D and unit production costs, in constant prices, has been upwards. For instance, the US F14 fighter costs five times as much as its predecessor, the F4 Phantom (in constant prices). Similarly, the R & D costs on a British combat aircraft such as the Buccaneer, Jaguar or Lightning were typically *eighty times* the unit price of the aircraft. On the later Tornado, R & D costs were *120 times* the 1977 unit price of the aircraft.

102 Nato Arms Co-operation

(b) For a given aircraft performance, costs and development time are negatively associated, as shown in Figure 6.1(b). In other words, faster development is costlier and this complicates international comparisons of industrial performance (Hartley and Corcoran, 1978). One study estimated that the average development time for American military aircraft was 6.25 years, compared with 8.3 years in the UK, with British aero-engines requiring up to 10 years (Elstub, 1969). But is the US industry faster at development because it applies more resources to R & D compared with Europe?

(c) Aircraft production work is characterised by productivity improvements through learning by doing (Figure 3.6). Labour learning curves can be converted into unit production cost curves by assuming that unit costs fall by one-half of the reduction in direct labour costs.

(d) Some of the employment implications of aircraft manufacture can be estimated by assuming that *airframe* work requires between 1 and 20 man-hours per pound (i.e. 0.5–10 man-hours per kilogram approximately) of airframe weight, depending on the size and complexity of the project and its output (UK evidence). Similarly, US studies show that the *first* unit produced usually requires 30 man-hours per pound (14 man-hours per kilogram) of airframe weight, with the labour input decreasing along a 75 per cent learning curve (Large *et al.*, 1974). Finally, it has been estimated that the production of fifty Mirage F1C aircraft generates about 40 000 man-years of employment (Dassault-Breguet, 1977, p. 25). This total consists of 17.5 per cent employed on

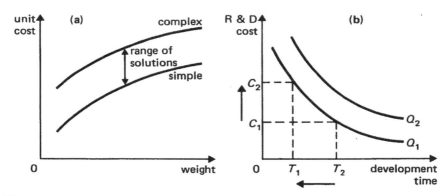

Figure 6.1 R & D costs (a) A range of solutions from simple to complex (Heath, 1979). (b) A set of time–cost trade-offs reflecting different levels of quality ($Q_2 > Q_1$).

airframe work and raw materials; 20 per cent on equipment and radar; 9 per cent on engines; 6.5 per cent on weapons, etc; and 47 per cent employed on overhauls and spare parts required over a twenty year period.

Market structure and performance

Aerospace markets consist of buyers and sellers within two major sectors, namely military and civil, each with a set of sub-markets. For example, firms specialise in fighters and strike aircraft, or transports, or helicopters, or missiles, or short- and long-range airliners. Governments dominate the demand for military equipment, whilst state-owned and privately owned scheduled and charter airlines are the major buyers of civil products. The supply side consists of aerospace firms involved in the design, development and manufacture of military and civil aircraft, helicopters, missiles and space vehicles. Typically, an aerospace industry consists of airframe, aero-engine and equipment firms, with the airframe companies acting as final assemblers. On a modern combat aircraft, the distribution of production costs might be 25–50 per cent for the airframe, 25–30 per cent for the engine and 20–50 per cent on avionics. Life cycle costs might be two to three times the initial equipment price (Appendix A, Section B2). Within NATO the major aerospace industries are located in the USA, the UK, France, Germany, Italy, Canada, the Netherlands and Belgium. American firms are dominant. An indication of their competitive advantage can be obtained by examining their shares in the world *civil* aircraft market, as shown in Table 6.1. Compared with military projects, the civil market is less subject to government protection. In 1979, US firms accounted for almost 99 per cent of the long-haul civil aircraft in service or on order, and some 81 per cent of the short–medium range airliner market; European manufacturers accounted for 1.4 and 19 per cent, respectively. However, during the 1970s, European firms, namely the collaborative Airbus Industrie, obtained an increasing share of the short–medium range airliner market, a trend which suggests that Europe has been improving its competitiveness in this product group. For defence equipment, 35 per cent of the value of military aircraft and helicopters in service in the EEC in 1978 were designed in the USA, with almost 65 per cent being of European design. In the rest of the world (excluding the USSR), American firms accounted for nearly 85 per cent of the military aircraft and helicopter markets, whilst the EEC share was 5 per cent (EEC, 1980). Predictably, some limited data on international trade in airframes and engines between the EEC and the USA shows that the American industry has a substantial trade surplus with Europe (cf. two-way streets; see Table

6.1). These figures on market shares and trade flows raise major doubts about the competitiveness of the European manufacturers in military and in civil markets. Explanations of this performance require an analysis of market structure.

Aerospace is an example of a dynamic market subject to government protection and regulation. The market has generated technical progress in the form of faster, larger and more productive military and civil aircraft, with the substitution of jet engines for propellers and missiles and rockets for fighters and bombers. The speed of combat aircraft increased from some 600 m.p.h. (965 km h) in 1945 to over 1600 m.p.h. (2575 km h) by 1975. Rapid technical progress means that any monopoly tends to be temporary. The emphasis on technical progress is a result of government demand for more advanced military equipment, the technological benefits being subsequently applied to civil aircraft and non-aviation products (i.e. technical spillovers). In fact, aerospace industries are greatly affected by the policies of their national governments. During the 1970s, military contracts accounted for 70–75 per cent of the total business of the EEC's aerospace industries, compared with 50–55 per cent in the USA (EEC 1981). Thus, governments are major buyers of military aircraft and missiles. They can use their procurement policy to determine the type of project

Table 6.1 *Market shares and trade flows*

Manufacturer	Short–medium haul airliners 1976 (%)	Short–medium haul airliners 1979 (%)	Long-range airliners 1979 (%)
Boeing	42.2	50.2	65.6
McDonnell-Douglas	29.6	20.0	28.7
Lockheed	15.5	10.0	n.a.
Airbus Industrie	2.6	12.6	n.a.
Total USA	87.5	80.5	98.6
Total Europe	11.9	19.2	1.4

Trade flows: airframes and engines, 1979 (1000 ECU)

EEC imports from the USA	2 386 357
EEC exports to the USA	855 785
EEC balance with USA	−1 530 572

Source: EEC (1981).

Notes: (i) Airliners are for aircraft in service and on order, by value, excluding the USSR. (ii) Trade flow figures are incomplete. They are for airframes and engines only and exclude UK data on trade in airframes. (iii) ECU = European currency unit. (iv) n.a. = data not available.

and hence technical progress, together with the size of any domestic aerospace industry, its structure, entry and exit, prices, profits, efficiency and ownership. When purchasing military aerospace equipment, governments have a complex choice problem. They have to determine the extent of the market, and select a project, a contractor and a contract. Whether contracts are cost-plus or fixed price, and the associated arrangements for policing and regulating profits on noncompetitive government work, can affect firm behaviour and contractor efficiency. Choices also have to be made on the point in a project's life cycle when competition should cease and selection occur (e.g. 'fly before you buy'). The solution of these procurement choices determines the efficiency of an aerospace industry. However, the choice set and government concern with wider 'ends' than the acquisition of military aerospace equipment raises doubts about the applicability of the economists' traditional market structure–performance framework. Aerospace markets are more appropriately analysed as political markets in which the relevant economic agents are governments, bureaucracies and contractors (Chapter 2). In such political markets, where competition is absent (e.g. European nations), firms receiving subsidies have inducements to pursue aims other than maximum efficiency and maximum profits. They might prefer to consume managerial 'perks' such as luxury offices, company cars, or increase expenditure on staff (e.g. pretty secretaries, empire building, employment of scientists). Governments might react by imposing profit controls on the recipients of subsidies; but firms are likely to respond by consuming even more managerial 'perks' and spending more on staff! Subsidised firms subject to profit controls could also have a reduced incentive to resist wage increases (a testable hypothesis). Indeed, the existence of state subsidies and other forms of government support and protection, including public ownership, might induce aerospace firms to become subsidy maximisers, seeking revenue from governments and bureaucrats rather than private markets (Hartley and Watt, 1981; Hartley and Tisdell, 1981, Chs 7 and 14). The results of government policy are reflected in a set of performance indicators for each nation's aerospace industry. These include profitability, market shares for civil and military products, productivity, and trends and variability in sales and employment (e.g. labour hoarding), as well as the time required to develop and produce an aircraft, and the extent of escalation in costs, time and quality. As always, international comparisons have their limitations. For example, international variations in productivity can reflect differences in the extent of bought-out equipment and in the amount of sub-contracting: hence value-added data are preferable to turnover or sales figures. Differences arise in the valuation of work-in-progress and in the proportion of R & D and production business (e.g. current R & D is reflected in future sales).

Table 6.2 NATO aerospace industries

Country	Sales (millions ECU, 1975 prices) 1970	Sales 1979	Total employment 1970	Total employment 1979	Employment in R & D 1979	Productivity (sales per man, ECU, 1975 prices) 1970	Productivity 1979	Concentration ratios (%) 1979
Belgium	66	152	4700	6272	230	14043	24235	29.7
Netherlands	209	233	8000	7935	1191	26125	29364	100.0
Italy	317	589	29500	36570	4742	10746	16106	29.9
West Germany	1291	1839	56206	60886	14200	22969	30204	40.2
France	2131	3572	103364	106297	22073	20616	33604	31.8
UK	2216	2883	235100	204381	42903	9426	14106	35.9
EEC	6230	9268	436870	422321	85339	14261	21945	17.4
Canada	722	956	36510	37700	n.a.	19775	25358	12.5
USA	24896	22992	1116000	1099000	n.a.	22308	20921	8.9

Source: EEC (1981).
Notes: (i) Sales figures are final *turnover* data in millions of European currency units in constant prices, using 1975 prices and exchange rates. Canadian sales of 722 are for 1972. (ii) Productivity figures are derived from the sales and employment data: ideally value-added figures are required. (iii) Concentration ratios are based on the largest firm's employment in each nation as a percentage of the industry's total employment (i.e. one-firm ratios). Employment data were used because of problems with sales figures.

There are also differences in relative factor prices which will affect the 'mix' of machinery and manpower and the proportions of skilled and unskilled labour used in an industry. As a consequence, there are limitations in using measures of *labour* productivity, especially where these are simply expressed as output per man (e.g. workers have different amounts of skill or human capital). Table 6.2 shows some performance indicators for the aerospace industries within NATO.

The major European aerospace producers are located in Britain, France and West Germany. Each is considerably smaller than the US industry, and even aggregate EEC output and employment are less than 50 per cent of the American. Nonetheless, in terms of employment and technology policy targets, aerospace in Europe is a substantial employer, particularly for R & D labour, which accounted for 20 per cent of the workforce. Also, relative to the USA, Europe's performance in terms of productivity improved markedly during the 1970s. Admittedly, sales data are only crude productivity indicators, but they provide a general ranking in which the UK industry's performance requires some explanation. Estimates using value-added and net output show that during the 1970s French aerospace productivity was 1.5–2.5 times that of the UK industry, whilst US productivity was three times that of Britain (Harvey, 1981). Evidence on firm size shown in Table 6.3 confirms the general difference in scale and productivity between the USA and Europe.

The major US companies are clearly much larger than their European rivals. Amongst the top five firms, the average American company employed almost twice the workforce and produced more than twice the output compared with the corresponding European enterprises (e.g. average employment of 83 570 in the top US companies compared with an average of 42 534 in the top five European firms). Within Europe, only British Aerospace, Rolls Royce and Aerospatiale, each of which is state-owned, had labour forces within the range of the top American firms. This is relevant to market performance, since critics and policy-makers often assert that European aerospace firms are 'too small' to compete with the large and successful US companies (i.e. Boeing, McDonnell-Douglas, Lockheed, General Dynamics). On this view, firms which are absolutely large are required to undertake complex R & D in a competitive time-scale, to achieve economies from large outputs and to spread the inevitable risks over military *and* civil products. In other words, the size hypothesis predicts that successful performance is positively associated with size and it is based on the observed correlation between bigness and success in the USA. But correlation does not necessarily imply causation, and there are ambiguities about the *direction* of causation (i.e. is size a function of success?). Moreover, the characteristics of currently successful US firms are the result of past and current decisions and procurement

108 *Nato Arms Co-operation*

Table 6.3 *Major aerospace companies in NATO, 1980*

Company		Sales (millions ECU, current prices)	Employment	Productivity (sales per man ECU, current prices)
USA				
Boeing		6772	106 300	63 707
McDonnell-Douglas		4358	82 550	52 792
Lockheed		3876	74 600	51 957
Pratt and Whitney	(E)	3874^e	70 000^e	55 343
General Dynamics		3407	84 400	40 367
General Electric	(E)	1800^e	24 000^e	75 000
Rockwell		1745^e	34 000^e	51 324
Grumman		1242	28 000	44 357
Northrop		1189	30 200	39 371
Cessna		718	18 024	39 836
Canada				
de Havilland		90^e	4 700^e	19 149
Europe				
British Aerospace	(UK)	2378	77 500	30 684
Aerospatiale	(F)	2244	34 422	65 191
Rolls Royce	(UK)	2102	58 800	35 748
Dassault-Breguet	(F)	1830	15 660	116 858
MBB	(WG)	1309	26 287	49 797
SNECMA	(F-E)	594	11 460	51 833
Matra	(F)	440	4 600^e	95 652
VFW	(WG)	427	12 185	35 043
Fokker	(NL)	409	8 862	46 152
Westland	(UK)	408	12 662	32 222
Dornier	(WG)	401	8 454	47 433
Agusta	(I)	378	9 358	40 350
MTU	(WG-E)	276	6 594	41 856
Aeritalia	(I)	233	11 500	20 261
Turbomeca	(F-E)	218	4 400	49 546
Casa	(S)	160	8 270	19 347
SEP	(F-E)	155	2 775	55 856
Shorts	(UK)	152	6 629	22 930
FN Herstal	(B)	131	2 282	57 406
Fiat Aviazione	(I)	124	3 555	34 881
SABCA	(B)	98	1 870	52 406

Source: EEC (1981).
Notes: Superscript e = estimate; E = aero-engine company; Canadian figures are for 1979.

policy, the structure of the market (i.e. competitiveness) and the level of technology, all of which might be inappropriate for future success. As a result, government policy towards aerospace has to be formulated under uncertainty, so that the fundamental question concerns the appropriate institutional and market arrangements for responding and adjusting to unforeseen and unexpected changes. Nonetheless, the size hypothesis raises questions relating to the optimum or most efficient size of aerospace firms and the causes of success, the answers to which might explain some of the differences in competitiveness between America and Europe.

The size of firms

The optimum size of a firm depends on its range and number of aerospace products (e.g. fighters or large transports), its 'mix' of R & D and production, relative factor prices, delivery time-scales and the existence of specialist and competitive sub-contractors. The interview study found that for similar aircraft types the minimum efficient scale, especially for R & D, was substantially smaller in Europe than in the USA. Employment was used as an indicator of size, although there are international differences in relative factor prices and in the definitions of R & D staff (e.g. scientists, engineers). Within Europe, technical staffs of about 1000 or less were regarded as the minimum for the development of a combat aircraft, with a minimum size of *firm* of around 8000 employees. For a similar project, American firms believed that some 2000 engineers was the *minimum* requirement for development work, although one estimate specified a lower bound of 4000 engineers; and the minimum size of *firm* could be some 20000 employees. However, US firms generally agreed that the *optimum* (best) size of a division was about 20000–25000 employees for combat aircraft and possibly 30000 for large transports, subject to the constraint that 150000 employees was regarded as 'too large'. Within Europe, the optimum size of firm for combat aircraft is probably best represented by Dassault-Breguet, with about 15000 employees, including 4000 engineers (Appendix A, Section B4). On this basis, the evidence on optimum size suggests a diversity of experience throughout NATO. The success of the relatively small companies, such as Dassault-Breguet in France and Northrop in the USA, casts doubts upon the case for large units. There were also indications that British firms might have a comparative advantage in R & D work. Some UK companies claimed that they could have *developed* American aircraft at a lower cost, and this view was further supported by a US firm. Apparently, the UK benefits from lower salaries for R & D work and a tradition of 'flexibility and inventiveness' which leads to higher productivity in the R & D functions. But, there seems to be general agreement that the UK is at a cost disadvantage in manufacturing (Appendix A, Section A3). The implications for a NATO free trade area in weapons might be that the UK would specialise on aerospace R & D work, leaving other nations, such as the USA, to undertake production. This raises the general question of whether it is necessary for R & D and production work to be associated and undertaken by one firm, and the cost implications of separating these activities. Opponents of any separation argue that profits are earned on production and not on R & D. If this is the main objection, there seems no reason why governments could not change the profit rates on R & D contracts. Some of the remaining objections to separating R & D and production seem dubious in view of the willingness of aerospace firms to accept licensed production and co-production (see Chapter 7).

Significantly for government policy towards aerospace industries, all the US firms interviewed claimed that size was *not* the major determinant of success (Appendix A, Sections A2 and B7). Indeed, there was general agreement amongst the US companies that a distinguishing feature of the American industry was its greater competitiveness, which was believed to have a variety of favourable effects on market performance. A competitive market in R & D, involving at least two to four national firms competing in designs and ideas, was valued as a source of technical progress. Moreover, the American industry benefits in price and delivery from competition amongst domestic sub-contractors, whilst the general competitive environment results in firms being more aggressive and responsive to customer requirements. These are, of course, the standard economic arguments for favouring competitive markets which European governments have sacrificed in creating larger domestic units, some being state-owned. There is support for the view that the American market is more competitive. Single-firm concentration ratios within each European nation are 30 per cent or more compared with under 10 per cent in the USA (Table 6.2). But competitiveness is only one aspect of industrial performance, and other factors have also contributed to the success of the US aerospace industry.

The efficiency of the American and European industries

The majority of firms interviewed agreed that the British and European aerospace producers were less efficient than the US industry. One American view was that, in the late 1970s, the US industry was probably some 20–30 per cent more efficient than the Europeans. Understandably, there were exceptions and qualifications to these broad generalisations. A few British firms felt that the UK was competitive and equally efficient in some product groups, such as engines, guided weapons and possibly helicopters. It was also suggested that in airframe manufacture the UK has a competitive advantage over relatively short production runs, but not for a large scale output (Appendix A, Section A1).

The firms interviewed offered four major explanations for the differential efficiency between the European and American industries:

(a) *Labour problems in the European aerospace industry.* There was considerable support for this explanation. The problems were reflected in lower labour productivity for a given output, greater labour hoarding, union opposition to hiring and firing, immobility, a concern with job preservation rather than production, and a general absence of shift working in Europe.

(b) *The European industry lacks the scale and learning economies associated with long runs.* This view also attracted substantial support. For combat aircraft US production runs of 1000 of a type are typical (e.g. F16, F18), sometimes extending to 5000 units (e.g. F4), at rates of 12–30 units per month, with monthly rates of up to 45–58 aircraft not unknown. Within Europe, a typical UK domestic order for a military aircraft might be 200–300 units at a rate of 2–4 per month. Similarly, the initial combined F16 order from Belgium, Denmark, the Netherlands and Norway totalled 348 units, compared with a USAF planned buy of almost 1400 for the same aircraft. Such major differences in scale emphasise the problems confronting the European producers and, at the same time, indicate the opportunities for cost savings through standardisation. Of course, the European producers can aim to raise their output levels, and hence their competitiveness, through exports. The Dassault Mirage is a good example, with output in the region of 1400 units, at a rate of 11–14 per month. Alternatively, joint projects such as the Tornado, with a planned output of some 800 units, enables the European producers to approach the American industry's scale of operations (Appendix A, Sections B1 and B6).

(c) *Capital intensity.* The European industry has less capital per worker and the vintage of its capital stock is believed to be older.

(d) *Europe lags in R & D and production technology.* It was estimated that the US industry has a technological lead of 7–10 years, with one suggestion that the UK industry might be some 20 years behind in *production* technology. Such a 'technological gap' between Europe and the USA is also likely to be a factor in explaining the generally shorter development time-scales for American aircraft. Most US companies claimed that they could have developed British and European collaborative projects (e.g. Tornado, Harrier) within shorter time-scales (Appendix A, Sections A1 and A3).

Some of the above explanations are related to the scale of aerospace output, whilst others reflect the structure and general competitiveness of labour and product markets in Europe and the USA. And in aerospace, European governments have been dominant in determining market structure. Even so, output has a major impact on labour productivity and aircraft unit costs. With the relatively short production runs in Europe, high R & D costs have to be spread over small outputs, there are fewer opportunities for learning economies in production and less incentive to invest in new machinery. The extent of the difference in scale between America and Europe can be seen from the output of some of the post-1945 military and civil aircraft. Examples are shown in Table 6.4, which also includes estimates of USSR production. Typically, US output levels are some three times greater than in Europe.

Learning curves, output and costs

Learning is a major source of productivity improvement in aerospace. Typically, US learning curves have steeper slopes than in Europe, implying greater savings on unit production costs for each doubling in cumulative output. American labour learning curves are usually 75 per cent for aircraft compared with 80 per cent in Europe. Actual curves vary around these averages. On the Phantom, the manufacturing labour learning curve was 72 per cent, compared with 78 per cent on the B52 and 82 per cent on the F111; the corresponding numbers of man-hours per pound required for the *first* unit of each of these aircraft were 60, 12 and 24, respectively (Large *et al.*, 1974) (1 man-hour per pound = 0.45 man-hours per kilogram).

A study of American and British production learning curves showed that unit man-hours are slightly higher in the United States during the early stages of output, possibly up to the fiftieth aircraft; but, thereafter the American's steeper learning curve gives them an advantage, especially since the UK curves tend to 'flatten out' (Jefferson, 1981). The interview study confirmed these relationships and trends, indicating that British learning curves (man-hours) tend to 'flatten out' when output exceeds 100 units. Relatively lower labour costs have been a traditional source of competitiveness for the UK and it was estimated that on unit production *costs*, British aircraft manufacturers could be cheaper than the USA up to an output of 150–200 units. Above 200 units, the USA is superior on man-hours and on unit production costs, as shown in Figure 6.2. One example was given where a US company

Free trade versus nationalism 113

Table 6.4 *Scale of output in America and Europe*

Type of aircraft	Total output	Type of aircraft	Total output
EUROPE		**USA**	
Military aircraft		*Military aircraft*	
Meteor	3788	F86 Sabre	9502
Vampire	3268	F4 Phantom	5195
Hunter	1985	Skyhawk A4	2960
Mirage	1400+	F100 Super Sabre	2294
Canberra	1376	F104 Starfighter	1958
Tornado	809	F16	1949
Mirage F1	649	Hercules	1600+
Aeritalia G91	557	A-7 Corsair	1570
Jaguar	583	F18	1500
Alpha Jet	486	Grumman Tracker	1281
Javelin	428	Vought Crusader	1259
Lightning	338	F15	1055
Harrier/Sea Harrier	297	F102 Delta	938
Hawk	263	A10	825
Super Mystere	180	F105	818
Buccaneer	143	B52	744
Atlantic	129	F14	601
Vulcan	124	F111	586
Valiant	108	Rockwell Vigilante	225
Victor	84	B1 bomber	100
Mirage IV	62	SR-71	30
Civil aircraft		*Civil aircraft*	
Fokker F27	517	Boeing 707	962
HS 125	500	Boeing 727	1811
Viscount	440	Boeing 737	867
HS 748	351	Boeing 747	564
Aerospatiale Caravelle	280	McDonnell-Douglas DC8	556
Airbus A300	227	McDonnell-Douglas DC9	1071
Airbus A310	79	McDonnell-Douglas DC10	362
BAC 1-11	245	Lockheed Tri-Star	249
Fokker F28	169		
Trident	117	**USSR**	
Comet I–IV	108	*Military aircraft*	
Britannia	83	Mig-19	10 000+
Vanguard	44	Mig-21	10 000
		Mig-17	5000+
		Su-9-11	2000+
		Tu-16	2000+
		Backfire bomber	450(?)

Sources: Gunston (1977); Green (1981).
Notes: (i) Output data should be regarded as approximations at end-1981. (ii) Military output can include licensed production; USSR figures are estimates. (iii) Civil output figures are for deliveries and orders.

114 *Nato Arms Co-operation*

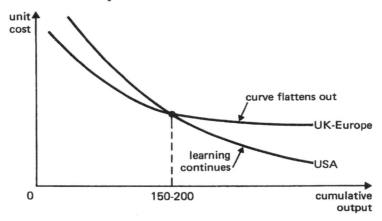

Figure 6.2 British and US unit production costs. British and European learning curves tend to 'flatten out', whereas learning appears to continue indefinitely in the USA.

claimed that, on the same aircraft, unit production costs would be identical when the American firm had produced 350 units and the British 450 units. Moreover, UK experience is not unique and learning curves for other European aerospace producers tend to 'flatten out'. In contrast, US learning curves are reputed to be 'continuously falling'. Various hypotheses have been formulated to explain the shape of European learning curves. Possible explanations include the payments system, reduced productivity at the end of the line, modifications, and the European concern with job preservation. Unfortunately, the interview study was unable to obtain conclusive support for any of those hypotheses (Appendix A, Section B6). Nonetheless, the evidence on learning curves has implications for weapons standardisation policies. It is misleading to apply US cost–quantity relationships to

Table 6.5 *Slopes of American and European learning curves*

European companies				US company	
A		B			
Wings only ($n = 500+$ units)		*Fuselage only*			
Assembly	80%	1–100	75%	Assembly of wings	70%
Wing box installation, sheet metal and related manufacturing	} 85%	100–300	80%	Major assembly	71–80%
		300–500	85%	Sub-assembly	72–81%
Mechanical manufacturing	90%	500+	100%	Fabrication	77–86%

Note: For the US company, the range of slopes reflects different categories of labour.

Free trade versus nationalism 115

European firms which have never experienced American scales of output and production rates.

Table 6.5 shows the slopes of learning curves on a given combat aircraft which was produced in the USA and in Europe. It can be seen that for similar tasks US learning curves have steeper slopes and that the curve for one of the European producers 'flattens out' once output exceeds 500 fuselage units.

Is competition possible?

Contrary to popular belief, a competitive aircraft market in NATO is technically possible. For each major aircraft type, there are a sufficiently large number of firms to create rivalry situations. With fighter-strike aircraft, it was estimated that there could be between three and eight US firms, with up to twelve in the rest of the world. In this market, the French Dassault company has been relatively successful with some 15 000 employees compared with McAir and General Dynamics where employment exceeds 80 000. The number of competitors was much smaller for large transport aircraft, engines and strategic missiles but, in each case, the firms interviewed estimated at least three rivals. Moreover, in a competitive market, there would be no barriers to new firms entering, so that it would be possible for, say, combat aircraft specialists to bid for large transport aircraft contracts. This is even more likely if, as the interviews suggested, the number of firms declines in the future. Companies expected a smaller volume of business, greater competition and more mergers, with the long term optimum number of three firms per sub-market. In this context, US firms were unanimous in emphasising that the competitive nature of their aircraft industry was one of its major features and a factor in its success, with competition requiring a minimum of two firms (Appendix A, Sections A2, B3 and B5). Thus, competition within NATO aerospace markets is technically possible and would lead to substantial gains from international specialisation and exchange. It was predicted that in a competitive market, the USA would specialise in advanced technology aircraft and missiles, with Europe and the UK having a competitive advantage in products such as strike and VTOL aircraft, ejector seats, electronics, engines, sub-contract work, sub-systems and small missiles (e.g. Harrier, Mirage, Shorts, Marconi-Elliott, Martin Baker, Rolls Royce). In return, Europe would benefit from lower unit prices, with one US company suggesting reductions of 20–30 per cent. Indeed, such gains from specialisation and exchange explain the existing pattern of international trade in civil products, where NATO nations import labour-intensive commodities from developing countries and export goods which rely upon machinery, technology and skills (i.e. physical and human capital). However, whilst competition in aerospace markets is technically possible, it is usually viewed as politically impossible. A number of firms expressed the belief that competition is unlikely not because there are too few firms, but because governments are involved in aerospace markets.

Fears of a US monopoly: dependence and the prices of spares

Opposition to a competitive aerospace market in NATO reflects beliefs about the desirability of the outcomes and the distribution of gains and losses. A free market was expected to result in a smaller European aerospace industry. Critics in Europe claim that a free market would lead to US technological domination, resulting in an American arms monopoly, cheap equipment but expensive spares, together with a loss of independence and technology. The fear is that Europe would become a metal-bashing sub-contractor to the USA. Interviews with firms provided empirical evidence on some of these claims, many of which have achieved the status of myths and are accepted as the conventional wisdom on *both* sides of the Atlantic.

Efforts to define the American monopoly suggested that it reflected a European worry about being 'dependent on the USA for supplies and spares'. It was believed that a US monopoly would mean less choice and a loss of independence in foreign policy, poor quality weapons, higher prices for aircraft and spares, and a dependence on US technology. Alternative views were also expressed about the accuracy and reliability of initial price quotations by US firms. A European view was that US price quotations are 'wildly inaccurate' until a contract is signed; but an American company made the point that initial prices change if the customer requests modifications and extras. There were, however, too few respondents for reliable generalisations on this issue (Appendix A, Sections A4 and B9).

Spares pricing is a further example of some of the myths of aerospace procurement policy. European industry often claims that US aerospace equipment sold abroad is cheap, but you 'pay for the spares'. Here, the interview study was informative in clarifying some of the issues in the debate and providing insights into the pricing behaviour of firms. It soon became apparent that the European view was frequently a belief for which there was little published empirical support: it was usually 'second-hand' or 'hearsay' evidence, often based on a single example of European experience with the US Lockheed F104 Starfighter. Nor is it obvious that even if profits are based on the export of spares that this policy is unique to US firms, and to aerospace industries (cf. cars, computers). In the circumstances, American companies were the obvious ones to question about the pricing of spares. Some US firms readily accepted that for aircraft sold abroad they raised the prices of spares on later orders, and examples were given of foreign spares prices being some 15–20 per cent higher than for sales to the American government. But the explanations for this policy were diverse. They included the search for higher profit rates, the fact that exports involve greater risks, or specific requirements which are costlier due to shorter runs, or because foreigners often buy spares at the end of a production run, or require them urgently, as well as US government policy which imposes a levy on foreign military sales. At least one firm regarded spares pricing as part of its general product pricing strategy, explaining that its export prices reflected the extra costs of foreign transactions and the 'full costs of doing business', including some cost items which are not recoverable on US government sales but which can be recouped on foreign work. Indeed, this firm stressed that since US procurement rules do not apply to foreign sales, its export prices for aircraft and spares tend to reflect 'what the market will bear', including any monopoly position. However, not all American firms raised prices on the export of spares. References were made to the loss of consumer goodwill and the fact that potential rivals can compete on spares and on new aircraft. There are also difficulties of the counter-factual, with some firms claiming that foreign nations benefited from *lower* spares prices resulting from the large scale orders for the American armed forces. Thus, whilst there was some support for the hypothesis that American companies raise the prices of spares on later orders for exports, this pricing policy was by no means universal. Moreover, in view of the frequent references to the F104 Starfighter case, it was interesting to consider the views of the companies involved. There was a general agreement that some European nations 'paid a high price for their F104 spares'. However, it was suggested that the West German F104G example should be regarded as part of the costs of re-entering the aircraft industry and providing experience to the air force and the procurement agency. For example, Germany relied upon US experience and advice in purchasing spares, with the result that 'too many' were ordered (Appendix A, Section A4). Even so, the life cycle costs of US aerospace equipment sold to Europe might still be substantially lower than purchasing from a small scale, inefficient European supplier. Paradoxically, to avoid dependence on the USA (with its competitive aircraft industry), each European nation has to be dependent upon a protected and inefficient domestic monopoly!

Spares prices are only one aspect of pricing in aerospace markets. The interview study also obtained some limited evidence on the pricing and profitability of exports and other aerospace products (Appendix A, Sections B10 and F). Export prices for military aircraft were usually higher than home prices, although exporting was not always more profitable. Elsewhere, there were mixed views about the relative profitability of military and civil aircraft; missile work was at least as profitable as military aircraft business; and there were indications that non-aircraft work was relatively more profitable. For our purposes, the basic point is that the profitability of military aerospace work will determine the willingness of firms to remain in the market and for new firms to enter. With a NATO free market in weapons, it is envisaged that competitively-determined, fixed price contracts will regulate profits, so that governments need not be concerned with profit rules and 'fair and reasonable' prices. Proposals for a competitive solution do, of course, require a more detailed specification, so that the implications can be predicted and assessed. Not surprisingly in view of US experience (e.g. Lockheed C5A), total package procurement policies have their critics. They are regarded as unsuitable and too risky for major technical advances, although there are the compensating aspects of a clearly specified deal which places the contractor at risk and, in principle, penalises optimistically low bids (Glennan, 1966). Given these reservations, an alternative solution would be competitive prototyping to reduce the uncertainties prior to arranging further competitions for the development and/or production work. Opponents of competitive prototyping point to the costs of duplication, its wastes, and the delays involved in arranging the competition and determining the winner. As with other aspects of aerospace procurement policy, this is an area where quantification has been conspicuously absent. The US experience with its 'fly before you buy' policy provides some evidence.

Competitive prototyping and a 'fly before you buy' policy

American and European firms generally agreed that competitive prototyping takes longer, involving at the most an extra one to two years. The additional time is required to organise the competition, evaluate the rival aircraft and select the winner. In the US lightweight fighter competition, the Request For Proposals was issued on 6 January 1972, bids had to be submitted by 18 February 1972 and the winners were announced on 14 April 1972. In other words, the USAF selected the two firms for the prototype competition in about two months (i.e. General Dynamics YF16 and Northrop YF17). The first flight of the F16 aircraft was twenty-one months later in January 1974, and the subsequent 'fly-off' between the F16 and F17 occurred between February 1974 and the announcement of the winner in January 1975. *Thus, a total of thirteen months was required to organise the competition and assess the rival F16 and F17 aircraft*. Moreover, there are two reasons why this is likely to be an upper bound estimate. First,

Free trade versus nationalism   119

some of the time spent in evaluation and flight testing would also be required with the alternative single developer strategy. Second, the actual results of competitive prototyping as in the F16 and F17 example are usually compared with an *ideal* single developer policy which assumes no problems; but problems always arise and the ideal is never realised. One US firm also claimed that competitive prototyping reduces the time taken to deliver a *fully operational* aircraft, with a possible time saving of up to three years (Appendix A, Section B8).

Competitive prototyping is further reputed to be 'costly and wasteful'. There were mixed views on the question of costs, with some US firms claiming that costs and cost escalation are likely to be lower with a competitive 'fly before you buy' policy. Here, competition for a production contract acts as an incentive and policing mechanism, providing firms with an inducement to beat their rivals. Nor is competitive prototyping necessary costly. The competition between the F16 and F17 cost the US government some $120 million (1972 prices). General Dynamics was awarded a $38 million contract (1972 prices) to produce two prototypes, on which the company earned a $2 million profit; Northrop was awarded a $39 million contract (Anon., 1977, p. 71). On this basis, the unsuccessful prototype and engine work cost between $50 million and $60 million (1972 prices), which is a relatively small proportion of total development costs, possibly in the region of 10 per cent (cost escalation on a single developer policy usually exceeds this figure). The US lightweight fighter competition had the further feature of allowing the contractors maximum freedom, the aim being to 'beat their rivals' and offer a low cost aircraft. In this context, the greatest opportunities for cost savings in designing, developing and producing a new aircraft exist at the operational requirements stage; fewer opportunities occur at the development stage and, by the production phase, there is little possibility of designing for cost savings (General Dynamics, 1974). Nonetheless, problems remain. Usually, the successful prototype is not representative of the production aircraft and requires further development work. And, once the contract has been awarded, competition no longer exists. In this situation, efficiency incentives can be retained by awarding a competitively determined, fixed price contract. Or, development and production work can be separated, with competition occurring for the production contract. Such a solution is opposed because of the alleged costs and difficulties for the government in acquiring the relevant technological information and transferring it to a different producer. But, in principle, this problem is soluble in the same way that profit-seeking companies willingly transfer technology to foreign firms in return for a licence fee or royalty (see Chapter 7).

Whilst firms generally accepted that competitive prototyping takes longer, they also agreed that the end result is higher quality in the form of a 'better' aircraft. It was stressed that prototypes and a 'fly-off' prove and confirm new technology, so reducing the risks of full scale development. On this view, competitive prototyping buys information, demonstrates new ideas and so reduces risks, thereby avoiding failures (i.e. there are no 'free lunches'). Even the unsuccessful prototype might provide valuable information and knowledge to producers and customers.

The preferences of producers

Competitive solutions and a NATO free trade area in weapons are obviously attractive to the potential beneficiaries, namely voters and taxpayers. Other groups in each nation's political market place are less likely to be persuaded. In particular, producer groups in the form of weapons firms likely to lose contracts have every inducement to oppose free market solutions. And since democratic governments are likely to be influenced by, and to favour, producer interests, it seemed appropriate to examine the views of companies on alternative procurement policies and their preferred solutions.

Predictably, firms expressed a preference for home weapons, although it was not always possible to deduce how much more nations would be willing to pay for a domestic supply. The American view was that they do not incur extra costs in buying from their own industry since it is the lowest cost supplier. For the UK, there was the example of a willingness to pay up to an extra 20 per cent for British inputs on the US Phantom 'buy'. In return, European firms argued that buying from the domestic industry provided advantages in the form of weapons designed for national needs and security of supply. In general, the answers to this question confirmed the views expressed about the European fear of a US monopoly (Appendix A, Sections A4 and C1). More interesting were the views of firms on the *minimum* size of domestic industry needed for defence purposes. American firms felt that the minimum size had to be sufficient to retain competition in R & D (ideas), namely some two to four firms. In contrast, the UK view was that a 'total capability' is required (i.e. airframe, engines and avionics), with estimated employment varying from under 100000 to a minimum of 8000 R & D staff for military and civil airframe projects, plus a similar number for engine and avionics work (see Table 6.2). A West German view expressed the minimum required in terms of the capability of developing a fighter weapon system. Other European firms felt that a minimum nucleus was required for wartime expansion and to continue acting as an intelligent customer. Interestingly, some of the replies suggested that the minimum required for defence purposes is below the current size of the American and European aircraft

Free trade versus nationalism 121

industries. Firms tended to agree on the need to maintain a minimum capability in R & D, with manufacturing capacity regarded as less of a problem. All of which raises the general question of whether the US and European aerospace industries are 'too large'. What would be the costs and benefits of, say, halving employment in these industries? In this context, it has to be recognised that budget-conscious Defence Departments and armed forces are also likely to produce 'too large' an output. As a result, there is a presumption that industries which are directly supported by monopoly government departments (e.g. Defence) will be 'too big'.

All firms were willing to enter collaborate military projects, but there were major differences between the US and European models, with implications for the development of NATO standardisation policies. The contrast resembles the debate between market forces and state solutions. American firms preferred a single prime contractor acting as a design leader (i.e. a US firm), with manufacturing shared through co-production, operating in *ad hoc* international consortia arranged on a commercial basis. In other words, American firms preferred collaboration and work-sharing on production but not design. They were opposed to government involvement and were extremely critical of European joint projects of the Panavia–Tornado type, mainly because of the lack of a single management and decision-making point. The Panavia–Tornado form of collaboration was regarded as an example of how *not* to proceed! The Americans were critical of the higher costs of European joint ventures and their poorer quality, resulting from their administrative problems, committee management and inefficient partners. In contrast, European firms favoured work-sharing and financing on the basis of the size of domestic orders, with collaboration organised through new or existing international companies (e.g. Panavia). They dismiss the American criticisms of the European model of collaboration as reflecting the US industry's total lack of experience of truly joint projects, sharing R & D and production work. Ultimately, these competing views on the efficiency and appropriateness of different forms of collaboration will be tested in the market place, as reflected in aircraft sales and profitability (Appendix A, Sections C2–C4).

American and European firms gave examples of the minimum size of order required for collaborative ventures. These ranged from under thirty NATO AWACS to 1000 units of the F16 type, together with the belief that on complex aircraft, more than three equal partners is 'too many'. But minimum orders are not the only problem. The list of major obstacles to collaboration was sufficiently diverse and extensive to explain the general failure of NATO weapons standardisation policies. Nationalism and government interference were given as major barriers. For example, each nation's contractors are known to its domestic bureaucrats and armed forces. Other obstacles included exchange rate problems, differences in efficiency, accounting and legal procedures, together with the European desire for balanced employment (Appendix A, Section C4). Some of these obstacles were reflected in the views of firms towards the choice of alternative procurement policies. Generally, firms agreed that a government would buy abroad for cheaper weapons, and that it would purchase at home or undertake licensed or co-production for the usual employment, technology, strategic and balance of payments reasons (Appendix A, Section D1). One view was that UK governments should use the following criteria:

(a) Buy abroad when small numbers are required and R & D costs are a relatively high proportion of total costs (e.g. the UK purchase of thirty-three US Chinook helicopters).
(b) Home purchases are justified where large numbers are required, and it is a relatively small, simple, low risk project, with export prospects (e.g. Hawk trainer). It was suggested that projects such as TSR-2 (between £240 million and £260 million in R & D in 1964 prices and a planned output of 100+ units), AWACS and space satellites were too costly to be developed and produced by the UK only. On the civil side, the break-even point for a new small jet airliner is in the region of 300 units, rising to some 500 units for larger airliners. Even the USA has found it costly to undertake projects such as the B-1 bomber, AWACS and the SST airliner (Appendix A, Section D1).
(c) Joint projects should be undertaken where high R & D costs can be made acceptable through sharing and where there is a desire to maintain industrial capability in the UK.
(d) Licensed or co-production should be used where R & D costs are relatively high but large numbers are to be produced.

Conclusion

Budget-maximising bureaucracies are likely to favour expensive weapons which can be presented as 'vital to meet the enemy's threat', thereby raising the bureau's budget. They will oppose low-cost aerospace equipment since the benefits of reduced spending are likely to accrue to rival services (e.g. Army, Navy) or to the Treasury. However, bureaucrats might adopt, say, a low-cost lightweight fighter and prototype competition (cf. F16 versus F17) as a means of 'buying into' an attractive new programme. Once the aircraft has been selected, it can be progressively modified to meet the demand for more complex weapons in response to the 'increasing sophistication of the enemy'.

Producers' views will be influenced by the expected profitability of alternative procurement policies, with overseas purchases regarded as least profitable for domestic contractors. Opposition to free trade and the rising costs of complete independence creates pressures to adopt intermediate policies, namely, some form of licensed production or joint projects. Firms were agreed that licensed production results in higher unit production costs. Disagreements arose over the cost implications of joint projects. Some European firms claimed that, compared with a domestic purchase, joint collaborative ventures resulted in lower unit costs, possibly in the region of 20 per cent. Nor was there much support for the hypothesis that collaborative contracts change a firm's behaviour. In contrast, US firms believed that joint ventures led to higher unit costs, longer development times and inferior aircraft (Appendix A, Sections C3–C4). Clearly, these views about joint endeavours and licensed production require more detailed consideration.

7
Licensed Manufacture and Co-production

Introduction: sharing production work

This has been a growth area for new jargon. Increasingly, references have been made to co-production, industrial collaboration, multinational programmes, offsets and work-sharing. All involve firms aiming to obtain business by offering customers aerospace equipment *plus* an industrial package of production work. Traditionally, a nation acquiring a foreign aircraft obtained manufacturing work for its domestic industries through negotiating a contract for licensed production. However, competition within the world military aerospace markets has led firms to offer different and new industrial packages designed to win more business. In the context of NATO weapons standardisation policy, American producers favour international collaboration through sharing production (but not design work) in the form of co-production schemes (Chapter 6). What are the possible differences between the various production sharing arrangements? How much work might a producer be willing to offer to obtain a foreign order, and what is a customer willing to pay in the form of any higher costs and the time taken to transfer technology? Here, case studies, together with the interviews, provided some orders of magnitude (Appendix A, Section E).

Definitions and examples

Many of the firms in the interview study have been involved in licensed manufacture and co-production contracts, as well as work-sharing arrangements. In particular, US producers have considerable experience of successfully competing for these contracts in Europe and Japan. American firms distinguished between licensed manufacture and co-production. With licensed production, the foreign nation builds for its own orders only. Co-production contracts allow the foreign nation a share of US orders, domestic production and third party sales. For example, the General Dynamics F16 European co-production contract was based on a sharing arrangement on an *initial* 998 aircraft programme. The USA originally ordered 650 aircraft (later raised to 1388 units) and the European consortium of Belgium, Denmark, The Netherlands and Norway ordered a further 348 aircraft (116, 58, 102 and 72 units, respectively). The European consortium was allocated manufacturing work on the following basis:

(a) Ten per cent of the initial US order, equivalent to sixty-five aircraft.
(b) Forty per cent of their own order, equivalent to 139 aircraft. Together with the US business, this gave the Europeans work to the value of 58 per cent of their order (equivalent to 204 aircraft). The total value of the initial European buy was $2.418 billion (May 1975 prices). Similarly, the US industry's share of the initial order for 998 units was equivalent to 794 aircraft – i.e. the USAF order plus an extra 144 units.
(c) Fifteen per cent of export sales to other countries, estimated at a further 500 aircraft and hence equivalent to seventy-five units. Achievement of such export sales would give the Europeans manufacturing business to the value of 80 per cent of their total order – i.e. equivalent to 279 aircraft (General Dynamics, 1977). An output in the region of 2000 units was required to give the Europeans a 100 per cent offset on their order. In other words, this part of the contract introduced a risk-sharing element, where Europe's involvement depended on the world market competitiveness of the F16.

Industrial collaboration, work-sharing and offsets are further variants on the same theme. A nation purchasing a foreign aircraft obtains some production work, usually on its own aircraft. For example, a number of European states have been involved in an industrial collaboration programme which provided them with some of the work for their jointly funded NATO order for AWACS, but they were *not* allocated a share in the US purchase of the same aircraft (i.e. a NATO order for eighteen aircraft plus a USAF order for thirty-one AWACS). Similarly, the British purchase of 170 US Phantoms (1965) incorporated a work-sharing arrangement whereby UK industry was allocated about 50 per cent of the value of its national order. Finally, nations purchasing a foreign aircraft might negotiate an offset under which the original manufacturer will offer to allocate an agreed proportion of work to the buyer, usually some sub-contract business which could be on a completely different project. Although the names are different (cf. brands of cars and soap powder), the basic concepts are identical.

Why do firms co-produce?

Economic theory would explain the variety of international arrangements for sharing production work in the world aerospace market as representing the response of profit-seeking firms to the different demands of national governments. The result is a set of voluntarily negotiated international contracts which are mutually beneficial. National governments willing to 'shop around' for aerospace equipment can allow rival firms to compete against each other, exerting downward pressure on prices, until prices tend to reflect the costs of producing the extra output (Demsetz, 1968). This generalisation applies to price defined to embrace contributions to R & D outlays, as well as the percentage share of co-production.

Most of the firms interviewed agreed that they would offer some form of licensed or co-production to enter a market that would otherwise not be available, particularly since foreign governments are increasingly demanding a share of manufacturing work. American producers were most willing to offer attractive work-sharing arrangements in an effort to obtain a contract. Examples included the 10, 40, 15 per cent share on the European F16 programme and the industrial collaboration on the AWACS for NATO. In the case of licence fees, a UK firm paid a fee of 5 per cent on sales, although the figure could approach 10 per cent. Other examples were given of US companies charging up to $10 million for the transfer of data packs and up to $100 million for technical assistance (1976 prices). Ultimately, of course, the size of licence fee and the amount of co-production will be determined by the market environment (competition) and a producers' desire for profits. Almost all the firms in the study regarded licensed production and co-production as being *at least as profitable* as domestic military work. Since the bias in responding to this question was likely to be towards lower profitability, the answers can be regarded as reasonably reliable (Appendix A, Sections E1–E3).

The costs of licensed production and co-production

Work-sharing, licensed production and co-production are not costless. Firms have to re-arrange their production plans and re-allocate some of their contracts. Understandably, they will aim to protect their own business, seeking to impose adjustments on suppliers through transferring sub-contract work to the purchasing government's domestic industries. And the purchasing government will have to be willing to pay a higher price – compared with buying directly 'off the shelf' from the main manufacturer. An indication of the magnitude of the cost penalty for licensed production is shown in Figure 7.1.

Licensed manufacture and co-production 127

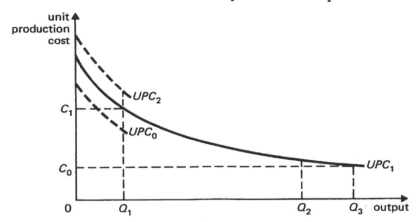

Figure 7.1 The cost penalties of licensed production. Consider unit production cost curve UPC$_1$. A nation wishing to license $0Q_1$ will pay a unit cost of C_1. Purchasing the same quantity 'off the shelf' from the main manufacturer would raise output to Q_3 (i.e. $0Q_1 = Q_2Q_3$) and result in unit costs of C_0: what is the magnitude of $C_1 - C_0$? If the assumption of a given cost curve is relaxed, the possibility arises of cost schedules at UPC$_0$ or UPC$_2$ – i.e. lower or higher cost positions, respectively, which will reduce or raise the cost penalty.

The interview evidence suggested that the typical cost penalties for any form of shared production work are in the range of 10–50 per cent, with the lower bound estimate applying to advanced nations and the upper figure to under-developed countries (Appendix A, Section E4). Usually, cost penalties reflect the absence of learning economies and relatively short production runs. However, there were exceptions, with at least one UK firm claiming that its licensed products were *cheaper* than the US main manufacturer, possibly up to 30 per cent cheaper. A similar result has been estimated from a study of Japanese experience with the licensed manufacture of the Lockheed F104 aircraft. An F104 airframe manufactured in Japan cost only 79 per cent as much as an airframe produced in the USA, and the unit costs for the Japanese aircraft (airframe and engines) were 88 per cent of US costs for a comparable aircraft. The difference reflected lower Japanese labour rates and some transfer of knowledge (learning) from Lockheed (Hall and Johnson, 1967, pp. 156–9). In this context, the interview study provided some support for the view that the unit costs of aircraft produced under licence were likely to be influenced by the previous experience with licensing work of the licensor and of the licensee (e.g. European experience with F104). One firm aimed to transfer experience so that its licensed producer's costs for the first unit would be 85 per cent of the level originally achieved by the main manufacturer. Learning curves for aircraft produced under licence could have slopes in the region of 80–85 per cent (cf. 75 per cent in the USA; Appendix A, Section E4). Nonetheless, firms generally believed that production sharing involved cost penalties. Three examples can be given:

(a) On the work-sharing arrangement for the US Phantoms, Britain was willing to pay a 20 per cent premium for UK inputs. The aim was for the UK to undertake work to the value of 50 per cent of its order for 170 units. Rolls Royce engines and UK avionics were specified as part of the contract. For the remainder, McAir was asked to accept UK bids for parts and equipment so long as they were no more than an extra 20 per cent above McAir's lowest bid. As a result, it has been estimated that the UK Phantoms might have cost at least an extra $600 000–$1 million per copy (1966–7 prices) or an additional 23–43 per cent per unit compared with purchasing directly from McDonnell-Douglas. On this contract, the US Government did *not* charge for previous R & D expenditure on the Phantom; but the UK had to pay for any modifications as well as for the development work on the British engine and avionics.

(b) The F16 co-production programme involves the Europeans in the manufacture of the airframe, engine and avionics. Efforts were made to divide the work on the basis of specialisation, so providing co-producers with a worthwhile production run allowing the exploitation of learning economies. For example, Fairey in Belgium will manufacture over 500 aft fuselages, whilst Fokker in the Netherlands will produce a similar number of centre fuselages. However, there are constraints on the efficient allocation of work. In addition to the 10, 40, 15 per cent rule, each European nation desired a 'fair' share of the work. The USA also required an autonomous production capability so that it would not be dependent on overseas suppliers: hence, there are two sources for most parts, which also provides a 'check' on the competitiveness of US and European firms. In other words, each major American supplier has a European 'twin' or co-producer. In the case of aft and centre fuselages, over 400 units of each will be built by General Dynamics. European co-producers were also required to be 'reasonably' competitive. This was defined as a price differential of under +15 per cent; an extra +15–25 per cent price differential was regarded as 'marginal', and over +25 per cent was not competitive. Such price differentials between the USA and Europe are, of course, likely to lead to departures from the least-cost method of producing the F16. There are also the extra organisational, travelling and transport costs associated

Licensed manufacture and co-production 129

with an international programme and the 'start-up' costs resulting from 'doing business with strangers' (see Chapters 8 and 9). A further constraint arose from the European desire for final assembly work. This is undertaken by Fairey–SABCA in Belgium and Fokker in the Netherlands. Thus, there are *three* final assembly lines for the F16. As a result, it has been estimated that Europe will pay at least an extra +20–25 per cent for its F16 co-production programme compared with an 'off the shelf' purchase from the USA. The Europeans agreed a 'not to exceed' price of $6.091 million per copy, including a pro-rata share of total R & D costs (0.47 million per unit), with co-production adding $1.07 million to the cost of each of their F16s (1975 prices). Flyaway prices for USAF aircraft were estimated at $4.55 million in 1975. By 1982, it was stated that the project was still within its 'not to exceed' price, although critics have suggested that this has only been achieved by allocating some costs

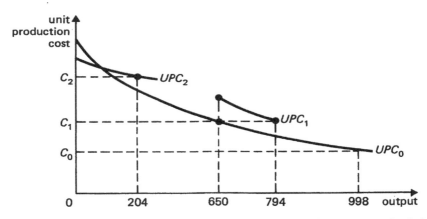

Figure 7.2 The cost penalties of co-production. The efficient cost schedule is shown by UPC$_0$. The output figures are based on the F16 example, with the USA producing the equivalent of 794 units out of the initial order for 998 aircraft. Least-cost production of all 998 units would result in a unit cost of C_0. If co-production imposes cost penalties on the USA, it is assumed that unit costs will be C_1, equivalent to the costs if America had produced only for its own order of 650 units (UPC$_1$). For the Europeans, the cost curve is assumed to be UPC$_2$, giving a unit cost of C_2 which also reflects a flatter learning curve. The relationships are illustrative only. In fact the Europeans are further down the cost curve than shown by the equivalent output of 204 units – e.g. they are manufacturing over 500 fuselage components, so exploiting the economies of long runs (i.e. specialisation). The cost penalties reported in this study are based on the difference between C_2 and C_1 (20–25 per cent or $1.07 million per unit; 1975 prices): the penalties would be greater if actual costs were compared with C_0.

to different budget headings. The cost penalties of co-production are illustrated in Figure 7.2.

(c) Industrial collaboration on the NATO order for AWACS. Originally, this was planned as a twenty-seven aircraft programme valued at $2240 million (1975 prices; North Atlantic Assembly, 1977, p. 142). NATO Ministers willingly accepted a 10 per cent cost penalty for some 25 per cent of European and Canadian industrial collaboration or work-sharing on the order. More collaboration would have meant increasing cost penalties, as shown in Figure 7.3. Indeed, the curve in Figure 7.3 reflects the higher costs of European and Canadian inputs and the fact that the new partners had to start learning compared with US suppliers who had already built some AWACS. It is possible that the curve might differ for other aircraft, for larger quantities and where industrial collaboration is *planned* at the start of the project.

With licensed production, it takes time to transfer technology from the original manufacturer to the licensee. Times for such transfers varied between a minimum of three to six months and up to ten years, with a typical period of between two and two-and-a-half years. Some of the variations in time-scales reflected different interpretations of the transfer process. The simple transfer and interpretation of drawings, or the assembly of an aircraft from 'knocked down' parts might require a minimum of three to six months. In contrast, independent local production of an aircraft or an aero-engine could take some five to ten years. For the European F16 consortium, the time-scale from the start of production tooling to the first aircraft totally manufactured by Fairey–Sabca was about forty months. Estimates suggested that the Europeans required some eighteen months longer than General Dynamics to start producing their own aircraft (Appendix A, Section E4).

The benefits of licensed production and co-production

Two potential benefits were explored, namely jobs and technology. Licensed manufacture and co-production provides extra employment to both parties in the transaction. Estimates of the jobs accruing to the main manufacturer varied from a 'small number' to 25 per cent of the total work, with one US firm suggesting that it retained 90–99 per cent of the jobs which it would have obtained if it had undertaken all the work. A producer of large transport aircraft suggested a 'rule of thumb' of 1 man-hour per pound of airframe weight (~0.45 man-hours per kilogram). In some instances, airframe firms protected their work loads by offering foreign customers the following:

Licensed manufacture and co-production 131

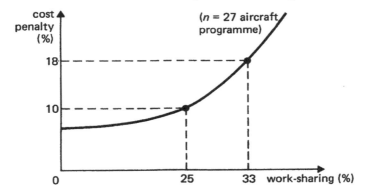

Figure 7.3 The cost penalties of industrial collaboration. The curve is illustrative only and might be more accurately represented as a series of steps. Nevertheless, it shows that the cost penalty becomes quite steep beyond 25 per cent work-sharing or industrial collaboration. An eighteen aircraft programme might be represented by an upward shift in this curve, meaning *less* industrial collaboration for a 10 per cent cost penalty.

(a) Final assembly work. Nations interested in production sharing might be offered a final assembly line, equivalent to some 5–6 per cent of total man-hours. Such arrangements are not 'too inefficient' and are an effective and attractive method of demonstrating a foreign nation's participation in aircraft production.

(b) Work undertaken by domestic suppliers and sub-contractors. One American firm manufactured 30 per cent of its aircraft, procured a further 40 per cent from domestic suppliers and received 30 per cent as government-supplied equipment. In other words, domestic sub-contractors and suppliers are likely to bear the employment losses of production sharing arrangements (e.g. simplest tasks).

(c) Technical assistance, advice, support and training.

Foreign nations undertaking licensed or co-production appear to gain jobs (see Chapter 4). Examples were given where a licensed producer undertook 75 per cent of the licensed business. Other estimates suggested that for every direct job lost in the USA, at least 1.15 jobs would be gained in Europe, and one executive put the figure as high as an extra three or four jobs gained for each one lost in America. Table 7.1 shows some of the estimated direct employment effects of the initial F16 European contract. Emphasis is placed on the initial estimates since these formed the basis of the European selection of the F16. On the original 998 aircraft programme, Europe's labour input was estimated at some 29 000 man-years, rising to 36 000 man-

Table 7.1 Jobs on the F16 European co-production programme

Country	Estimated number of man-years	
	998 aircraft	1500 aircraft
Europe	28 900	35 900
General Dynamics	25 000	n.a.
Total for USA	74 000	98 000

Notes: (i) A 998 aircraft programme consisted of 650 units for the USA and 348 for Europe. A 1500 unit programme assumed an additional 502 export sales (10, 40, 15 per cent). (ii) Figures are for direct employment only and exclude additional multiplier effects. For example, 25 000 man-years of work at General Dynamics might represent 3000 workers employed at the Fort Worth plant. General Dynamics estimates suggest an employment multiplier of at least 2.5.

years on a 1500 unit programme. Europe planned to manufacture six aircraft per month over much of the period 1979–85. Similarly, the USA expected to gain jobs from its involvement in the European order. The sharing arrangements meant that it would manufacture the equivalent of an *extra* 144 units on a 998 aircraft programme and an additional 571 aircraft on a 1500 unit programme (i.e. compared with a USAF order only). As a result, American producers expected some 74 000 man-years of work from their involvement in the European contract, possibly rising to almost 100 000 man-years with the more successful programme. General Dynamics initially planned to produce fifteen units per month, with the possibility of rising to forty-five units per month if necessary. Indeed, by 1981, General Dynamics' Fort Worth plant employed 16 500 workers and the average number of production man-hours required for the F16 had declined from 130 000 to 32 000 per unit and was continuing to decline (General Dynamics, 1982).

Licensed manufacture and co-production are often justified in terms of the technical benefits which are obtained by the purchasing nation. All firms interviewed agreed that licensees and co-producers acquire such technical benefits, particularly in manufacturing technology. American firms believed that Europe was some five to ten years behind the USA in production technology. Examples were given where US firms had supplied European industry with the experience of working with new materials, precision machining and new management techniques (Anon., 1977, pp. 99–101). But these technology transfers from, say, the USA to Europe (or vice versa), are not 'free gifts': they have to be paid for. Aerospace firms will willingly supply technology on the basis of the profitability of the transaction and the result is an international market in technology transfer as reflected in different arrangements for production sharing. Predictably, firms will aim to establish property rights in their valuable ideas (technology) through patents and by linking technology with the sale of aerospace equipment. They will tend to offer a purchasing nation their less valuable and more dated technology, especially if they are entering new technologies. For example, if European producers are, say, ten years behind, then their American rivals have every incentive to offer technology which is, say, 7–9 years old. Airframe firms might also aim to shift any technology transfers to their suppliers, so that sub-contractors 'lose' technology. Nor must it be forgotten that firms generally obtain new technology at their government's expense through the state funding of new weapons projects. In other words, firms acquire much technology at zero price and have considerable opportunities of influencing budget-conscious bureaucracies and vote-sensitive governments to fund new advances in technology. And governments are involved in the demand and the supply sides of the international market in aerospace technology (Udis, 1979).

Whilst there was universal agreement that licensees and co-producers gained technically, no firm could place a value on these technical benefits. References were made to Europe gaining 5–8 years technology on the F16 contract, so enabling some firms to remain in business as competitive suppliers. Examples were also given of European firms which had started as licensed producers and had subsequently developed either as competitive suppliers with the USA and/or as major partners in joint projects (e.g. Westland helicopters, West Germany's involvement in the three-nation Tornado). In contrast, few US firms felt that as the original manufacturer or licensor they gained any technical benefits from licensed and co-production business (Appendix A, Section E5).

How valuable are the benefits?

Policy-makers rarely reveal the valuations which they are placing on the benefits of licensed and co-production. In these circumstances, an indication of the magnitudes involved in a procurement choice can be deduced from the extra costs which are willingly and voluntarily incurred. For example, if co-production involves an extra $\$x$ compared with the least-cost method of purchasing, does the buyer value the resulting benefits at $\$x$ or greater? In other words, for a purchase to be worthwhile, the additional benefits have to be at least equal to the extra costs. Three case studies can be used to illustrate this choice framework, namely the UK work-sharing arrangement on its Phantom purchase, the F16 co-production contract and Britain's selection of the Nimrod AEW rather than the Boeing AWACS. It is recognised that these examples provide only broad approximations, since benefits are aggregated, some are difficult to value and others are vulnerable to subjective valuations by the choosers!

The work-sharing on the UK Phantom buy was a direct consequence of the cancellation of the TSR-2 and other major projects, with the resulting loss of business for the British airframe, engine and avionics industries: was this an example of producer groups influencing government policy in their favour? The UK's 50 per cent share comprised sub-contract work on the aft fuselage and outer wings, undertaken by the British Aircraft Corporation and Shorts, respectively; ejector seats were provided by Martin Baker; whilst Rolls Royce engines and Ferranti avionics were also used. As a result, the UK paid *at least* an extra amount of between $0.6 million and $1 million per copy compared with purchasing directly from the USA, thereby adding between $102 million and $170 million to the total bill for 170 units (1966–7 prices). In addition, there was a delay of fifteen months in delivery due to the problems of incorporating some of the UK inputs. In return for these extra costs, many experts believe that the UK received an aircraft which in terms of *overall* performance was about the same as the USAF Phantoms, possibly 'a little better'. Furthermore, the UK obtained a set of benefits in the form of 'savings' in jobs and foreign exchange, plus a contribution to retaining some of the major firms in the industry. One justification given for the work-sharing arrangement was that it provided the UK '. . . with a large measure of expertise and self-reliance which could have important strategic consequences'. Technical benefits have also been claimed in the form of engine technology later applied to the Tornado and fuselage design knowledge eventually used on the Jaguar. But were such benefits worth between $102 million and $170 million – or possibly more (say, an extra £50 million or more in 1966–7 prices and exchange rates)? And, were some of the benefits planned or are they now used as an *ex post* justification of the work-sharing programme? In other words, was work-sharing the least-cost method of purchasing Phantoms and retaining a UK aerospace capability (i.e. would there have been more jobs and/or more technology if the resources had been used elsewhere in the UK)?

From a European perspective, the F16 co-production programme is often justified in terms of its jobs and technology benefits. The original European choice of the F16 was partly based on a *certainty* of 29 000 man-years of work in Europe. There was a *probability* of additional employment depending on export sales, up to an initial upper limit of a 100 per cent offset against the order for 348 units. Assuming a six year programme, the guaranteed 29 000 man-years of work might provide almost 5000 jobs between 1979 and 1985. These jobs and the probability of others, plus the technical benefits, were reflected in the initially estimated co-production premium of $1.07 million per unit, giving a total additional cost of at least $370 million on 348 aircraft (1975 prices). In other words, the Europeans were willing to pay $12 760 for each man-year of aerospace employment and the associated production technology (1975 prices). A further cost was incurred in the form of delays in the delivery of the European F16s. At a rate of six per month, the initial order for 348 units will require almost five years. By producing an extra fifteen per month, the USA could probably complete the European order within two years (i.e. a saving of three years)! Although co-production is a higher cost solution than acquiring F16s directly from the USA, it is almost certainly cheaper than an independent programme by a European nation. If the European consortium had undertaken an idential project independently, they would have incurred R & D costs, and learning economies would have been restricted to an output of 348 units. Instead, co-production meant the sharing of R & D, with the Europeans initially agreeing to pay a total of $164 million (1975 prices) as a contribution towards the F16 development costs. Also, the Europeans benefited from the economies of a larger output and the competitive 'policing' from US rivals. In contrast, when the UK purchased American Phantoms, it made no contribution to the previous R & D costs of the aircraft. Did the different R & D contributions on the European F16s and the British Phantoms reflect the existence of a well established rival aerospace industry in the UK?

The purchase of AWACS for NATO is a classic example of a public good where there are benefits from *collective* action. NATO believed that AWACS would provide a general warning and command system of value to the Alliance as a whole (cf. NATO common infrastructure). However, to any individual country, the aircraft was regarded as 'too costly' in relation to the benefit to that nation. In other words, the aircraft provides benefits to all members so that an individual nation is likely to under-invest in AWAC provision. Thus, a sub-group of NATO members, all of whom will share in the collective benefits, joined together to fund the programme jointly (cf. the formation of a club and the benefits of group action). The proposal for a NATO force developed through a variety of stages, beginning with a planned force of thirty-two AWACS, later reduced to twenty-seven units, with a final choice of eighteen aircraft. By 1976–7, the UK was confronted with a major choice between an involvement in the co-operative proposals for a NATO fleet of twenty-seven AWACS or to 'go it alone' with its own Nimrod AEW aircraft. The subsequent UK decision to buy the Nimrod provides some insights into the valuation of its domestic policy objectives, particularly the employment benefits. In fact, the analysis is illustrative rather than conclusive since, at the time, the choice was hypothetical. The UK had an urgent requirement for an early warning aircraft; it was willing to participate in the NATO plans for an AWACS force but member states were unable to reach an agreement in the time required by Britain: hence the decision to proceed with the Nimrod.

In 1976–7, the UK had to choose between a 20 per cent involvement in the planned NATO force of twenty-seven AWACS or an independent development of the Nimrod. The choice involved judgements about the quality of the two aircraft and their associated jobs and balance of payments benefits. Inevitably, such choices are surrounded by a confusing array of conflicting estimates and claims! Domestic defence contractors and bureaucrats obviously have every incentive to try to influence government policy in their favour. Table 7.2 shows examples of some of the elements which are likely to have entered the UK's choice set. Once again the empirical magnitudes should be regarded as illustrative and suggestive of the type of information on which the UK government had to make a decision. Both projects were estimated to cost the UK some $450 million, either in direct expenditure on the Nimrod or the 20 per cent share of the AWACS fleet (comparing like with like, 1976–7 prices). However, since the AWACS were already in existence, whilst the Nimrod had to be developed, the latter was regarded as a *riskier* project, so affecting the reliability of its estimated costs and delivery date. Indeed, some early cost estimates for the Nimrod were as high as $540 million, giving a unit cost figure of between $41 million and $49 million per copy, compared with an estimated cost of $83 million per copy for a fleet of twenty-seven AWACS (at a total cost of $2.24 billion, 1976–7 prices). In terms of relative qualities, and to some experts, AWACS appeared to be superior, although it has to be asked whether their additional superiority was worth an extra amount of between $34 million and $42 million per copy. After the UK Nimrod decision, NATO eventually proceeded with a fleet of eighteen AWACS at a total programme cost of between $1.8 billion and $2 billion (1977–8 prices). Thus, it might be concluded that a NATO force of eighteen AWACS plus eleven Nimrods is roughly equivalent to the original NATO plan for twenty-seven AWACS. This implies that one AWAC is equivalent to 1.2 Nimrods, with the latter seeming to be a relatively cheaper buy.

Jobs and balance of payments arguments also entered the UK choice. It was estimated that the UK's involvement in the original NATO plan for twenty-seven AWACS would have resulted in installation and check-out work on the electronics, probably equivalent to 1000 direct British jobs over a five year period. There were expected to be a further 2000 jobs associated with the basing of the AWACS fleet in the UK, resulting in an estimated total of up to 43 000 man-years of employment for the UK between 1977 and 1997 (North Atlantic Assembly, 1977, p. 143). In contrast, the development of the Nimrod was estimated to involve 4500 UK jobs between 1978 and 1982, plus a

Table 7.2 *AWACS or Nimrods?*

Item	Nimrod	AWACS for NATO
Quantity	11	27
Estimated cost to UK	$450 million to $540 million	$450 million
Estimated delivery	mid-1981	end 1980–early 1981
Jobs		
Development and production	4500 (1978–82)	1000 (1979–84)
Operations and maintenance	500 (1982–97)	2000 (1980–97)
Balance of payments		
Add $ spent in UK		
Acquisition	(450 million)	119 million
Operation and maintenance	(210 million)	935 million
Total	($660 million)	$1054 million
Minus $ payments by UK		
Acquisition		450 million
Operation and maintenance		210 million
Total		$660 million
Net balance of payments	($660 million)	+$394 million
Quality of aircraft		
A UK view	6/10	8/10
A US view	4/10	9/10

Notes: (i) Figures in brackets are $ saved by UK, equivalent to the $ payments on AWACS. (ii) Aircraft quality was measured by asking American and British experts for a mark out of 10. (iii) Expenditure data in 1976–7 prices. (iv) Some of the estimates might be regarded as indicative of a non-UK view and hence could be biased against Nimrod.

further 500 jobs on operations and maintenance work, giving a total of 32 000 man-years of employment up to 1997. Whilst the AWACS force seemed to offer the UK more jobs, the estimated employment effects were subject to three qualifications. First, the Nimrod project offered the UK considerably more jobs in the short term (probably more than twice as many between 1977 and 1982). Predictably, the rival UK and US firms disputed each other's employment estimates. For example, it was claimed that Nimrod would provide some 6000–7000 UK jobs during its development and production phase, whilst AWACS would offer only 450 in the acquisition stage. Such differences can reflect the effects of rival interest groups aiming to influence UK Government policy, as well as each firm using its own knowledge to estimate its competitor's labour inputs. Second, British firms argued that the Nimrod provided the UK with more technically demanding and more

138 Nato Arms Co-operation

highly skilled jobs than would have been available on the AWACS. In other words, man-years of work can be a misleading indicator of employment benefits since it ignores the market value of the jobs. Third, the estimated life-cycle jobs on the Nimrod are subject to considerable uncertainty, depending on the eventual reliability of the aircraft after the completion of its development programme. Finally, efforts were made to calculate the balance of payments implications of AWACS and Nimrods. Table 7.2 shows one set of estimates. Britain's involvement in the AWACS scheme would have meant foreign currency receipts exceeding $1000 million and payments of $660 million, giving a net dollar inflow. It might then be argued that Nimrod 'saved' the UK $660 million of foreign currency. However, this 'saving' needs to be related to the sterling expenditure on Nimrod so enabling a comparison to be made with the ruling exchange rate between pounds and dollars. For example, if Nimrod was estimated to cost £660 million, the shadow rate of exchange for the project would be £1 = $1, and this would indicate the UK government's valuation of foreign currency and hence the extent to which it believed that the ruling exchange rate was 'incorrect'. Nor must it be forgotten that if the data in Table 7.2 are reliable, a decision to 'buy British' meant the sacrifice of dollars which would otherwise have been spent in the UK. Perhaps all this illustrates the complexity of choice in weapons procurement.

Conclusion

Work-sharing arrangements such as licensed manufacture and co-production are not without their problems. There are international differences in accounting procedures, depreciation policies, attitudes towards exports, government arrangements for policing and monitoring defence contracts, together with currency fluctuations and varying inflation rates. Drawings have to be interpreted and not all licensors are willing to co-operate and offer advice and information (Appendix A, Section E4). There are also the inevitable demands for a 'fair' share of co-production work, including access to new technology. Such problems have arisen with the F16 project where the European partners have received different shares of the work and where, by 1980, their aggregate share had failed to reach the original 58 per cent target. Offsets can be a major source of controversy. They have to be clearly and unambiguously defined, and care has to be taken to ensure that they represent *net* additions and new business rather than transactions which would have occurred anyhow. For example, a main contractor has every inducement to claim its existing or planned overseas orders as new business qualifying as an offset against a foreign purchase of aerospace equipment. And if licensed manufacture and co-production involve problems, the difficulties must be considerably greater where two or more nations agree to share development and production work. European producers favour such joint projects.

8
Joint Projects

Introduction: standardisation and collaboration

Inefficiency in NATO weapons markets is reflected in 'excessive' product differentiation resulting in 'wasteful duplication' of R & D and relatively short production runs, so that economies of scale remain 'unexploited'. European defence industries are particularly criticised for being 'too small and too fragmented' to be able to compete with the USA (Callaghan, 1975, p. 71). It is often argued that an efficient '. . . two-way street will only be possible insofar as sufficient industries in Europe rally to achieve a size which will enable them to deal under better conditions with the American partner' (Lefevbre, 1978, p. 5). European producers believe that joint projects are the appropriate solution. They are preferred since they enable the major European aerospace industries to retain and develop their technology: 'building of components under licence could . . . be a short-cut to third world status' (Heath, 1978, p. 41).

Joint or collaborative ventures involve two or more nations agreeing to share the *development and production costs* of a new project. Collaboration is undertaken where independence is regarded as 'too costly', usually because of the scale of R & D required (or 'too risky' in the case of civil projects). Consideration of the range of collaborative European ventures provides an indication of the scale and type of project which some nations can no longer afford to undertake alone (e.g. supersonic airliners, space satellites, complex strike aircraft). Such joint projects enable a nation to retain its domestic defence industry and reap the benefits of continued involvement in high technology work. In this form, collaboration resembles a *club*, with a small group of nations combining to purchase a set of benefits (e.g. technology, weapons, jobs) which each would be unwilling to finance independently. Such joint arrangements are believed to be an appropriate solution to 'greater rationalisation, less wasteful duplication and increased weapons standardisation' within NATO, particularly for the traditionally 'small, fragmented and inefficient' defence industries in Western Europe. At its simplest, it is argued that joint projects result in major savings in R & D if a group of nations combine, so avoiding duplicate development programmes. Further savings arise from lower unit production costs as the partner nations pool their orders and purchase a single product. But do joint ventures result in cost savings and are they the 'best' method of creating a competitive European aerospace industry?

This chapter presents an economic evaluation of joint aerospace projects based on European experience. The central hypothesis concerns the magnitude of any cost savings from collaboration and this provides a basis for a general assessment of the efficiency of joint ventures. The study is based on interviews with the major aerospace companies in America, Britain, France and West Germany and the detailed results are presented in Appendix B. Consideration is given to the criteria used to allocate work on international ventures, the form of organisation, the behaviour of firms and the influence of the political market place. The chapter begins with some examples of joint projects and an outline of the case for a *European* aerospace industry.

The case for a European aerospace industry and examples of collaboration

Europe has considerable experience of government-supported collaboration in advanced technology aerospace work, particularly in the military sphere. Some examples of the international sharing of R & D and production work are (a) Anglo-French projects, namely Concorde, Jaguar and the helicopter package; (b) the UK–German–Italian Tornado multi-role combat aircraft; (c) the French–German Alpha Jet trainer and Transall transport aircraft; (d) the French–German–UK–Dutch–Spanish participation in the civil Airbus; (e) other joint European projects, which have embraced missiles and space – e.g. the UK–French Martel, the French–German Roland, together with the French–German–UK Euromissile Dynamics Group and the European Space Agency.

Joint projects can be regarded as 'clubs', with nations participating so long as membership is expected to be worthwhile. The benefits are diverse and their valuation will differ between nations. Such diversity of 'end' outputs makes it extremely difficult to evaluate the performance of joint projects and also increases the opportunities for discretionary behaviour by politicians, bureaucrats and firms. Within Europe, it is claimed that collaboration results in cost savings for each partner and allows a nation to undertake aerospace projects which would be too costly to develop on a national basis (a benefit?). It is also suggested that collaboration enables European firms to compete with the USA, with favourable effects on European jobs, technology and the balance of payments. Indeed, fears are often expressed about US technological domination of Europe, with the aerospace industry

142 *Nato Arms Co-operation*

regarded as one of the commanding height technologies and vital for the future economic development of the EEC (Nobbs, 1979). Moreover, some industrialists believe that joint work provides a stimulus to each nation's suppliers, as well as reducing the probability of cancellation! But joint projects are not costless. They can involve substantial transactions costs, delays in development, compromises in operational requirements for military aircraft and possible losses of property rights in national technology. Clearly, there are opportunities for a critical evaluation of joint projects. An assessment of their costs provides orders of magnitude which policy makers can use to compare with the expected benefits.

The central hypothesis

Compared with an independent venture, a nation's involvement in a joint project was reputed to result in two sets of cost savings: (a) the sharing of R & D costs; (b) scale and learning economies from the longer production runs associated with the pooling of orders.

The ideal case comparing cost savings under a joint project with an independent solution is shown in Figure 8.1, which can be developed to incorporate alternative assumptions and complications. Cost curves for R & D and production are shown separately, each based on *X-efficient* behaviour. For simplicity, it is assumed that prices depend on unit costs (i.e. full-cost pricing) and that a government wishes to purchase 200 units of an aircraft. If a nation prefers independence, it will bear all the fixed R & D costs, namely R_1 in Figure 8.1(a). Average manufacturing costs at an output of 200 units are C_2, as in Figure 8.1(b). Alternatively, two nations each requiring 200 units could combine to share equally the R & D costs, so halving each nation's development outlays ($0.5R_1$). In addition, a doubling of output for a joint project should reduce unit manufacturing costs to C_1, compared with C_2 for an independent venture (Figure 8.1(b)). Clearly, evidence is required on the magnitude of these cost savings. Two questions are considered. First, what are the conditions (assumptions) required for cost savings on joint projects? Second, how large are such savings? One view is that the cost-sharing arguments for collaboration provide an *ex post* rationalisation and justification for joint ventures, thereby concealing the real underlying political reasons – i.e. that once started, they are harder to cancel!

Joint Projects 143

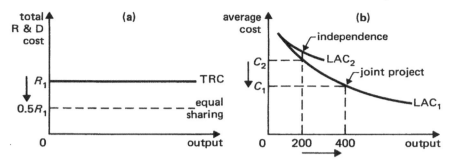

Figure 8.1 Cost savings on joint projects: the ideal case. R & D is a fixed cost shown by TRC in (a); unit production costs are shown by the long-run average cost curve LAC_1 in (b). Compared with a national independent venture, a joint project results in cost savings of $0.5R_1$ and $C_2 - C_1$ in the *ideal case*. In fact, a large planned output is likely to result in additional economies: hence, the unit cost curve for an independent venture might be LAC_2.

Some methodological problems

The economic analysis of joint aerospace projects raises a basic methodological issue, namely the *counter-factual*. *In the absence of a joint venture, what would have been the policy choices of each of the participants?* To illustrate the problem, consider the three-nation Tornado aircraft with a planned output exceeding 800 units (Angus, 1979).

Tornado is a multi-role combat aircraft (MRCA) with varying strike, reconnaissance and air defence capabilities. It is being developed and produced by the UK, West Germany and Italy, and it will replace six different aircraft types in the three nations (standardisation). Collaboration has required the creation of new international organisations representing the purchasing nations and contractors:

(a) Administration, management and monitoring on behalf of the *buyers* is the responsibility of the NATO MRCA Management Organization (NAMMO). This represents the participating nations. It is a committee of senior officials located in each country's Ministry and Services which meets frequently. Detailed management of the programme and the allocation of contracts is delegated to the NATO MRCA Management Agency (NAMMA) which is located in Münich and consists of seconded officials from each partner nation. In effect, NAMMA represents the partner governments or customers with their requirements for 385 aircraft for the UK (220 of the strike version and 165 of the air defence version or ADV), 324 for West Germany and 100 for Italy. At various times, specialist monitoring and procurement arrangements were added to this basic framework. For example, an Engine Monitoring Group comprising technical officers of the three governments was created to assist NAMMA. The selection and procurement of avionics and general equipment was controlled by panels comprising representatives of NAMMA and the partner governments. National procurement agencies have also assisted NAMMA in monitoring work in the individual countries. Throughout, a major aim is to ensure that common development and production costs are shared between the partner nations in proportion to their aircraft orders, with each country being entitled to receive common work in the same proportions.

(b) Airframe development is undertaken by Panavia (located in the same building as NAMMA), an international company specially formed by three aircraft manufacturers. Its partner companies are British Aerospace in the UK, Messerchmitt-Bolkow-Blohm in West Germany and Aeritalia in Italy: participation is 42.5, 42.5 and 15 per cent, respectively. Engines are produced on a similar basis by another international company, namely, Turbo-Union whose partner companies are Rolls Royce, MTU and Fiat. Since 1977, Panavia has been the prime contractor for the entire weapon system, including the engine and gun. As such, it is involved in regular meetings with its customers – NAMMO and NAMMA – and with its main contractors on the engine and avionics. The international organizational arrangements for Tornado are summarised in Figure 8.2.

The methodological difficulties associated with the counter-factual can now be stated. Without this joint project, would the UK (and each partner) have built an *identical* aircraft, using the *same* contractors and procurement policy and purchasing the same quantity in a given time-scale; and would the project have been affected by domestic economic conditions? *One British view is that a UK-only project would have been cancelled* (cf. TSR-2). Indeed, a reduced probability of cancellation is often presented as one of the major 'benefits' (to whom?) of collaboration! To simplify the analysis, it will be assumed that an independent national venture would have been identical to the joint project, receiving the same domestic order (e.g. 385 units for the UK). However, this is a restricted analysis of cost 'savings' because:

(a) It excludes comparisons with the savings which could be achieved by purchasing from the least-cost suppliers within world markets.

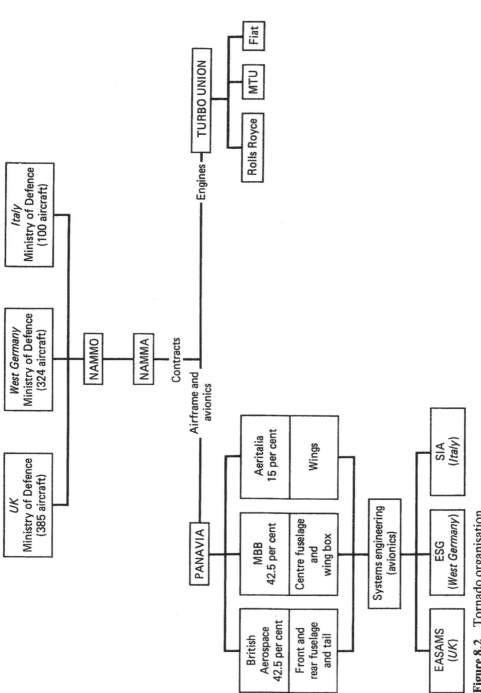

Figure 8.2 Tornado organisation.

146 Nato Arms Co-operation

(b) Cost savings are not the only element in collaborative European projects. Other elements cannot be ignored, namely the concern of European governments with the acquisition of advanced technology and a collective desire for military and political independence from the USA. Some nations have also participated in joint programmes in order to extend their aircraft design and development capability (e.g. Germany and the Tornado), or as a means of entering the EEC (UK and the Concorde and Tornado projects). Such objectives mean that collaborative European projects involve wider policy aims than the acquisition of aircraft and produce group benefits which might not be available to any nation acting independently (at reasonable cost). In other words, the nature of the benefits might differ between collaborative (club) and independent ventures (see Chapter 9).

A further methodological difficulty arises from the limited population of European aerospace projects. The small numbers have also involved different projects, various partners and alternative forms of organisation, all of which reduce the opportunities for reliable generalisations. Moreover, if a learning process operates, experience on some of the earlier ventures is likely to give a misleading impression of the costs of collaboration. Table 8.1 shows examples of collaborative organisations involving the UK.

The small population and the diversity of projects, partners and organisations (Table 8.1) create major problems for researchers. Statistical tests are constrained by the limited population of projects (a small sample): hence this chapter reports the results of the interview–questionnaire study (Appendix B). Here, the researcher is faced with a major task in assembling alternative views into a coherent framework which can also be critically assessed. At various points, specific views are reported: hence the use of such phrases as 'it was said that', 'supporters claimed', 'critics alleged', ... These phrases illustrate the type of arguments which emerged from the interview study, without implying that any particular view is 'correct' or in 'error'. Nonetheless, economists have an obligation to be critical of all the views which are encountered in any research study.

Alternative assumptions on joint projects

Ceteris paribus, joint ventures are believed to result in cost savings for each member of the club. But other things are rarely equal and departures from the ideal case arise because:

(a) On joint military aircraft, each nation might require modifi-

Table 8.1 Examples of collaborative organisations

Project	Partner nations	Major companies Airframe	Major companies Engines	Collaborative organisation for Buying	Collaborative organisation for Development and production	Date of start
1. Concorde	UK	British Aircraft Corporation	Bristol Siddeley	Supervision by a committee of UK–French officials (later the Concorde Management Board)	Committee organisation	1962
	France	Sud-Aviation (Aerospatiale)	SNECMA			
2. Jaguar	UK	British Aircraft Corporation	Rolls Royce	Supervision by a set of joint committees	Creation of joint company (SEPECAT) for airframes but no separate staff	1965
	France	Dassault-Breguet	Turbomeca			
3. Helicopter package (Puma, Gazelle, Lynx)	UK	Westland	Rolls Royce	Major decisions by a joint helicopter management committee. Supervision by national government of the country of the prime contractor	Prime contractor–sub-contractor relationships. UK is prime contractor for Lynx, with France as sub-contractor. France is prime contractor on Puma and Gazelle	1967
	France	Aerospatiale	Turbomeca			
4. Tornado	UK	British Aerospace	Rolls Royce	New management organisation: NAMMO and NAMMA	New International companies – Panavia and Turbo-Union – with separate staffs	1968
	West Germany	MBB	MTU			
	Italy	Aeritalia	Fiat			

cations, so raising research and development (R & D) expenditure and possibly reducing the economies from a long run of one type.
(b) Nations will demand their 'fair' share of each sector of advanced technology and production work. Consequently, development and production on collaborative projects will tend to be allocated on equity, rather than efficiency, criteria. The result will be a departure from the least-cost solution (X-inefficiency or a collaboration premium).

Inevitably, there are mixed views on collaborative ventures and these can be used as the basis for alternative assumptions in estimating the magnitude of any cost savings. These views will be presented as generalisations. However, where the arguments can best be illustrated with specific examples, references will be made to the three-nation Tornado aircraft and comparisons are made between the joint venture and an identical UK-only programme.

Three schools of thought or viewpoints exist on the value of joint European projects. Each is distinguished by its beliefs about the effects of collaboration on total R & D and unit production costs compared with a national venture (i.e. collaboration premia):

(a) There are the enthusiastic supporters of joint projects who argue that they result in substantial gains to a country. This view approximates the ideal case (Heath, 1979).
(b) There are those who claim that there are some relative inefficiencies or collaboration premia. Even so, this group believes that there are net gains to participation, particularly savings in R & D costs.
(c) Opponents of joint ventures claim that there are major inefficiencies and net losses from participation (i.e. the UK is worse off).

Economists can contribute to the policy debate about collaboration by identifying and critically analysing the different views and, where possible, assessing their predictive accuracy (i.e. testing hypotheses). In the absence of empirical verification, the analyst can at least clarify some of the issues in the controversy (e.g. the questions which have to be answered).

The case for joint European projects

The advocates of joint ventures maintain that compared with a national project there is little, if any, increase in *total* R & D outlays, and that unit production costs are lower. Their arguments *approximate* the ideal case shown in Figure 8.1. Presentation and evaluation of their views can be simplified by considering development and production costs separately.

What happens to R & D costs?

Here, it has to be reported that there was universal agreement amongst all the firms interviewed that collaboration results in *higher* R & D costs compared with a national development. But, opinion differed on the magnitude of the extra costs (Appendix B, Section A3). The supporters of collaboration argue that *total* R & D costs on joint projects are about the *same* as for a national venture. Indeed, about 25 per cent of the firms interviewed suggested that the extra R & D costs on joint projects were 'very little'. They ask the critics to identify the sources of extra development expenditure. Critics claim that higher R & D costs on joint projects result from the following:

(a) *Duplicate organisations.* Often there appear to be duplicate organisations for procuring, managing and constructing a joint aircraft project. About 60 per cent of the firms interviewed mentioned the administrative costs of international work (Appendix B, Section A3). Critics point to such examples as the creation of a separate procurement organisation and a new company (NAMMA and Panavia, respectively) for the three-nation Tornado. It is then claimed that the individual governments and the partner companies of Panavia also become involved in the *same* problems at the *same* time. But appearances can be deceptive, and the supporters of collaboration argue persuasively that many of the tasks performed by the international organisations represent *net* additions to output. In other words, the international agencies on joint ventures are defended as undertaking functions which would be necessary for a national project, as well as providing the required co-ordination between partner governments and partner industries. One view is that, without NAMMA and Panavia, there would be greater problems of co-ordination. Indeed, the NAMMA–Panavia 'set up' is sometimes presented as the logical outcome of learning from the experience gained in organising previous joint programmes (see Table 8.1 – e.g. Concorde, Jaguar). Earlier ventures suffered from *ad hoc* committee organisations and the lack of a single decision maker representing the partner nations, and the absence of a clear commercial relationship on the supply side. In contrast, NAMMA represents the three governments and Panavia represents all three nation's industries, so that there is a *single* agent on each side, rather than three! Furthermore, Panavia is an *equal* partnership with unanimity voting rules designed to avoid any of the leadership problems which characterised previous joint ventures. Also, the international organisations on collaborative work are managing a large scale project which exceeds the recent experience of an individual European nation's aircraft industry and procurement authorities. If, say, the UK were undertaking the Tornado project at a scale of output exceeding 800 units, a correspondingly greater organisational input would be required by the industry and the procurement agency. Moreover, since NAMMA is devoted to Tornado only, it claims to be exploiting the gains from specialisation. In total, NAMMA and Panavia might be viewed as an organisational framework aimed at minimising transactions costs on a complex, high technology, multinational programme.

(b) *Duplication of R & D work*, including duplicate flight test centres and too many (costly) development aircraft. Five firms in the study mentioned duplication as a source of higher costs (Appendix B, Section A3). Examples have arisen where a nation with a low technical capability has been given work as part of its 'fair share': hence the joint venture bears the costs of entry into a new technology. In reply, it is claimed that on the Tornado programme there is little, if any, duplication of R & D tasks. For example, it is maintained that there is no duplication of jigs, tools and testing. Each firm is supposed to specialise in solving an agreed and clearly specified problem, thereby avoiding substantial overlap. Indeed, at the outset of the Tornado project, work was allocated on the basis of specialisation, with each firm given responsibility for all aspects of a specific task, namely the design, development and production of part of the aircraft. This meant that there was no confusion about the responsibility for the work and for any failures. Also, each developer aimed to design parts for a planned output of 800 units. The existence of three flight test centres is also explained by the scale and complexity of the Tornado development work, with each centre specialising by comparative advantage on particular aspects of flight testing and operating in different climates. It is argued that one flight test centre would be unable to cope with the fifteen Tornado development aircraft.

(c) *Delays* due to the need to harmonise different operational requirements and national standards. Disputes also arise over management, language, measurement and more time is required to reach agreement between two or three nations. Overelaborate designs might emerge and there can be greater escalation of performance requirements, all of which contribute to delays and higher development costs. About half of the firms interviewed claimed that joint projects take longer, with estimates in the region of an extra 20 per cent to more than three years (Appendix B, Section A2). The supporters of collaboration reply to their critics by pointing out that the result of the extra time and cost is a better project. It is also suggested that some of the extra costs might be regarded as a worthwhile investment in creating a European aerospace industry capable of competing with the USA. And collaboration costs have fallen as partner nations have been learning from past experience.

(d) *Extra travelling costs*, including the value of travelling time. Supporters claim that these are trivial when related to the total R & D budget. Estimates suggest that travel costs might represent 3 per cent of development outlays (Heath, 1979, p. 341). Moreover, the advocates of European collaboration make the point that American firms incur travelling and transport costs between suppliers and procurement agencies in the geographically larger US market. European distances between the UK, West Germany and Italy are much less than in the USA! None of the firms interviewed mentioned travel as a major source of extra costs on joint programmes (Appendix B, Section A3).

In total, the supporters of collaboration maintain that *if there are any extra R & D costs they are under +20 per cent*; and even this is regarded as 'too high'. A number of firms suggested that the collaboration premium could be 'very little' and that it has been falling with greater experience of joint European programmes. The point is also made that there are possibilities of substitution between R & D and production, so that higher development expenditures might lead to lower production outlays. There are even some who claim that the total R & D cost of the Tornado could be *less* than a UK-only venture. Such a result could arise if Tornado resulted in (a) better selection procedures; (b) greater competition in technical ideas using the knowledge available in three nations rather than one (competing ideas from each partner act as a 'check' on the project and can result in a better aircraft); (c) more competition for work (e.g. with UK firms not guaranteed contracts); (d) less 'gold plating' (it can be much more difficult to change requirements since *international* approval is required: two or three nations have to be convinced rather than one).

The interview study tested some of these hypotheses. Where answers were given, most firms felt that, compared with a national programme, collaboration has resulted in either the same or *lower* escalation of costs and quality, and the same or *higher* time slippages (Appendix B, Section A5). Concorde was mentioned as an example of a joint venture which was characterised by greater escalation of costs and time-scale. However, there were mitigating circumstances. Concorde was the first experience of a collaborative programme involving a major technical advance. As the first SST airliner, it was subjected to a rigorous flight-testing programme and further delays arose since every decision had to go through a committee (Table 8.1).

On balance, the supporters of collaboration argue that the total R & D costs on joint projects are about the same as for a national venture. Some 40 per cent of the firms interviewed suggested a collaboration premium of 20 per cent or less (Appendix A, Section A3). Even with a 20 per cent premium, the UK's share of Tornado R & D means that it benefits by paying about 50 per cent of the bill it would have incurred on an independent programme.

What happens to production costs?

Supporters of collaboration claim that unit production costs are *lower*, mainly due to the learning and scale economies associated with longer production runs. There was substantial support for this hypothesis (Appendix B, Section A4). On the Tornado, each nation specialises in manufacturing parts for *all* 809 operational aircraft, so obtaining the maximum learning economies (i.e. greater than if each nation built only its own order). West Germany manufactures all centre fuselages, the UK produces the front and rear fuselages and Italy is responsible for the wings. A large planned order, already announced, enables firms to tool-up for a greater scale of output and adopt capital-intensive methods, which further reduces unit costs. A large order also means more competition from components firms, so resulting in lower prices. US evidence suggests that a large planned order can result in cost savings of some 10 per cent (Appendix A, Section B6). In other words, the Tornado allows European aircraft firms to approach the US scale of output. Assuming a *given* 90 per cent unit cost curve, the Tornado project could result in savings in unit production costs of about 10 per cent for the UK, 15 per cent for West Germany and possibly 30 per cent for Italy. The savings could be greater if a joint project follows a steeper and continuously declining learning curve (e.g. a 87.5 per cent unit cost curve) compared with a flatter UK curve where learning eventually ceases (see Chapter 7). However, these are ideal or best case estimates. Usually, there are policy constraints on the extent to which all potential production economies are realised. Nations prefer to maintain a 'total capability' rather than specialise according to comparative advantage. In the production of Tornado, the result has been a multiplication of final assembly facilities, with each nation assembling and testing its own aircraft. Critics claim that this raises unit production costs and is a source of inefficiency.

A substantial number of firms mentioned duplication of final assembly as a source of higher costs on a collaborative programme. Within Europe, final assembly can represent between 10 and 30 per cent (say 15–20 per cent) of total production costs and such duplication might add as little as an extra 1–2 per cent to manufacturing outlays. Nor is it necessarily valid to regard duplication as an extra cost since national ventures require a final assembly line and such facilities are also needed for repair and overhaul work. Moreover, the evidence cannot be ignored. About half of the respondents claimed that joint projects result in *lower* unit production costs. Compared with a national programme, savings of between 10 and 30 per cent were mentioned (Appendix B, Section A4).

Departures from the ideal case: some inefficiencies

A substantial body of opinion believes that collaboration does not provide the major cost savings indicated by the ideal case (Figure 8.1). This middle view on European projects argues that total R & D outlays are significantly greater than on a national programme and that production is characterised by inefficiencies. Indeed, one UK official has concluded that collaboration results in only marginal savings on production and that the main aim is to save on R & D costs (Commitee of Public Accounts, 1978, p. 30).

How inefficient is collaborative R & D?

Six firms in the study felt that R & D on joint European projects cost 30–50 per cent more than on a national venture. For this group, the median figure was an extra 30–35 per cent (Appendix B, Section A3). One 'rule of thumb' states that the collaboration premium on R & D is equal to the *square root* of the number of partners, with total development time approximated by the *cube root* of the number of participants. On this basis, total R & D outlays on a three-nation project might be some 1.7 times greater than on a national aircraft, with development time some 45 per cent longer. The corresponding figures for a two-nation project are 1.4 on R & D costs and 1.26 on time. However, such 'rules' are no more than tentative hypotheses, lacking an underlying analytical framework and empirical support. Generalisations are restricted by the small size and diversity of the population of collaborative ventures. And, if the supporters of joint projects are correct, a collaboration premium of 20 per cent or less appears to refute the 'square root rule'. Such a rule might reflect earlier experience with European collaboration, when a 30 per cent premium was regarded as typical: this premium could have fallen with learning and experience to a figure of less than 20 per cent. In contrast, there appears to be some support for the 'cube root rule', with a number of firms suggesting that collaboration takes longer, say, an extra 20 per cent or one to two years for development work.

The six firms indicating a median collaboration premium of 30–35 per cent on R & D generally agreed that administrative costs were a major source of extra expenditure. Duplication and harmonisation of different national standards were also important. Mention was made of extra testing, modifications taking longer to agree and of instances where a nation undertaking only one project would allocate all its overheads to the collaborative programme. But even with a collaboration premium of 30–50 per cent, equal sharing on a two-nation project will still lead to savings of 25–35 per cent on each partner's R & D bill (i.e. compared with a national venture).

How inefficient is collaborative production?

Seven firms believed that joint projects resulted in higher unit costs for a *given output*.[1] Estimates of X-inefficiency ranged from an extra 1–2 per cent for aero-engines to 5–10 per cent for airframes. On one project it was suggested that the unit production costs of manufacturing 200 units in one country might be about the same as producing 400 units on a collaborative basis, shared between two assembly lines. Once again, duplication of production and final assembly facilities were major sources of inefficiency. There are also the costs of transport and matching parts at different factories in Europe. Nor can joint partners be treated like sub-contractors and organisational problems arise between two or three nations. Thus, collaboration might result in production inefficiencies ranging from 1 to 10 per cent. As a result, a joint venture with twice the output of a national project might result in savings in unit production costs of between 9 per cent and zero (i.e. assuming a 90 per cent unit cost curve). In the zero case, the savings on collaboration are restricted to R & D. Some firms also agreed that unit production costs would be lower if collaborative work were allocated on a competitive basis within the partner nations (Appendix B, Section A4).

The case against European collaboration

Critics claim that joint European projects do not result in the expected cost savings. Indeed, for the UK it has been suggested that collaboration leads to over-elaborate designs and *higher* costs than if it had 'gone alone'. Significantly, politicians and bureaucrats advocate joint European projects on the basis of cost savings, but there is little published evidence on the magnitude of *expected* and *realised* savings

Joint Projects 155

from collaboration. References are made to the UK's experience with TSR-2 and the need to collaborate when undertaking expensive projects (Cmnd 2853, 1965, p. 92). Rarely is consideration given to the costs of simple prototyping, licensed manufacture or buying from abroad as alternative procurement policies (see Chapters 6 and 7). The opponents of European collaboration maintain that:

(a) When two equal partners collaborate, each nation's R & D effort is not reduced to 50 per cent of the level required for an independent national programme. Instead, 100 per cent sized R & D teams are used in each country for two to three times longer than on a national venture! On the Tornado, feasibility studies started in July 1968, with the first aircraft delivered to the Services' training unit in July 1980: a total development period of twelve years. Critics claim that a national programme would have been completed in less than half the time.
(b) There is excessive government bureaucracy. The slow decision-making process by 'over-involved' governments delays the joint companies. Delays are inevitable where all the partner nations have to be consulted and must agree before a decision can be taken. In this context, newly created and specialist procurement agencies such as NAMMA are criticised as inefficient due to a lack of general 'across the board' experience in project management. Indeed, NAMMA requires the assistance of national agencies to monitor work in the partner countries.
(c) There is design by committee, particularly where decision making has to be unanimous.
(d) Meeting arrangements and paperwork tend to escalate. The number of people attending meetings can be inversely proportional to the gravity of the decisions involved, whilst the amount of paperwork required for a small piece of equipment can be as great as for a major item! It is further claimed that comparisons between the distances in the USA and Europe are misleading. American firms and procurement agencies do not spread their daily management and decision-making across the continental USA, as happens with European collaborative ventures. Indeed, critics of joint European projects believe that the real problem is that several tiers of decision-making committees meet in turn in each other's countries and few critical decisions are made and even fewer are implemented. In order to proceed, firms have to make decisions which then require more meetings to discuss (bargain) and agree the costs incurred! As a result, two partners make a decision in about the time it would have taken either to complete the job. If the number of partners increases from two to three, the time taken to reach decisions may start to

increase by the square of the number of participants or greater (Heath, 1979; Howard, 1976). Nor is it wholly convincing to argue that new international organisations reflect the benefits of previous experience on joint ventures. Few people have worked on *all* projects and, even where the companies are the same, the teams are different.

(e) Problems also arise from differences in language, measurement, managerial practices, traditions and national pride. Inevitably, new international companies lack the long experience and 'tight' management required to produce competitive aircraft. Also, where a new joint company is created it will lack an established reputation in export markets.

(f) Each partner demands a proportionate share of the total work. Within this share it will wish to be involved in the development of each part of the aircraft (i.e. airframe, engine, avionics). It will also demand its own flight testing centre, a final assembly line and the right to modify the aircraft for national requirements. Further complications arise since the major firms and their partners are selected on *political*, rather than *commercial*, criteria. On the Tornado, once the leading suppliers had been selected, some reward still had to be given to the runners-up (Heath, 1979, p. 338). The result is a time-consuming bargaining process in which the partner governments allocate work on equity, rather than efficiency, criteria. A country might also lose its technical advantage if work on new technology has to be given to its partner.

(g) Collaborative ventures have been used as a means of pursuing other policy objectives. The UK's involvement in some projects (e.g. Concorde, Tornado) has often been justified in terms of establishing closer links with Europe and as part of the price of entry into the EEC. But are joint aircraft projects the most appropriate method of achieving foreign policy objectives? Such objectives hardly seem conducive to creating a competitive product (Heath, 1979).

(h) Joint projects cannot be controlled. They involve a complex set of international transactions and contracts between governments and firms, and they are difficult (costly) to cancel. For example, an official report on the Anglo-French Concorde project concluded that 'We were left with an uneasy feeling that the inherent difficulty of the multiplicity of contracts, the number of interested parties and the participation of two sovereign states had meant that the project had acquired a life of its own and was out of control' (HC265, 1981, p. xx).

(i) The design of joint projects is over-elaborate due to the involvement of different national governments and industries. The operational requirement for a collaborative venture is inevitably more complex since it has to satisfy the technical aspirations of the military and scientists in each partner nation.

The net result is reputed to be perverse, since higher costs, overelaborate technical requirements and delays are unlikely to generate competitive products in world markets. It seems that the sharing of development costs and production economies which were the major arguments for joint projects ignored two factors. First, the national constraints on the choice of least-cost suppliers. Each partner requires a share in *each* sector of advanced technology. Indeed, nations sometimes regard joint projects as a means of establishing, protecting and sharing property rights in technology: such contractual arrangements are not costless. In some cases, there are substantial learning costs (which are allocated to the joint project) as new entrants are awarded a nation's 'fair' share of the work. Moreover, partners of different experience and capability might see different problems whereas experienced partners might see fewer problems. Critics have alleged that the Tornado project resulted in a net transfer of technology from the UK to West Germany, so enabling the Germans to establish a competitive, and potentially rival, aircraft industry. Whilst West German airframe firms accept that they have derived some technical benefits, they claim that on the aircraft, including equipment, the technical flows are about 'balanced'. Such a view might be further supported by the continued *voluntary* participation of the original partner nations. Continuation suggests that the project is believed to be worthwhile to each participant, although partners might differ in their perceptions and valuations of the 'benefits'. Second, the ideal case ignored the transactions costs associated with collaboration. There are costs in searching for partners with similar preferences towards projects and a 'willingness to pay'. Subsequently, there are the bargaining costs of two or more partner nations and users which have to reach detailed decisions on the type of project and work-sharing (horse-trading). Additional costs arise from collaboration between 'partner' firms selected on political criteria. New international organisations will have to be created so that the governments can administer and monitor the project and similar arrangements will be required between the contractors. But political constraints might prevent the selection of the most efficient form of international organisation. In the case of Tornado, the Panavia arrangement arose because the nations could not agree on the prime contractorship going to one country (Committee of Public Accounts, 1974, p. 150). Finally, equitable work shares have to be continuously assessed in the light of changes in expected orders, relative prices, exchange rates and productivity levels. It is not unknown for a nation in a joint venture to be allocated a substantial share of prestigious R & D work on the basis of a large initial order which is subsequently reduced. Adjustments in work-sharing then take place on the remaining (and less preferred) production work.

To the critics, the inefficiencies inherent in European joint ventures have been reflected in a sizeable collaboration premium on R & D, with two respondents suggesting a figure of 50–70 per cent, rising to a factor of 2.5–3.0 on some equipment items. For example, it has been estimated that the *equipment development costs* on a two-nation European collaborative military aerospace project can be 2.6 times more than on an equivalent national programme, rising to 4.4 times greater with three partners (Howard, 1976; Walker, 1974).

How can the arguments about joint projects be evaluated?

An analytical framework is required to clarify some of the cost concepts used in comparing collaborative and national ventures. Are joint projects relatively inefficient, resulting in costs additional to those which would have been incurred by one nation only *after standardising for output*? Collaboration *cannot* be condemned because it incurrs costs: there are no costless projects, nor policies! The *appearance* of easily identifiable features such as duplicate organisations and travelling cannot *per se* be presented as conclusive evidence of relative inefficiency in joint ventures. A collaborative project would be inefficient if it used higher cost methods of development and production for a *given* output. A simple framework for clarifying the issues is shown in Figure 8.3. It compares the three-nation Tornado with an independent UK programme, showing the positions of the different viewpoints on European collaboration.

In figure 8.3 the least-cost development and production is shown by the total cost curve, TC_1 and the corresponding long-run average cost curve, LAC_1. Assume that the UK industry is efficient. Output Q_1 reflects a UK only buy of 385 aircraft whilst Q_2 represents the Tornado production of 809 units. If the Tornado organisation operates on TC_1, it is *not* inefficient even though total costs are higher at Q_2 than Q_1 (unit costs are lower at Q_2). Inefficient projects are those operating on higher cost curves than TC_1 and LAC_1. Cost curves TC_2 and LAC_2 would reflect some inefficiency in collaboration (X-inefficiency), but unit costs at Q_2 would be lower than for a UK firm operating at Q_1 on LAC_1 (i.e. compare C_1 and C_0). Cost curves in the region of TC_1 represent the views of the supporters of collaboration, whilst curve TC_2 represents a middle position. Opponents of joint projects claim that TC_3 is a more accurate representation of the cost levels on collaborative ventures, with unit costs greater than shown by LAC_1 at Q_1. However, predictions about relative costs depend on the empirical validity of the assumption that the UK industry is efficient (TC_1).[2] The British government's traditional support for its domestic aircraft suppliers, non-competitive bidding and cost-based defence contracts means that this is likely to be an unrealistic assumption (Hartley, 1974). So, there is a danger that *nirvana* or ideal, but never achieved, UK cost levels will be compared with actual costs for joint projects, ignoring the realised costs on British programmes. In the final analysis, the relative position of the different cost curves shown in Figure 8.3 is an empirical matter (Greenwood, 1975; Saul, 1975).

What is the evidence on the possible magnitude of collaborative inefficiency? All firms interviewed agreed that joint projects involve higher R & D costs compared with a national programme, *and the median estimate was an extra 30 per cent*. However, the median reflected a range of estimates from 'very little' to figures of 70 per cent and over. Moreover, it might be that the estimate of an extra 30 per cent reflects the conventional wisdom and generally accepted beliefs based on earlier UK experience with collaboration (Harvey, 1980). Interestingly, the French and West German respondents believed that the collaboration premium on R & D ranged from a 'little extra' to 30 per cent, with a median estimate in the region of 10 per cent. On this basis, the estimate of an extra 30 per cent on collaborative R & D might be too high.

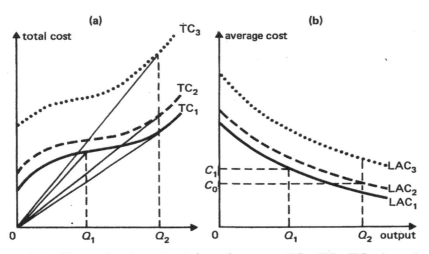

Figure 8.3 The evaluation of collaborative costs. TC_1, TC_2, TC_3 show three different total cost curves, with LAC_1, LAC_2, LAC_3 being the corresponding long-run unit or average cost curves. For simplicity, costs embrace R & D and production. Output Q_1 reflects a national buy (e.g. UK) whilst Q_2 is the output of the joint project.

Joint production work also raises efficiency questions. A substantial number of firms felt that collaborative production involved inefficiencies (Appendix B, Section A4). Such beliefs raise two possibilities:

(a) Since they are based on interviews, they could be wrong, reflecting bias or ignorance. For instance, how do we interpret the views of firms which have lost work as a result of joint projects or of those without experience of international collaboration?
(b) The beliefs could be valid, in which case we need to know why scale and learning economies are not being achieved.

A critical evaluation and evidence is required so that governments can appreciate the logical and empirical basis of these conflicting views. Assume that higher administration costs on joint programmes reflect genuine inefficiencies rather than the costs of managing a large output in an international organisation. Why does inefficiency exist? It could reflect inexperience, with joint European procurement agencies and contractors lacking the knowledge and experience of large scale operations characteristic of the USA (Table 6.4). Or, inefficiency arises where there are political constraints on the allocation of work by comparative advantage. Here, it has to be remembered that the distribution of production work is planned and agreed at an early stage in a project's development and will reflect each nation's *estimated* orders and ruling exchange rates. Attempts to re-allocate work to reflect changing comparative advantages due to unforeseen variations in national productivity, orders, inflation and exchange rates, can be costly. An example occurred during the development of the Tornado. In the 1970s, West Germany had to adjust to changing exchange rates and higher wages by introducing more advanced, capital-intensive production technology which reduced man-hours on its share of the work and enabled the country to remain 'reasonably' competitive on project unit costs. Interestingly, at the start of the Tornado project, Germany had planned to buy 600 units, so that it qualified for major development work on the centre fuselage and wing box; later, the order was reduced to 322 units.

Inefficiency is also likely where international procurement agencies and joint companies in non-competitive markets are more concerned with pursuing other objectives such as sales, staff and a 'quiet life' rather than maximum profits. If such inefficiency is worth eliminating (it is not costless to increase efficiency), is the more appropriate policy to change the procurement and contracting arrangements for collaborative projects, or to introduce more competition into national aerospace markets? The American aircraft industry provides some relevant evidence. US firms usually produce over 800 units, typical of the Tornado programme (Chapter 6). Their competitiveness in the US and world markets suggests that managerial dis-economies are not an inevitable feature of large scale output. But, when interviewed, American firms were unanimous in stressing that the competitive nature of their aerospace industry was one of its major characteristics and a factor in its success (Appendix A, Section A2).

The interview study of European firms provided evidence on the efficiency of collaborative production. Out of fifteen respondents, eight believed that joint projects resulted in savings on unit production costs. However, this part of the interview study was by no means unambiguous. It was difficult to determine the output assumptions being made by the respondents. Some firms were clear that for a *given output*, collaborative production involved higher costs than if the work had been undertaken in one nation. The estimated inefficiency ranged from an extra 1–2 per cent to an additional 10 per cent, but the sample was too small to provide reliable single point estimates. In the circumstances, it seems reasonable to conclude that collaborative production involves inefficiencies, although their magnitude is such that joint projects are likely to result in savings in production costs compared with a national venture (i.e. compare unit costs at (C_0, Q_2) and (C_1, Q_1) in Figure 8.3).

Conclusion

Joint European projects are likely to involve departures from the 'ideal case'. Compared with a national venture, they can result in higher R & D costs, possibly approaching an extra 30 per cent, and production inefficiencies in the region of an additional 1–10 per cent for a given output. Much will depend on the number of partners, their previous experience with collaboration and the complexity of the project. Nonetheless, such collaboration premia mean that a joint programme results in savings for each partner. *If two equal partners combine their national orders, each will save at least 35 per cent on R & D and up to 10 per cent on production costs.* An indication can be given of the budgetary implications of such percentage savings. It has been estimated that compared with a UK-only venture, collaboration on the Tornado could, in the ideal case, result in maximum savings to Britain of some £800 million (1976 prices). Assuming a collaboration premium of 40 per cent on R & D and 10 per cent on production reduces the estimated savings to £360 million (1976 prices; Hartley, 1982). Savings also accrue to other partners. On the basis of each nation's share in the Tornado, *total* savings on the project might be in the region of between £850 million and £1.9 billion (1976 prices), and further savings are likely over the aircraft's life cycle. Obviously, these estimates are only illustrative orders of magnitude but they show that the savings from collaboration could be substantial. Expressed in 1982 prices, collaboration on the Tornado might have saved the UK between £700 million and £1.56 billion, which is equivalent to between £35 million and £78 million *per annum* over a twenty year development and production horizon (equal to an extra three to seven Tornado aircraft annually). For all three partners, the total savings could be between £1.65 billion and £3.67 billion in 1982 prices. Such estimates provide an indication of the budgetary savings of collaboration compared with independence. Impressive though the savings appear, there are some outstanding questions:

(a) Can the efficiency of collaborative projects be improved, so that they resemble the ideal case? Possible solutions include improving the organisation of international projects, expanding competition especially amongst suppliers, and considering collaboration with US firms.
(b) Are there lower-cost solutions? The estimated savings are based on a comparison between collaboration and an independent national project. Ideally, a comparison is required between a joint project and the lowest cost source of supply, which is most likely to be the USA.
(c) Are there any other benefits from collaboration? This requires a wider cost-benefit evaluation of joint projects.

Notes

1 The seven respondents consisted of four who replied 'higher' and three who indicated the 'same'; but the latter group were comparing a *joint* output of, say, 400 units with a *national* programme of 200 units. Interviews can give misleading results in this area, with the respondents providing answers based on different output assumptions.
2 The analysis is identical if the UK industry is inefficient, but less so than on collaborative programmes.

9
How Can Joint Projects Be Evaluated?

Introduction: alternative criteria

Various NATO organisations are concerned with collaboration and by 1980 there were some fifty examples of joint ventures, 60 per cent of which involved aerospace projects (Cornell, 1980). Such evidence is used to conclude that large scale international collaborative organisations can be created and managed successfully. However, the criteria for success often concentrates on inputs rather than outputs, efficiency and profitability. Clearly, government-supported collaborative ventures will usually be completed; but completion is not necessarily evidence of success in terms of creating a marketable and profitable project and organisation capable of competing for, and winning, military contracts in open international competition.

Any evaluation encounters major problems because of the diversity, vagueness and subjectivity of the benefits of joint European aerospace programmes. Nations have different objective (subjective) functions containing different arguments, valuations and trade-offs. One country might place a high valuation on employment whilst another might prefer balance of payments or technology benefits. Nations are also subject to different comparative advantages and resource constraints, as well as to variations in their political markets. For example, there are international differences in constitutions, voting arrangements and competition between political parties. Nonetheless, some criteria are required for assessing the performance of collaborative ventures. There is a range of possibilities, embracing *planned* and *realised* economic and technical criteria:

(a) *Profitability*. What was the rate of return on the project (estimated and actual)? Since domestic military work is subject to government-determined profit rates, this criterion is more appropriate for civil ventures. In other words, it has to be recognised that profit controls and specific government requirements can impose constraints on the performance of international organisations.

(b) *Net social benefits.* Did the project result in *net* social benefits in the form of, say, extra jobs, new technology and balance of payments contributions? Other possible benefits include the preservation of a domestic defence industry. The emphasis is on *net* benefits, meaning the contribution over and above that which would have been obtained if the resources had been used elsewhere in an economy.

(c) *Orders.* The extent to which orders from club members and from abroad (exports) exceeded the initial estimates would be an indicator of market performance.

(d) *Cost criteria.* Do collaborative ventures result in cost savings?

(e) *Contract criteria.* To what extent does a joint project achieve its contractual estimates of cost, time and performance and how do such achievements compare with a typical national project?

(f) *Pairwise comparisons.* Using the criteria outlined above, comparisons can be made between joint ventures and similar national projects. Such comparisons are not without their difficulties, particularly the need to hold constant all other relevant influences. For example, early generation collaborative ventures might be compared with the fiftieth, and fastest, national project. Management emphasis also differs between programmes, some concentrating on fast development, ignoring life-cycle costs. And what is the appropriate comparison for a collaborative multi-role aircraft (Tornado) which replaces several types and which, as a national project, would probably have been cancelled?

This chapter will examine alternative criteria for assessing joint European aerospace projects. Initially, evidence is presented on the views of American and European firms on the general benefits and costs of collaboration, without attempting to determine whether the policy is regarded as worthwhile (e.g. do the benefits exceed the costs?). Consideration is then given to the results of joint projects in terms of development time-scales, exports and costs in relation to the USA. Efforts are made to identify the characteristics of any successful joint ventures and to analyse performance in the context of the European political market place.

The views of firms on the benefits and costs of joint projects

In formulating policy towards joint projects, vote-sensitive governments will be influenced by the attitudes of producer groups (Chapter 2). Some of the benefits mentioned by firms were not unexpected. There was substantial support for benefits in the form of more aircraft for a given budget, the ability to undertake projects which would be

How can joint projects be evaluated? 165

too costly for one nation (i.e. the benefits of a club) and the creation of a competitive European industry, plus standardisation and interoperability. Other perceived benefits were more surprising. Considerable numbers of European and US firms stressed that joint projects are less likely to be cancelled: a benefit which seems to favour producers rather than voters and taxpayers! There was also support for the view that joint projects provide a stimulus, with the partners pooling knowledge and competing in ideas. Surprisingly, little mention was made of any employment and balance of payments benefits, nor was much attention given to the prevention of a US monopoly (Appendix B, Section C1). Of course, some of these attributes might be reflected in the list of other benefits. For example, if a joint project is less likely to be cancelled, it will have associated employment effects. Alternatively, some of the benefits might be more highly valued by *governments* than firms. For example, governments are more likely to be concerned with jobs and balance of payments objectives. In this context, a limited number of firms claimed that, compared with a joint venture, employment on a UK-only project would have been lower or the same. Two examples were given. On the Anglo-French helicopter package, sales of the joint projects had exceeded 2000 units by 1982 compared with an estimated 400 units on a UK-only venture. Also, in the 1980s, Tornado was likely to involve over 70 000 jobs in three nations, with some 30 000 located in the UK. In the absence of a joint Tornado project, it was suggested that the UK would never have built a similar aircraft (see Chapter 4).

Amongst the benefits, firms on both sides of the Atlantic referred to standardisation, although this might be more beneficial to society than to producers. Seven respondents believed that standardisation would result in lower unit support costs. Examples were given of economies of scale in spares production, and savings through using common training facilities (e.g. Tornado). Most firms were unable to quantify the likely savings, although one mentioned a figure of over 20 per cent (Appendix B, Section B).

Joint projects are not costless and there was substantial agreement on the major costs. Administration, compromises in operational requirements and delays (e.g. of one to two years) were most frequently mentioned, and some of these costs were evaluated in Chapter 8 (Appendix B, Section C2). Not all compromises in operational requirements were regarded as undesirable. Examples were given where a nation's technical staff had been restrained and the 'lunatic fringe eliminated'. Little support existed for the view that collaboration results in a domestic industry losing technology. When this issue was examined in greater depth, most respondents recognised a two-way flow of technology, with technical benefits accruing to firms in each partner nation. Of course, individual firms might have lost a technical

166 *Nato Arms Co-operation*

lead to rivals, with Tornado avionics a frequently quoted example. This might be part of the price which has to be paid for joining a club and consuming the benefits of membership. And for every joint project, a nation's officials are likely to bargain vigorously for a 'fair share' of each sector of advanced technology. Two examples were given where collaboration has improved the competitiveness of a partner nation's industry. It was suggested that as a result of the Tornado project, West Germany has established a competitive aerospace industry, and that the Anglo-French helicopter package has improved the competitiveness of the UK helicopter industry. Some of these propositions can be tested by considering the evidence on the performance of joint projects.

Performance indicators for joint projects

Data on joint projects and national ventures can be used to check some of the questionnaire evidence (Chapter 8 and Appendix B). National programmes provide a 'benchmark' and comparisons can be made in terms of output, exports, and the length of time for pre- and post-flight testing, as well as total development periods. Some examples are shown in Table 9.1, which includes two joint civil aircraft so as to increase the data set for collaborative programmes.

Table 9.1 shows that the output of joint military projects reflects the pooling of national orders in an effort to approach US scales of production (see Table 6.4). For example, the planned Tornado output substantially exceeds that of its American counterpart, the F111. More importantly, exports in terms of levels and shares of output provide an indicator of international competitiveness. On this basis, the Jaguar, the Alpha Jet, plus the civil Airbus, have achieved varying degrees of success (cf. Concorde and Tornado). However, the export record of some national projects such as the French Mirage, the UK Hawk, the Phantom, F16 and the civil 747 are even more impressive. Only the Anglo-French helicopter package shows an equally impressive export performance. Admittedly, this is only a partial analysis which focuses on some of the successful national ventures. A more complete appraisal requires data on the average export performance of the total population of each nation's independent projects.

When considering the evidence on development time-scales, three standards of comparison are available:

(a) Pairwise comparisons can be made between a joint venture and a similar national project. On this basis, Tornado took more than *twice* as long to develop as the US F111 and F15 aircraft. Similarly, the Alpha Jet required almost an extra four years

How can joint projects be evaluated? 167

compared with the UK Hawk (cf. also Airbus and Boeing 747).
(b) Joint projects can be compared with the *average* development time for American aircraft. On this basis, all the joint European aircraft projects shown in Table 9.1 required longer development periods, ranging from an extra nine months on the Jaguar to almost six years on the Tornado.
(c) Joint projects can be compared with the *average* development time for *UK* aircraft. The Alpha Jet was slower by eight months, and Tornado needed an additional three years and eight months. Only the Jaguar proved to be *faster* than the UK average time for military aircraft.

Thus, the data suggests that joint European aircraft projects involve longer development time-scales compared with similar national programmes: a finding which supports the questionnaire responses reported in Appendix B (Sections A2 and C2). In general, UK military aeroplanes have taken about one-third longer to develop than American combat aircraft (Table 9.1). A comparison between development times for joint European ventures and UK projects suggests an *average* delay of about one year on the three collaborative military programmes (Alpha Jet, Jaguar and Tornado), possibly eight months on the civil Airbus, and some five to ten years on Concorde depending on whether it is compared with military or civil programmes. Of course, other relevant influences have to be considered. Projects differ in their priorities, resource costs and complexities (see Figure 6.1). For instance, a study of sixty-one US and European aircraft and missiles developed in the 1950s and 1960s concluded that Concorde involved the greatest technological advance in the sample. It was a basically new and radically different system design and the project was given a score of eighteen on a numerical scale of technical advance ranging from two to eighteen (Perry *et al.*, 1971). In such circumstances, the estimates presented above might be regarded as upper bounds for the delays on collaborative ventures.

Table 9.2 shows some limited data on cost escalation for joint projects. On this criterion, Jaguar and Tornado appear relatively successful, with escalation factors below those of national and other joint programmes. Note that the estimated escalation on Tornado is substantially less than on its predecessor, the TSR-2, and its US rival, the F111. Furthermore, cost escalation on Concorde and the Lynx helicopter is similar to that for UK projects, with Concorde involving a major technical advance. Thus, the limited data shows that European collaboration does not necessarily result in higher cost escalation than on national ventures: a finding which reinforces the questionnaire results (see Appendix B, Section A5).

Comparisons of cost escalation between joint and national projects

Table 9.1 Performance indicators

Project	Total output	Exports	Date of Start	Date of First flight	Date of In service	Total development time
Joint projects						
1. Concorde	16	0	November 1962	March 1969	January 1976	13 years 2 months
2. Jaguar	583	181	May 1965	September 1968	May 1972	7 years
3. Tornado	809	0	July 1968	August 1974	July 1980	12 years
4. Alpha Jet (Franco-German trainer)	446	86	July 1969	October 1973	Summer 1978	9 years
5. Airbus (A300)	316	250+	September 1969	October 1972	September 1974	5 years
6. UK–France helicopter package:						
(a) Puma	679	462	Pre-1967	Pre-1967	May 1969	n.a.
(b) Gazelle	1038	517	January 1967	1968	January 1972	5 years
(c) Lynx	310	76	January 1967	March 1971	July 1976	9 years 6 months
National projects: Europe						
1. TSR-2 (UK)	100+ (planned)	0	January 1959	September 1964	Cancelled 1964	n.a.
2. Hawk (trainer, UK)	263	70	October 1971	August 1974	November 1976	5 years 1 month

3. Mirage III (F)	1380	n.a.	November 1956	Late 1961	n.a.
4. Mirage F1 (F)	649	Early 1964	December 1966	March 1973	9 years
USA					
1. F111 (GD)	586	24	November 1962	December 1964	May 1967	4 years 6 months
2. Phantom (McAir)	5195	1334	October 1954	May 1958	December 1960	6 years 2 months
3. Grumman F14	601	80	January 1969	December 1970	October 1972	3 years 9 months
4. F15 (McAir)	1055	185	December 1968	July 1972	November 1974	5 years 11 months
5. F16 (GD)	1949	561	April 1972	February 1974	January 1979	6 years 9 months
6. Boeing 747	564	400+	April 1966	February 1969	January 1970	3 years 9 months

Average development times (1955–69) for

(a) US military aircraft 3 years 7 months   2 years 8 months   6 years 3 months
(b) UK military aircraft 4 years 10 months 3 years 6 months   8 years 4 months

(c) US civil aircraft   2 years 8 months   11 months   3 years 7 months
(d) UK civil aircraft   2 years 6 months   1 year 10 months   4 years 4 months

Sources: Elstub (1969), Taylor (1981).

Notes: (i) Output includes orders and licensed production, 1981. Export figures are approximations. (ii) Dates of start and in-service are sometimes approximations – i.e. it is often difficult to identify the point at which work on a new project actually starts. (iii) The Hawk and Alpha Jet are trainers. TSR-2 preceded Tornado (cf. times from start to first flight). The F16 was the result of a 'fly before you buy' policy: note the development time. (iv) Comparisons can also be made between time-scales from start to first flight and the duration of flight testing.

Table 9.2 *Cost control on joint ventures*

Project	Total cost (£m)	Cost escalation
Joint projects		
1. *Concorde* (UK–France; equal sharing)		
(i) (a) First R & D cost estimate, November 1962	150–170	
(b) R & D costs estimated at June 1973	1065	
(c) R & D costs estimated at June 1980	1134	
(d) Net production costs at June 1980	377+	
(ii) Causes of R & D cost escalation, 1962–73		
(a) Changes in wages, prices, exchange rates	307	
(b) Programme slippage	46	
(c) Revision of estimates	175	
(d) Additional development tasks	328	
(e) Other adjustments	39	
(f) Total cost increase, 1962–73	895	
(iii) Cost escalation in development:		
(a) Current prices 1962–73		6.27
(b) Constant prices 1962–73		2.23
(c) Current prices 1962–80		6.67
2. *Tornado*		
(i) Unit production cost, December 1973	2.9	
(ii) Unit production cost, 1981	11.4	
(iii) Escalation in		
(a) Unit production costs – current prices		3.93
(b) Unit production costs – constant prices		1.27
(c) R & D costs to 1976 – constant prices		1.4
3. *Jaguar*		1.1
4. *UK–France Lynx helicopter* Escalation in R & D costs, 1967–73 (constant prices)		
(a) Airframe		2.06
(b) Engine		2.8
Comparative data: national projects		
5. *TSR-2 (UK)*		
(a) First R & D cost estimate: December 1959	80–90	
(b) R & D costs at January 1964	240–260	
(c) R & D cost escalation (constant prices)		2.8
6. *F111 (USA)*		1.98
UK 1965 sample: military aircraft and missiles ($n = 16$)		2.7
UK 1977 sample: military aerospace projects ($n = 13$)		2.34
USA 1965 sample: aircraft and missiles		2.9

are complicated by the effects of changing exchange rates and which country's perspective is being used (Table 9.2; Concorde). Exchange rate changes also create a more general problem for the sharing arrangements on joint ventures. This can be illustrated by considering a two-nation collaborative project which aims at equal sharing of work and costs. What will be the effect of a change in exchange rates on the originally agreed sharing arrangements? For simplicity, assume that (a) the total work on the project is estimated at 100 units, where the units are either man-hours or numbers of aircraft (volume), and productivity is given; (b) the aim is equal sharing of work (volume) and costs – i.e. 50 : 50; (c) initially, the costs are £1 per unit in the UK and DM4 in Germany and the exchange rate is £1 = DM4 – at the outset of the programme, work and costs are shared on the basis of these unit costs and exchange rates, and the whole project is priced in German currency (Deutschemarks); (d) after the project has started, the exchange rate changes to £1 = DM2, *ceteris paribus* (i.e. depreciation of sterling and appreciation of the Deutschemark).

The results are shown in Table 9.3. It can be seen that equal sharing requires a re-allocation of work between the two nations. Once a project has started, such re-allocations are not costless and adjustments might have to be made in production rather than development work, or in the spares business, or there might have to be an international financial transfer. Alternatively, adjustments might occur through other offsets or via some future project. Uncertainty complicates any re-adjustment process. Problems arise in responding to changes in exchange rates, inflation and economic conditions (e.g. productivity differences) between partner nations for a project requiring a time horizon of twenty or more years for R & D and production. Today's appreciating currency might be tomorrow's depreciating currency (e.g. UK sterling 1975–81). Furthermore, which is the appropriate currency for pricing a joint project between, say, the UK and West Germany: pounds, Deutschemarks, or a special unit of account?

The competitiveness of joint European programmes can also be assessed in terms of their effects on unit costs in relation to American aircraft. Only three European firms claimed that US aerospace equip-

---

Sources: HC 265 (1981), Perry *et al.* (1971), Table 4.1.
Notes: (i) TSR-2 was a UK strike aircraft which preceded Tornado. It was developed by newly formed airframe and engine companies; hence, it is an example of the problems associated with collaboration between *domestic* aerospace firms. (ii) For Tornado, the initial planned in-service date (at 1969) was 1975–85. Actual first deliveries were 1980: time slippage = 1.8. (iii) For TSR-2, the initial planned in-service date (at 1959) was 1966. By 1964, the revised in-service date was end-1969 to mid-1970: time slippage = 1.5.

Table 9.3 Exchange rates and joint projects

Assumptions	UK share	West German share	Total cost
Initial plans			
(a) 100 units of work at £1 and DM4 per unit and an exchange rate of £1 = DM4	£50 (DM200)	DM200	DM400 (£100)
(b) Share of costs	50%	50%	100%
Change in exchange rate: £1 = DM2 (ceteris paribus)			
(a) Costs at new exchange rate	£50 (DM100)	DM200	DM300 (£150)
(b) Share of work at new exchange rates	33⅓%	66⅔%	100%
(c) Share of work required for equal sharing of costs (50:50)	£75	DM150	DM300
(d) Adjustment of work required	+£25	−DM50	DM300

ment was *not* lower priced compared with similar items produced jointly. Engines and helicopters were given as examples of competitive collaborative ventures. In contrast, four respondents claimed that American aircraft were lower priced than joint projects, possibly up to 30 per cent cheaper. However, in testing hypotheses about relative competitiveness, difficulties arise because nations have different policy objectives, and *identical* US and joint European aircraft rarely exist within the same time-scale. Nevertheless, evidence on relative prices is available from the UK evaluation of the American F14, F15 and F16 fighters as alternatives to the Tornado ADV. By late 1975, Britain had decided that the 'difference in cost between the ADV and the possible alternatives was probably not very great' (HC254, 1977, p. 5). *At the time*, the evaluation showed that the F14 was the closest substitute but that it was a costly aircraft, probably 50 per cent more expensive than the Tornado. The cost of an F15 alternative seemed to be similar to the ADV but it was felt that its single crew member would be incapable of coping with the complex UK air defence tasks; and the F16 lacked the required long-range, all-weather capability, although it was a cheaper alternative. Independent estimates by the author gave a unit cost of £13.1 million for the F14; £8.2 million for the F15; £3.7 million for the F16 and about £8.5 million for the Tornado ADV (1976 prices; Hartley, 1982). In the event, the UK decision to proceed with the collaborative Tornado ADV rather than 'buy American' was taken after considering '. . . operational, industrial, financial and foreign exchange considerations . . .' (HC254, 1977, p. 5). If the F15 was regarded as a close substitute (is it?), the UK preference for the Tornado ADV suggests that policy makers 'valued' these operational, industrial and other 'benefits' at a minimum of £56 million (£0.34 million × 165 aircraft). Such benefits are equivalent to a tariff rate of 4 per cent (alternative assumptions indicate that it could rise to 12 per cent) on the F15, which is by no means penal for weapons markets.

The organisation of joint European projects

Significantly, for the UK, the procurement and development of joint aerospace projects has involved a variety of partner nations, companies and international arrangements. Examples have ranged from single project committees of varying degrees of formality, to the prime contractor–sub-contractor Anglo-French helicopter package, and the project specific joint company of the Panavia type (Table 8.1). Such variety can reflect experimentation or the benefits of learning and experience from previous projects, or the influence of budget-maximising bureaucracies. Whatever the explanation, one short term result of this variety might be higher costs associated with new searching and new learning as different partner nations, procurement agencies and companies have to adjust and familiarise themselves with the basic techniques of 'doing business with strangers'. It takes time for industrialists of different nations to know, understand and trust each other; they have to establish common management procedures, an agreed language and an acceptable location for meetings. Costs are also likely to be higher if some firms are selected by governments rather than by competition. Clearly, some criteria are required for assessing the success of alternative organisational forms for collaborative ventures.

The interview study of European firms produced roughly equal support for the Anglo-French helicopter package and the Panavia solutions. The latter was regarded as an evolutionary development reflecting previous UK experience with Concorde and Jaguar. Concorde relied on a committee organisation, with joint committees representing the purchasing governments and the partner airframe and engine firms. The Jaguar programme was felt to be an improvement on Concorde in that it was based on joint companies for the airframe and engine (Harvey, 1980). However, both nations' airframe firms maintained independent design staffs for the project, so resulting in duplication. Also, the government procurement organisation for Jaguar was criticised for its committee structure. Some of these organisation problems were reduced on the Tornado, with the creation of single companies responsible for airframe and engine contracts, together with a single organisation to represent the partner nations (i.e. Panavia, Turbo-Union and NAMMA). Supporters of the NAMMA–Panavia solution claim that it benefits from 'national pride': no one wants to be the cause of project failure and there is access to a greater variety of expertise and knowledge for decision-making. Ultimately, of course, the success of NAMMA–Panavia will be determined by its end-product, namely Tornado. It is not sufficient to claim that the organisation has been successful because it has brought together three nations and produced an advanced technology aircraft. Such an achievement is possible so long as the partner governments are willing to pay. Ideally, the Tornado organisation needs to be judged in terms of its profitability, but there are government profit constraints on non-competitive defence contracts. Export orders are a further possible criterion, but it might be argued that Tornado is a specialised aircraft like the F111 and hence has little prospect of overseas sales (which raises the interesting question of why three European nations have such a unique operational requirement?). Given these problems, the NAMMA–Panavia organisation might be judged in terms of the performance of the Tornado aircraft against the original contract targets or it might be compared with a national programme (see Tables 9.1 and 9.2). Alternatively, it might be deemed to be successful if the partner governments increase their orders for the aircraft or if the organisation is retained for a future collaborative project. There is another 'benchmark' which could be used, namely the results achieved by alternative collaborative organisations (Table 9.1). Here, there is a substantial body of opinion which supports the arrangements used for the Anglo-French helicopter package.

The UK–France helicopter package has two distinct features. First, it embraces *three* helicopter projects, namely the Puma, Gazelle and Lynx. Work-sharing is distributed over the three projects. Second, it is based on a prime contractor–sub-contractor organisation, with Aerospatiale acting as prime contractor on the Puma and the Gazelle, and Westland as the leader on the Lynx. Each leader was chosen on the size of the partners' orders and is responsible for *all* aspects of each helicopter, namely design, production and marketing. In other words, the arrangement resembles the model of a single company, and responsibility can be clearly defined (cf. US views on collaboration, Chapter 6). Government procurement is undertaken by a joint helicopter management committee, with supporting sub-committees having technical, production and administrative tasks. Project monitoring and policing is the responsibility of the country which controls the firm acting as leader. Initially, it was agreed that France would undertake 90 per cent of the production work on the Puma, 60 per cent on the Gazelle and 30 per cent on the Lynx, with export sales providing a basis for any subsequent adjustments in work-sharing. The results of the Anglo-French agreement are shown in Table 9.4. It can be seen that by

Table 9.4 *Anglo-French helicopter package*

Predictions and results	Puma	Gazelle	Lynx
1. Initial sales predictions, 1967			
France	130	170	55
UK	40	250	190
Exports*	85	210	120
Total	255	630	365
2. Sales position, end 1981			
France–UK	217	521	234
Exports	462	517	76
Total	679	1038	310

Sources: Legrand (1976), Westland (1982).
*Exports estimated at 50 per cent of initial national orders.

1982 national and overseas sales had substantially exceeded the initial predictions. Both nations had purchased 972 units compared with an initial plan for 835 units. And exports were 1055 units compared with a forecast of 415 units: such figures are evidence that joint European ventures can produce internationally competitive products. But to what extent does the success of the Anglo-French helicopter agreement reflect the choice of projects, the prime contractor organisation, collaboration or the package deal?

Economic analysis offers limited guidance on the 'best' form of organisation for collaborative projects. Different forms of organisation involve different transactions costs (i.e. the costs of doing business), with individual managers subject to varying amounts of risk. *In general, profit-seeking firms will select the organisational form 'best' suited to achieving their objectives.* Managers and workers are employed on a contractual basis and firms will recognise that incomplete employment contracts provide opportunities for employees to pursue discretionary behaviour (e.g. on-the-job leisure; Hartley and Tisdell, 1981, Ch. 7). Economic analysis provides further insights into the appropriate form of organisation for joint ventures. It seems a reasonable presumption that the formation of a new international organisation for procurement, development and production will be a costlier method of solving a given set of problems than using an established organisation, with clearly defined management responsibilities and previous experience of working with each other. New international organisations for procurement and development will inevitably incur 'set up' and learning costs. Some indirect support for this presumption can be obtained from evidence on the performance of newly merged firms. Studies show that take-overs and mergers can involve substantial adjustment costs with adverse effects on efficiency and profitability (Meeks, 1977). Since these effects arise where private firms influenced by commercial criteria can select their partners, they are more likely to be present in collaborative projects where governments determine the major contractors. Moreover, equal partners in a joint venture cannot be treated like sub-contractors and subjected to the same penalties and sanctions which would be applied for 'poor performance' by suppliers. Thus, the formation of a new international company and procurement organisation to solve complex technical problems is likely to increase transactions costs or the costs of doing business.

Collaboration and the political market

Choices of projects, partner nations, firms and organisational arrangements will be made in the political market place. Indeed, it is possible to formulate an international public choice explanation of joint projects. Such ventures provide discretionary power to politicians and bureaucrats in each nation's political market. They are attractive to vote-sensitive politicians as a means of 'protecting' high technology producer groups as well as providing opportunities to these groups for satisfying their technical aspirations at the expense of the taxpayers. This model predicts that such projects are likely to be 'over-elaborate' and 'too complex', as each national group insists upon applying its own ideas and maximising the technical benefit to its country and company. After all, these groups are experts, so that their views on technology, development costs and time are likely to be decisive. Joint projects also provide bureaucracies with larger budgets, together with opportunities for international travel, bargaining about each nation's 'fair share' of the work, allocating contracts and monitoring the programme. Treaties have to be negotiated between member states. Agreements are needed on the exchange rate adjustments necessary to avoid international financial transfers, and 'policing' is required to ensure that the work-sharing plans are actually implemented. Indeed, budget-maximising bureaucracies have every incentive to under-estimate the costs of joint ventures: this might explain the myth (there is little published official evidence) that independent UK projects are 'too costly' and that joint programmes are the *only* method of reducing the UK's costs of developing and producing modern military and civil aircraft. Bureaucrats supported by producer groups can also overestimate the social benefits of collaboration, especially when the alternative would be to 'buy from abroad'. They can negotiate international contracts which make it costly for any partner nation to the agreement to withdraw unilaterally. In other words, the economics of public choice predicts that budget-maximising bureaucracies in partner nations, supported by scientific interest groups in the form of weapons contractors, are likely to exaggerate the benefits and cost savings on joint ventures in order to persuade vote-conscious governments to undertake such work. And collaborative European ventures are attractive to governments seeking re-election. Each national government can be seen to be providing jobs for its own people, 'protecting' the balance of payments and preventing 'undue' dependence on American technology and military equipment.

Conclusion

In any evaluation, care must be taken to avoid the *nirvana* approach, comparing actual joint projects with a perfect, but never achieved, national venture. Joint projects are attractive to industry because they are believed to be more difficult to cancel; they take longer to develop but cost escalation appears to be the same or even lower compared with national programmes. Whilst European collaboration can lead to lower unit costs, the effects on relative competitiveness will depend on the American industry's scale of output and the non-price characteristics of European and US aircraft. Europe cannot assume that the US aerospace industry will remain static and will fail to respond to efforts to improve the competitiveness of European producers.

10
Conclusion: Some Policy Guidelines

A number of policy guidelines can be formulated for improving the performance of NATO weapons markets.

Guidelines for competition

There are considerable opportunities for introducing competition into NATO weapons markets. The creation of a competitive free trade area in weapons and civil goods would lead to gains from international exchange based on specialisation and comparative advantage. In this way, resource allocation would not be distorted through restricting free trade to military products. For weapons, cost savings of 20–30 per cent are likely to be typical. To achieve such gains requires the abolition of major barriers to the operation of weapons markets:

(a) Governments would have to act as competitive buyers, shopping around for weapons. For example, each nation's armed forces might be given a *fixed* budget for, say, a five to ten year period and instructed to buy equipment for its needs. In this way, weapons choices would not be dominated by domestic jobs and technology arguments which are the proper concern of *other* government agencies. Nor would this exclude the possibility of a group of nations forming a voluntary purchasing consortium, aiming to secure a more favourable transaction, so contributing to standardisation.
(b) Entry barriers into national markets would have to be abolished, so allowing foreign firms to compete for defence business. This would require the removal of tariff barriers and government preferential purchasing policies.
(c) Information would have to be more widely circulated, so that rival foreign producers would be aware of contract opportunities.
(d) Competitive bidding could be extended to the prototype and production stages, with a greater use of fixed price contracts.

Conclusion: some policy guidelines 179
Guidelines for a limited change (improvement)

A competitive solution requires radical changes which are unlikely to be implemented in the foreseeable future. Thus, policy makers might concentrate on limited changes consistent with a long term movement towards the competitive model. In this context, there are opportunities for improving the efficiency of the current variety of collaborative arrangements:

(a) Apply the principles of specialisation and comparative advantage to collaborative ventures, whether they be co-production, work-sharing or joint programmes for R & D and manufacturing.

(b) Allow firms to select their partners on a voluntary basis, using commercial and competitive criteria, embracing American and European producers. Firms would have to be subject to clear contractual incentives, placing them at risk. Efficiency on a joint programme might require one firm to act as the prime contractor for development, leaving it to determine whether to sub-contract some R & D work to other firms in the club or even outside it. Equity in work-sharing might then be achieved by allocating production work to other club members, with each specialising in a specific task (e.g. one firm might manufacture all the wings for the combined order, with another specialising in the production of all forward fuselages). If efficiency dictated one flight-testing centre and one final assembly line, any nation requiring duplicate facilities would have to bear the costs of duplication and compensate its partner(s) for the associated loss of scale economies.

(c) Aim for package deals embracing a number of projects. For example, a group of nations might aim to share R & D and production work over, say, three major weapons projects: this would permit greater opportunities for specialisation by comparative advantage. This package arrangement would have to be incorporated into an internationally-enforceable contract, with clearly specified compensation (e.g. financial payments) in the event of one nation refusing to fulfil its agreed obligations. Such a scheme might be attractive at the NATO level, with international agreements between the USA and Europe. For each aerospace project, there could be a prototype competition between a US and European design: this would guarantee each set of producers a continued involvement in high technology. The winning firm (how would it be selected and by whom?) would be responsible for completing the development tasks and allocating manufacturing work to American and/or European producers on a co-production basis. In this system, production would be used as the balancing item for achieving equitable work-sharing, subject to efficiency requirements (i.e. see the preceding guideline (b) on voluntary selection of partners).

(d) Introduce more efficiency incentives into the employment contracts of bureaucrats working in procurement agencies and the armed forces. Bureaucrats require inducements to search for substitutes and to economise. In the absence of such inducements, they have every incentive to spend (e.g. gold plating). Thus, employment contracts need to provide rewards for not spending (i.e. for saving or economising) and for providing governments with more information on the efficiency implications of alternative weapons procurement policies. For example, in considering joint ventures such as Tornado, governments, voters and taxpayers need to be aware of the 'sacrifices' incurred. Britain's share of collaborative R & D expenditure was equivalent to the sacrifice of between 110 and 160 F16 aircraft before a single operational Tornado was received. Information presented in this form would make governments and the military more aware of the sacrifices incurred in accepting a particular operational requirement and procurement policy.

Closing remarks

It is recognised that these policy guidelines provide no more than a framework which requires further elaboration. However, their philosophy should be clear. Market forces and the increasing costs of weapons will compel nations to reconsider nationalism. NATO nations seeking to economise on defence spending cannot ignore the costs of maintaining independent weapons industries. The armed forces need to recognise that costly domestic weapons mean that the defence budget buys less of the latest products, so that they have to rely increasingly on obsolete equipment. If voters were presented with more information on the costs of alternative weapons policies, they may well question the wisdom of the current methods of buying weapons.

Part III
Appendices

Appendix A

Survey of European and US Firms: A Summary of Responses to a Questionnaire

Name and status

(a) Number of companies visited:
 (i) USA, $n = 5$
 (ii) Europe, $n = 15$
(b) Number of executives and officials interviewed:
 (i) USA, $n = 20$
 (ii) Europe, $n = 26$
 (e.g. vice-presidents, directors, program managers).

Address

US Aerospace Companies

Boeing; General Dynamics; Lockheed; McAir; Northrop.

European Companies and Agencies

Aerospatiale; British Aerospace (Brough, Kingston, Warton, Weybridge, Dynamics at Hatfield); Dassault-Breguet; EMI Electronics; Groupement des Industries Françaises Aeronautiques et Spatiales; Marconi-Elliott Avionic Systems; MBB; Panavia; Rolls Royce; Westland; Ministry of Defence Procurement Executive (UK); Ministry of Defence RAF (Phantom, Tornado and Nimrod Offices); NATO (AWACS Program); NAMMA; General Dynamics F16 Program Office in Brussels.

Date

Interviews held 1977–80.

Duration

Typically 2½–5 hours.

184 Nato Arms Co-operation

A guide to interpreting the questionnaire results

(a) US results are based on twelve completed questionnaires (i.e. some executives were interviewed on a group basis). European results are based on twelve firm questionnaires plus extracts from the joint projects questionnaire, giving a total of twelve to fifteen questionnaires for the European sample.

(b) It was not always possible to obtain answers to *all* questions – e.g. interviews were limited by time constraints or by the knowledge of the respondent. A completed questionnaire required some 5 hours.

(c) Some answers were difficult to interpret, although this was not always apparent to the researcher until after the event!

(d) Remember that the questionnaire was used as the basis for a *structured interview*. With repeated use and experience, it became apparent that some questions were redundant, or too obvious, or 'distorted' the flow of the interview-discussion; and hence were omitted.

(e) In addition to firms, the US sample also included interviews with senior officials at the Department of Defense, the British Embassy in Washington and the Rand Corporation: these results are not reported in this summary of responses.

(f) G, L, S = greater, less, same; E = Europe and reflects European responses.

(g) Information was also requested on employment, output and exports.

(h) Reliable results and generalisations require a large number of identical responses. For example, if all fifteen European respondents agreed on an issue, it was regarded as a reasonably reliable result (i.e. an indication of European beliefs).

Appendix A 185

A. **Views on US, UK, European aircraft industries**

1. UK–Europe aircraft industry: what are its distinguishing features as seen by your organisation?

    (i) Less efficient than US?

	YES	NO
US responses	9	2
European responses	11	6

Number of responses	
Europe	USA*
6	5
1	
7	2
4	4
1	
4	5
1	
2	6
	3
	2
1	2
3	

    If YES, why?
    (a) Lacks scale economies from long runs
    (b) Smaller R & D teams (why)
    (c) Lower labour productivity for a given output (why)
    (d) More labour hoarding (why)
    (e) Poorer weather in UK
    (f) Less capital per worker (why)
    (g) Behaviour, organisation and attitudes of UK procurement agency (explain)
    (h) Others (specify)
      (i) Lags in R & D and production technology
      (ii) Lack of shift working in Europe.
      (iii) Higher labour costs and less mobile labour in Europe
      (iv) US unions don't interfere with hiring –firing
      (v) Decreasing competitiveness of Europe due to inflation and exchange rates.

    (ii) Longer time scales for similar military aircraft?

	YES	NO
US responses	4	
European responses	3	1

    IF YES, how much longer for same projects? (Compare F111 and MRCA Tornado; F15 and Tornado.)
    Why?

---

*Throughout Appendices A and B, the numbers refer to the number of responses. At some points, numbers of responses is shown in brackets (e.g. $n = 1$). The fact that there were seventeen European respondents to the question on the efficiency of the US –European industries is explained by two respondents who replied YES on long runs and NO on short runs.

186 Nato Arms Co-operation

Europe	USA
1	1
2	
1	
2	1
	3
	1
	1

(a) Poorer weather
(b) Poorer flight testing facilities
(c) Fewer resources loaded on to project
(d) Slower decisions by UK procurement authorities
(e) Others (specify)
    (i) UK lacks aggressive management and not as schedule conscious
    (ii) UK lacks R & D knowledge
    (iii) Longer UK manufacturing cycle

2. Main features of US industry as seen by your organisation?

Europe	USA
7	2
2	1
3	1
3	7
	2
1	1
2	2
1	1
1	

(i) More efficient (why)
(ii) Shorter time scales (why)
(iii) Cheaper aircraft (why)
(iv) Higher priced spares
(v) More competitive (why) (e.g. competition in ideas)
(vi) Others (specify)
    (a) US management and companies more aggressive and responsive to customer
    (b) US has technical lead
    (c) Less labour hoarding and more labour mobility in USA
    (d) Larger US home market
    (e) Hidden subsidies

3. What would be *costs* and *time* scales for you to develop (G, L, S – how much)

	R & D cost	Production cost	Time
(i) UK firms			
(a) F15	L2	G1	G1
(b) F16	L3	G1	G1
(c) Boeing AWAC	L1	G1	
(d) F111	L1	L1	
(ii) US firms			
(a) Tornado	{L1 / S1	{L2 / S1	L5
(b) Jaguar	L1	L1	L1
(c) Harrier	G1	L1	

Appendix A

4. Fear of US monopoly
   (i) Definition

Europe	USA
2	1
	1
1	

   (a) One US company
   (b) Dependence on US for supplies and spares (where US has a number of competing companies)
   (c) Others (specify)
       (i) Temporary monopoly by one company (e.g. Phantom)
       (ii) Fear of US domination of civil market

   (ii) Implications of US monopoly

Europe	USA
1	
2	
1	NO
1	
2	
1	

   (a) Poorer quality weapons for UK
   (b) Loss of independence in foreign policy
   (c) Monopoly prices for aircraft
   (d) Higher prices for spares
   (e) Less choice
   (f) Others
       (i) Dependence on US technology

   (iii) Monopoly prices for aircraft
   (a) Without a UK aircraft industry, would US aircraft prices be higher?

	YES	NO
US responses		3
European responses	1	

   (b) If YES, how much higher (in per cent)?
   (c) With a UK industry, how much higher are UK prices compared with US for similar types?
   (d) Are any UK aircraft lower priced than US?

	YES	NO
US responses	1	1
European responses	1	

   IF YES, which and how much cheaper
   (i) Possibly cheaper on small scale, medium technology missiles
   (ii) HS 125

   (iv) Higher prices for spares
   (a) For US military aircraft sold abroad do prices of spares rise on later orders?

	YES	NO
US responses	4	3
European responses	4	1

188 Nato Arms Co-operation

(b) How much do they rise compared with first deliveries (constant prices)?
   Example: from + 15–20 per cent to + 50 per cent.
(c) Why – reasons and ranking (i.e. *why spares prices rise*)?

Europe	USA
2	3
	2
	2
	2
	1
	1
	1
	1
	1
1	

   (i) Profits earned on spares (profit rates)
   (ii) Specific foreign requirements are costlier due to shorter runs
   (iii) Foreigners buy at end of production run
   (iv) Others (specify)
      (a) Foreign business costlier
      (b) Greater risks
      (c) Monopoly pricing
      (d) Spares wanted quickly
      (e) Costs which can't be charged to US government can be recouped on spares
      (f) US government policy on spares pricing
      (g) Prices not raised for fear of loss of future orders
(d) Are prices of US spares supplied to UK or Western Europe higher than similar spares for USAF?

	YES	NO
US responses	2	3

If YES, how much higher (constant prices)
Comments (quotations):
   (i) US foreign military sales policy is relevant
   (ii) Foreign sales allow recovery of items not allowable or recoverable on US government contracts
   (iii) Prices identical where government operates military and civil versions of same aircraft
   (iv) No clear evidence either way: spares only a small part of life cycle costs
(e) Do UK firms increase prices of spares once they have sold to US?

	YES	NO
US responses	1	
European responses	1	1

Comment:
With a temporary monopoly, prices can be raised on firm–foreign government sales, but less so on government–government sales.

B. **Economics of aircraft manufacture**

1. What is a typical production run for

		Europe		USA	
(a)	First order	MRCA = 40 Harrier = 60 Hawk = 175		9–30 aircraft F111 = 69 F16 = 446	
(b)	Total output (approx. 1981)	Hunter Canberra Tornado Jaguar Lightning Harrier/ Sea Harrier Hawk Buccaneer Mirage III/5 Mirage F1 Alpha Jet Nimrod	1985 1376 809 583 338 297 263 143 1400+ 649 486 49	Fighters Phantom F5/T38 F16 F18 F15 A10 C5 C141 Orion Hercules	500–1000 5195 3400 1949 1500 1055 825 81 281 366 1600+

2. Typical breakdown of aircraft costs (combat aircraft):

	Europe		USA
R & D			$3 million unit cost (1977)
Production			$12 million unit cost (1977)
Production costs only (range):			
Airframe	30–50%		25–40%
Engine	25–30%		15–35%
Avionics	20–40%		25–50%

Examples

(i) Life cycle costs on a European helicopter are some three to four times its unit price.
(ii) For UK combat aircraft, life cycle costs are typically three times the initial equipment cost.
(iii) For a 1960s UK combat aircraft, the division of unit production costs was: airframe structure 25 per cent; basic systems (undercarriage, ejector seats) = 25 per cent; engines and support = 25 per cent; operational systems (navigation, weapons system) = 25 per cent.

190 *Nato Arms Co-operation*

3. (a) Number of potential rivals in USA and world for

		Present		1985–90	
		USA	World	USA	World
(i)	Fighters	3–8	2–12	Less	Less
(ii)	Strike–ground attack	4	5		
(iii)	Engines	2	1		
(iv)	Transports (large)	2	1	1	1(?)
(v)	Anti-submarine aircraft	2	2		
(vi)	Helicopters	5	3+		
(vii)	Missiles				
	(a) Strategic	1–2	1	1–2	2(?)
	(b) Tactical	12–15	5+	12–15	Less

Europe	USA
	1
	2
	2
1	
	3
	2
	1

(b) If numbers expected to decline, why?
  (i) Larger firms required for increasing technology
  (ii) Smaller volume of business
  (iii) Greater competition
  (iv) New firms unlikely to enter
  (v) Others (specify)
    (a) Mergers
    (b) Continuation of secular decline – long term optimum number is three firms per sub-market
  (c) Civil aircraft business is unprofitable = exits

4. Minimum efficient scale and ideal size for different types?
   (i) *Range of replies* (employment data)

	Fighters	Strike	Transport	Missiles Strategic	Tactical
USA					
(a) Minimum efficient scale					
(i) R & D	700–4000	5000–20000	Under 27000	5000	500–1000
(ii) Production	3000; minimum of 200 units				
(b) Ideal size					
(i) R & D	14000–25000		1000–3000		
(ii) Production			30000 per division		
Europe					
(a) Minimum efficient scale					
(i) R & D	8000	500–1200	8000 on civil and military R & D		
(ii) Production					
(b) Ideal size					
(i) R & D	15000	750–4000			
(ii) Production		11000			

(ii) *Additional points*
   (1) Answers on minimum scale depend on assumptions about number of aircraft types – the US MES of 20000 assumes three or four aircraft types.
   (2) A development team of 3500 on a large US military transport was regarded as 'too large (diseconomies).
   (3) Optimum size of *plant* could be 25000–30000 employees for USA.
   (4) It was suggested that a *firm* size of 150000 employees in the USA was '*too large*' (diseconomies of scale).
   (5) For Europe, a minimum size of 8000 was required for R & D on civil and military airframes.

5. Is competition possible in world military aircraft market?

	YES	NO
US responses	4	2
European responses	1	

192 Nato Arms Co-operation

USA
2
2
1
1

(i) If NO, why not?
   (a) Too few firms – how many required for competition?
   (b) Government involvement in market (nationalism – independence.)
   (c) Projects are too costly and complex
   (d) Others (specify)
      (i) Competition possible but unlikely – government barriers to trade
      (ii) USA has technical lead – rest of world can't compete
      (iii) US has large domestic market

(ii) If YES, which types?
Example: see answers to question B3(a) and markets with more than three firms in total

(iii) If we had a free market in weapons in the West (e.g. governments shopping around) what would happen to

No. of responses:
Europe and USA

		Larger	Smaller	Same
(a)	Size of			
	(i) UK industry*		5	
	(ii) USA	4		
	(iii) Western Europe		6	
(b)	Number of aircraft firms in			
	(i) UK			
	(ii) US		1	1
	(iii) Western Europe		2	

*Some respondents believe that the USA is the lowest cost source of supply, probably 20–30 per cent more efficient than Europe. One view was that a free market would leave prices *unchanged in the USA*.

(c) Who would specialise on what?
Examples:

UK and Europe:	Fighter, strike and VTOL aircraft; engines; electronic and sub-systems; small airliners; small missiles
USA	Advanced technology aircraft and missiles. USA would dominate world market.

Appendix A   193

6. Costs

   (a) Learning curves
       (i) Own firm

	USA (%)	Europe (%)
Airframes	75–85	77–80
Assembly	70–80	70
Fabrication	80–92	n.a.
Other parts	95	90–95
Jet engines	87–93	90
Missiles	87	n.a.
Helicopters	n.a.	80–85
Avionics	87–95	n.a.

       (ii) Joint projects; co-production

USA	Europe
85 per cent for Europe tending to flatten	Joint = same or better than for national venture

   (b) Is your learning curve S-shaped on log–log paper?

	YES	NO
US responses	1	2
European responses	2	

   If YES, why?
   (i) Payments system
   (ii) Reduced productivity at end of line
   (iii) Inferior equipment–materials used on last aircraft
   (iv) Others (specify)
       (a) Labour turnover
       (b) Need to buy small quantity of extra parts
       (c) Accounting reasons – i.e. recovery of remaining costs
       (d) Modifications and changing order pattern

Europe	USA
2	
2	
	1
1	
	1
	1
2	

   (c) (i) Maximum production run achieved since 1960?

	USA		Europe
F4	= 5195	Hunter	= 1985
F16	= 1949	Mirage	= 1400+
F15	= 1055	MRCA	= 809

194 *Nato Arms Co-operation*

(ii) Rate per month?

	USA	Europe
(i) Typical	12–30	UK = 2–4 MRCA = 7–14
(ii) Maximum since 1960	F4 = 58 F102 = 42 Boeing = 28	Mirage = 13–14 French helicopters = 30–40

(iii) What is typical unit production cost for one of your aircraft?

	F15	F16
Output	729	998
Rate (per month)	9	15–30
1975–6 Prices	$10 million	$3.8 million

(d) (i) How do unit production costs vary with scale of output under ideal conditions?

Unit production cost curve =
$$\begin{cases} 85 \text{ per cent } (n = 1, \text{ USA}) \\ 87\text{–}90 \text{ per cent } (n = 1, \text{ composite of assembly, fabrication, etc., cost curves, USA}) \\ 90 \text{ per cent } (n = 1, \text{ USA}). \end{cases}$$

US curves should be BELOW UK unit cost curves ($n = 1$, USA)

Examples:
(a) Phantom – manufacturing labour learning curve = 72 per cent (output = 5057)
(b) F111 – manufacturing labour learning curve = 82 per cent (output = 586)

(ii) What rate per month is assumed? If rate were doubled, what would happen to unit production costs?

Greater	
Less	3
Same	

85–88 per cent unit cost curve compared with 87–90 per cent curve; USA

Appendix A 195

If lower, how much lower?
Example:
Approx. −2 per cent (USA)

(iii) What are main reasons for lower unit costs with greater volume?

Europe	USA
1	2
1	4
1	2
	1
	2
	1
	1
1	

(a) Greater capital per worker
(b) More labour learning
(c) Can justify purchase of highly specialised equipment
(d) Spreading of overheads
(e) Others (specify)
  (i) Economies of bulk buying
  (ii) Suppliers obtain economies of scale
  (iii) Learning might reflect management and economies of bulk buying rather than direct labour
  (iv) Labour markets are a constraint

(iv) Having discussed scale economies under ideal conditions, what is effect on unit costs of not knowing *in advance* the total production order?

Greater	3
Less	
Same	

(US and Europe)

Example:
500 aircraft ordered initially compared with an initial order of 100 and four re-orders of 100 each

Examples of replies:
(a) Minimum of 100 orders required to launch a new civil aircraft (USA)
(b) Minimum production run for a fighter = 200 units (USA)
(c) It was estimated that one US firm could produce about 200 units per annum with the capital and labour being used to produce about 110 units per annum
(d) One UK firm claimed that if it had been given a large order initially, it could have produced at least *twice* as many combat aircraft with a given plant and labour force

7. How important is size of (i) R & D and (ii) production unit for success in (a) military and (b) civil aircraft business? US responses only.

	No (n=4)
Very	
Quite	1
Little	1

Explanation
(i) Four US firms claimed that size was *NOT* important for success – i.e. size = f(success) and not vice versa
(ii) Market structure – i.e. competition in R & D – was more important.

8. (a) What have been effects of introducing competition? Classify as greater, less, same (G,L,S) (USA and Europe).

	Costs	Time	Cost escalation	Time slippage	Quality
(i) Up to flight-testing stage ('fly before buy')	G2	G5	G1	G1	G5
(ii) For sub-contracting work	L2		L3	L3	(i.e. better)
	L2				

Note: Extra time = +12–24 months ($n = 4$).

Europe	USA
	2
	1
1	
1	

	1
	1
1	
1	

(b) Total procurement package: main lessons
  (i) Unsuitable for major technical advances (e.g. C5)
  (ii) Unsuitable where customer (buyer) is inflexible
  (iii) Advantage of a clearly specified deal, but risky
  (iv) Problems of inflation and threat of nationalisation

(c) 'Fly before you buy': main lessons
  (i) Demonstrates performance of concept
  (ii) Reduces risks of project failure (buys information)
  (iii) Only if time available
  (iv) Military opposition: they fear they will have to buy the prototype

Appendix A 197

9. It is argued that US quoted costs and prices are inaccurate until a contract is signed.
   (i) Is this correct?

	YES	NO
US responses	1	2
European responses	1	

   (ii) If YES, what is relationship between initial quoted price and final contract price?
   Responses:
   (a) Depends on competition: monopoly = higher prices
   (b) Depends on modifications and extras
   (c) US quotes are wildly inaccurate until a contract is signed
   (d) Unless costs differ by a factor of two or more, they are unreliable as a basis for choice.

10. Profit rates (Europe and USA)
    (i) Are profit rates on capital (or any asset test) higher on military than civil aircraft?

YES	NO
3	3

    (ii) Are profit rates on capital higher on aircraft than non-aircraft work?

YES	NO
	2

    (iii) Are profit rates on capital higher on military aircraft than missiles?

YES	NO
	3

    Explanations:
    (a) *Successful* civil aircraft more profitable than military aircraft
    (b) Missiles as profitable or more profitable than military aircraft

C. **Alternative policies**

1. (a) Do you prefer home to foreign weapons?

	YES	NO
US responses	2	
European responses	5	1

(b) How much more are you willing to pay for home weapons?

Examples:

Up to 5% ⎫ (i) Inapplicable to USA since USA is lowest cost supplier for advanced weapons systems.
5–10%   ⎬
10–20%   ⎪ (ii) Up to 20% extra for UK equipment on US Phantoms.
Over 20% ⎭

Europe	USA
4	1
1	
4	
1	
	1
2	
1	
1	
1	
1	
1	

(c) What are the advantages of buying from the domestic industry?
  (i)   Security of supply
  (ii) Better quality weapons
  (iii) Weapons designed for national needs
  (iv) Lower prices (of spares)
  (v)   Others (specify)
        (a) Unfavourable experience with joint projects
        (b) Avoids dependence on US high technology
        (c) Freedom of choice
        (d) Avoids dependence on foreigners
        (e) Control over supplies of spares
        (f) Saves jobs
        (g) Saves dollars

Europe	USA
	3
	1
3	
1	

(d) If a domestic aircraft industry is needed for defence, what is the *minimum* size required?
  (i)   Competition in IDEAS (R & D) required (i.e. minimum of two and possibly three or four firms)
  (ii) Size needed to supply US forces
  (iii) Retain a *total* capability
  (iv) Sufficient to be an intelligent customer

Appendix A   199

2. (a) How would you rank alternative policies (US responses)?

USA
4
8
4
6

		Rank
(i)	Buy USA	First choice
(ii)	Buy UK – Europe	
(iii)	Joint collaborative projects (which nations)	Least preferred – rejected by all eight respondents
(iv)	International consortium (Tristar – private commercial collaboration)	Preferred to (iii) (joint)
(v)	Licensed production, co-production/ industrial collaboration	Usually second choice

USA
2
1
2
2
1
2

(b) Reasons for ranking (US responses):
 (i) Relative profitability
 (ii) Ideal policy would be to specialise by comparative advantage and trade
 (iii) Joint projects disliked because
    (a) Too slow
    (b) Lack of a single management decision-maker
    (c) Committee aircraft
    (d) Government involvement and lack of profit motive

(c) If you had to choose a mix of these policies, which would you select?

	US responses
*Home	*Mix of home–consortium–/ licensed manufacture–co-production: $n = 7$
Abroad	Little support: $n = 1$
Joint	No (disliked): $n = 6$
*Consortium	
*Licensed manufacture	Mix of home–consortium– licensed–co-production $n = 7$
Co-production/ industrial collaboration	

200 *Nato Arms Co-operation*

3. (a) For you as a buying nation, what would you expect to happen to
   (i) Unit R & D costs
   (ii) Unit production costs
   (iii) Total unit costs
   (iv) Aircraft quality
   for each of these policies compared with buying domestically (G,L,S – how much), *US responses only*.

	Unit R & D cost	Unit production cost	Total unit costs	Quality
Buy abroad	USA is lowest cost supplier for most aircraft ($n = 2$)			
Joint collaborative	G4	G5	G3	Poorer (inferior) 5
	L1			
International consortium	G1	G3	G1	Poorer 1
	L2			Same 1
Licensed production	G1	G7	G2	Same 5
	L2			

(b) Reasons for (US responses):
Higher costs

6	(i) Administrative–organisational
	(ii) Labour hoarding
4	(iii) Inefficient partners
	(iv) Geography
	(v) Others (specify)
2	(a) Lack of one clear decision-maker
2	(b) Management by Committee
1	(c) Tough technical projects chosen
1	(d) Fighting for project control on joint projects
1	(e) Joint projects take longer and cost more

Lower costs

2	(i) Comparative advantage and greater efficiency
2	(ii) Longer runs
	(iii) Best ideas pooled
1	(iv) Others (specify)
	(a) Spreading R & D over longer runs

4. (a) Are you willing to enter joint collaborative military projects?

	YES	NO
US responses	8	1
European responses	10	

Appendix A 201

(b) If YES,
   (i) On what terms and for which projects?

Europe	USA
3	5
6	2
1	
1	
	4
	3
	2
	1
1	
1	

      (1) Design leadership
      (2) Work-sharing and financing according to size of domestic order
      (3) Willingness to compromise on OR
      (4) Large, complex, costly projects (examples)
      (5) Others (specify)
         (a) Desire for some technical involvement by each nation
         (b) Co-production–industrial collaboration
         (c) Share design effort by comparative advantage
         (d) International consortia of Lockheed–Rolls Royce type
         (e) Any joint project needs to be at risk
         (f) Desire to retain a European capability
         (g) Select risky projects

   (ii) Minimum size of order
      Examples:

      F16 type = 1000   bomber = 400
      airliner = 350–500   NATO AWACS = 18–27

      On complex aircraft, more than three equal partners is 'too many'

Europe	USA
4	
3	6
1	No (n = 3)
	4
	1
2	
	1
2	
1	

   (iii) What form?
      (1) Formation of new international companies (e.g. Panavia model)
      (2) *Ad hoc* international consortia
      (3) Government–government relationship
      (4) Other (specify)
         (a) Co-production/industrial collaboration
         (b) Possible partners limited to UK, West Germany, France, Japan
         (c) Build on existing joint projects organisations
         (d) Exclude governments
         (e) Prime contractor, government leader on joint projects – avoid equal partners
         (f) Prefer known firms for collaboration rather than strangers

Europe	USA
2	5
	1
	1
1	1
	1
1	1
1	3
1	

(iv) What major obstacles do you envisage?
- (1) Nationalism
- (2) Limited range of partners
- (3) US bureaucrats will not sacrifice or share power
- (4) Exchange rate problems
- (5) Collaboration is costly
- (6) Differences in accounting, contracting procedures, international law, etc.
- (7) Government interference with profit motive and choice of partners
- (8) Efficiency requires a single leader; equity requires equal partners

(v) Would a joint project change your firm's behaviour?

	YES	NO
European responses	1	3

If YES, how (prices, output, diversification, efficiency)?

Examples:
- (a) Joint projects lead to political criteria and interference with profit motive (US view)
- (b) Joint projects add an extra incentive – each nation has its pride
- (c) No effect on cost controls
- (d) Firms become less competitive

(vi) Minimum size of order for co-production (e.g. F16)

F16 = 348 units   NATO AWACS = 18 units

D. Benefits and costs of collaboration

1. (a) Under what circumstances would you expect your government to select each of the alternative policies (US and European responses)?

	Balance of payments	Strategic	Technology	Employment	Cheaper weapons	For complex costly weapons	Others
(i) Buy home	2	4	5	4		1	
(ii) Buy abroad					6	1	Less gold plating; better weapons
(iii) Joint collaborative			1	1		1	Where high R & D can be made acceptable via sharing
(iv) Licensed production; co-production; industrial collaboration	4	4	4	7	3		Standardisation; entry to new markets

Note: Replies refer to NUMBER of responses – e.g. seven respondents felt that JOBS were a relevant factor in licensed manufacture and co-production.

(b) Compared with your current experience, what do you expect to happen to escalation under each alternative policy?
(G,L,S – USA and European responses).

	Buy abroad	Joint	Consortium	Licensed
Cost escalation*		G 1 L 1	S 1	
Time slippage		G 1 S 1		G 1
Quality escalation		G 1		S 1
Total development time		G 3	G 2	

*Do not assume zero cost escalation on national projects – i.e. when comparing them with joint ventures.

204 Nato Arms Co-operation

(c) Profits. Compared with present, what would you expect to happen to your profits under alternatives (G,L,S)?
A US view only.

		Answer	Rank: most–least profitable
(i)	Buy home	Most profitable ($n = 1$)	1
(ii)	Buy abroad	Least profitable ($n = 1$)	5
(iii)	Joint		4
(iv)	Consortium	Consortium more profitable than joint projects ($n = 1$)	3
(v)	Licensed manufacture Co-production	Same ($n = 2$)	2

(d) For joint projects, are there any weapons which are

(i) Politically too sensitive

YES	NO
1	

Example: Strategic missiles

(ii) Technically too intricate

YES	NO
	1

(e) Are there any projects which are too costly to be developed and produced by (US and European responses)

(i) UK only?

YES	NO
5	

Examples: TSR-2; AWACS; Chinook helicopter; space satellites

(ii) US only?

YES	NO
5	

Examples: AWACS; B1 bomber; SST; next generation airliners

(f) Details of maximum R & D budget per project
Examples: B1 bomber; AWACS; TSR-2 for UK (between £240 million and £260 million, 1964 prices) space satellites (£20 million to £60 million per copy, 1982 prices)

(g) Details of maximum ratio of R & D to total production costs per project
Examples: TSR-2 for UK; B1 bomber; AWACS

E. **Licensed production (including co-production)**

1. (i) Do you have any licensed production?

	YES	NO
US responses	5	
European responses	5	

(ii) If YES, approximate value of business to your firm?
Examples:
- McAir: F4, F15 Japan
- Boeing: Roland-Europe
- General Dynamics: F16 Europe
- Lockheed: P3 Japan
- Northrop: F5 Taiwan, Spain, Canada, Switzerland
- European firms: Finland, India, Romania, Yugoslavia

(iii) Is there a difference between licensed production and co-production and industrial collaboration (US responses only)?

	YES	NO
US responses	2	

If YES, explain
(a) Licensed = foreigner builds for its own nation only
(b) co-production = foreigner shares in US and domestic production + third party sales. US company acts as prime contractor, with foreigners as sub-contractors
(c) Industrial collaboration = foreigners build some of their aircraft but none of USA's

206 *Nato Arms Co-operation*

2. Why do/would you license production (or co-produce)?

Europe	USA
2	7
	1
1	4
1	1
	1
1	

(i) To enter market that otherwise would not be available
(ii) To obtain extra income when at capacity
(iii) To enter a market which firm had not previously been successful in entering
(iv) Others (specify)
   (a) Foreign governments require licensed or co-production (otherwise no order)
   (b) Extra work and production
   (c) Means of economic development for UDCs
   (d) Buys ready-made R & D – shortens time scales

Examples of behaviour:
(1) Offer final assembly work: assembly = 5–6 per cent of total man-hours
(2) Offer co-production or work-sharing for business which would otherwise be undertaken by US components suppliers. One airframe firm claimed that it did not lose any work; another claimed that it might lose 1–10 per cent of jobs (work) which it would otherwise have undertaken.

3. (a) How are licensing fees determined (including determinants of work-sharing)?

USA
2
2
1

(i) Size of order
(ii) Competition
(iii) Extent to which R & D already recovered on government sales
(iv) Extra costs incurred in LP.

Appendix A 207

USA
1
1
1
1

(v) Others (specify)
    (a) Aim for equal profitability of work
    (b) Costs of transferring technology
    (c) Modify collaboration arrangements to obtain order
    (d) Profits *should* be higher on co-production–but are same

(b) What is typical license fee?
Examples (1976 prices): Between $3 million and $10 million for transfer of data packs: between $1 million and $100 million for technical assistance; typically, 5 per cent on sales, but could be up to 10 per cent.

(c) How much would you be willing to pay to break into a large NATO market (US responses only)?
    (i) Specify size of market
    Example: Work-sharing on NATO AWACS

USA
1
4

    (ii) Would you
        (a) Waive R & D reimbursement for an inferior aircraft?
        (b) Reduce prices of components?
        (c) Waive or reduce license fees?
        (d) Others (specify)
            (i) Offer attractive co-production–collaboration deal (e.g. F16 European programme: 10, 40, 15 per cent)

(d) Is licensed production more profitable, less profitable or about the same degree of profitability as domestic work?

	More	Less	Same
US responses	2	1	7
European responses	1	1	3

4. Are unit costs of licensed production aircraft higher than those of main manufacturer?

	YES	NO
US responses	9	1
European responses	3	2

(i) If YES, how much higher
    Examples:
    (a) UK work-sharing on F4 = +23–43 per cent
    (b) At 100 units, for (i) an ADC = +10–12½ per cent (ii) a UDC = +25–40 per cent
    (c) +10 per cent for 25 per cent industrial collaboration
    (d) For USA = +10 per cent; for UDC = +40–50 per cent
    (e) −30 per cent to +300 per cent

    Range: +10–50 per cent

Europe	USA
1	4
2	5
1	3
	2
	1
	1
	1
1	
1	

(ii) If YES, why?
    (a) Shorter production lines
    (b) No learning economies from earlier production
    (c) Transactions costs of transferring technology (how much)
    (d) Others (specify)
        (i) Start at higher point on learning curve
        (ii) Duplicate tooling
        (iii) Duplicate assembly lines
        (iv) Modifications to aircraft
        (v) Previous experience, skill levels and capital of licensee (e.g. UDC)
        (vi) Depends on labour rates

(iii) What is typical learning curve for a licensed producer (licensee)? US and European responses:
    80 per cent ($n = 1$); 85 per cent ($n = 1$);
    80–85 per cent ($n = 1$)

(iv) Do unit costs for licensed production aircraft (licensee) vary with (US and European responses):
    (a) Main manufacturers (licensor) production?
    (b) Licensor's previous experience with licensing?
    (c) Licensee's previous experience with licensed production?

	YES	NO	How much?
(a)	2		Less; $n = 1$
(b)	4		Less; $n = 1$
(c)	5		Less; $n = 1$

Appendix A   209

(v) For licensed production, what are
  (i) Costs?
    Example: Between $5 million and $6 million on F4 for one nation (1976 prices)
  (ii) Time scales for transferring technology to licensee (US and European responses)?

Minimum of 3–6 months	2
6–24 months	3
2 years	1
2½ years	1
Up to 3 years	1
Under 5 years	1
Up to 7 years	2
Up to 10 years	1

(vi) On a typical licensed production job, how much extra work do you obtain?

Range: { 25–33 per cent of total licensed production
90–100 per cent of work at main *airframe* firm }

(vii) How much work and how many *jobs* are obtained by licensee?
  Range: Jobs *gained* = (1.15–4) × US jobs *lost* (mainly in supplying industries)
  European firms: some extra jobs gained – e.g. small numbers

(viii) Main problems of licensed production?

Europe	USA
	2
	2
	2
2	1
2	
1	

  (a) Differences in accounting, depreciation, government policing – monitoring and inflation
  (b) Exchange rate problems
  (c) Need for *fair* sharing of work, including access to technology
  (d) Different attitudes to exports and constraints on exports
  (e) Problems of interpreting drawings; willingness of licensor to co-operate and offer information–advice
  (f) Licensee has to go through a lot of learning

5. Benefits of licensed production
  (i) Does the licensee gain any technical benefits?

	YES	NO
US responses	10	
European responses	6	

210 Nato Arms Co-operation

Europe	USA
4	5
1	2
	2
	1
1	

Examples:
(a) Manufacturing technology (but at a price)
(b) Design ideas
(c) Commercial fall-out
(d) Management–organisational benefits
(e) Started with licensed production, but now partner in European projects and competing with US

(ii) If YES, how highly would you value these?
Examples:
£1 million ⎫
£1 million to £5 million ⎬ Europe gaining 5–8 year on F16 deal
£6 million to £10 million ⎪
£10 million or more ⎭

Can't say: $n = 5$

(iii) Does the licensor gain any technical benefits?

	YES	NO
US responses	2	5
European responses		1

(iv) If YES, how highly would you value these?
(a) Not very much ($n = 1$)
(b) Difficult to value ($n = 1$)
(c) Some knowledge acquired ($n = 1$)

F. Exports

Europe	USA
1	
1	2
1	2
1	1
	1
1	

(a) How would you describe profitability of exports as compared with home sales?
  (i) Exports less profitable
  (ii) Same
  (iii) Exports more profitable
(b) Why difference?
  (i) Firms can charge higher prices and recover costs not allowable or recoverable on national government business
  (ii) Higher margins offset by higher costs
  (iii) Often price is less important for exports

2. (a) Are export prices of military aircraft (*ex* factory) identical to home prices?

	YES	NO
US responses		3
European responses		2

Appendix A 211

(b) If NO, are export prices higher or lower?

	Higher	Lower
US responses	3	
European responses	1	

(c) If NO, what determines export prices?
- (i) Competitors prices
- (ii) Volume of domestic business
- (iii) Size of order
- (iv) New customer
- (v) Others (specify)
    - (a) Government policy and levies
    - (b) Price reduced when product at end of life

Europe	USA
2	1
2	
2	1
1	
1	1
1	

Appendix B

Joint Projects: Summary of Responses to a Questionnaire

Sample

(1) Number of executives and officials interviewed, $n = 18$
(2) Aerospace, helicopter and electronic firms in Western Europe:
    (a) *UK*: British Aerospace (Warton, Weybridge, Kingston, Dynamics at Hatfield); Rolls Royce; Westland; EMI Electronics; Marconi Avionics; Ministry of Defence
    (b) *France*: Aerospatiale; Dassault; GIFAS (trade association)
    (c) *West Germany*: MBB; NAMMA; Panavia.

Date

Interviews held 1977–9.

Duration

Interviews lasted 1½–4 hours.

Notes

(a) Results are based on eighteen completed questionnaires (e.g. interviews with directors, managers and senior civil servants).
(b) The joint projects questionnaire was twenty pages in length. This section reports the results of only a *part* of the larger questionnaire.
(c) The results are based on European companies with actual experience of joint projects (e.g. Concorde, Jaguar, MRCA, helicopters, etc.). Many of these firms and others also replied to the firm questionnaire (Appendix A).
(d) See also 'A guide to interpreting the questionnaire results' on page 184.
(e) Some questions referred to the UK. For joint projects, this embraced the partner nations included in the interviews – i.e. France and West Germany.

A. Economics of joint European projects

1. Percentage cost breakdown of project compared with typical UK project

R & D	Joint project (see 3. below)	UK only (see 3. below)
Unit production costs		
(i) Airframes	Joint projects are similar to UK only on % cost breakdown – no major differences	50% 30%
(ii) Engines		30% 30%
(iii) Avionics		20% 40%
		100% 100%

2. What were initial (original) costs of project?
   Example:
   In 1978 tornado was within 5–8 per cent of its 1970 forecast man-hours for production

   Estimated delivery: Joint projects take longer:

	No. of responses
(i) +20 per cent	1
(ii) 1–2 years extra	3
(iii) 3+ years extra	1
(iv) Delays (unspecified)	3

3. (a) Does joint project involve higher R & D costs than if work had been undertaken in UK (or in France–West Germany)?

YES	NO
17	

   (b) If YES, how much higher?

Very little	4
+10–20 per cent	3
+30–50 per cent	6
+50–70 per cent	1
+70 per cent or over	1

No. of responses	
10	
3	
1	
3	
2	
2	
2	
1	
1	
1	
1	
1	
1	

(c) Why?
  (i) Administrative costs of international work
  (ii) Harmonisation of different national standards and operational requirements
  (iii) Greater escalation of performance requirements
  (iv) Less cost control
  (v) Others (specify)
    (a) Duplication
    (b) Each partner insists upon having a prototype and test rigs
    (c) Disagreements over management, language, measurement, national pride
    (d) More time required – e.g. modifications take longer to agree
    (e) Over-elaborate design
    (f) Overheads shifted to joint project
    (g) Political constraints on efficient allocation of work
    (h) Better project is costlier
    (i) Costs of creating a European industry to compete with USA
    (j) Travel costs are trivial part of total R & D

4. (a) Does joint project involve higher/lower unit production costs than if all the work had been done in UK (or one country)?

	YES	NO
Higher	4	
Lower	8	
Same	3	

(b) If YES, how much higher/lower

Range:		
+1–2 per cent	2	for a given output
+5 per cent	1	
+10 per cent	1	
−10 to −30 per cent	2	

Appendix B. 215

USA
2
6
5
2
2
2
1
1

(c) If YES, why?
   (i) Duplication of production lines
   (ii) Duplication of final assembly (including loss of learning economies)
   (iii) Economies due to longer runs in one plant and greater learning.
   (iv) Others (specify)
      (a) Exchange rate variations
      (b) Political constraints on production by comparative advantage
      (c) Transport costs and costs of matching-up at different factories
      (d) Organisation problems over partners
      (e) Challenge from partner

(d) If the production work were to be allocated on a competitive basis but still within the partner nations, would unit production costs be lower?

YES	NO
4	1

(e) If YES, how much lower?

Under 5 per cent	
5–10 per cent	
10–20 per cent	1
Over 20 per cent	1

5. (a) Is cost escalation higher, lower or the same compared with typical UK (or partner) projects?

Higher	1
Same	4
Lower	5

(b) Is time escalation higher, lower or the same compared with typical UK (or partner) projects?

Higher	3
Same	3
Lower	1

(c) Is quality escalation higher, lower or the same compared with typical UK (or partner) projects?

Higher	1
Same	1
Lower	3

216 Nato Arms Co-operation

B. Standardisation and support costs

1. (a) Effect on unit support costs?

G	L	S
	7	

(b) How much?

Under 5 per cent	
5–10 per cent	
10–20 per cent	
Over 20 per cent	1
Can't say	2

Examples of replies:
   (i) Life cycle costs exceed twice production costs over 15–20 years ($n = 1$)
   (ii) Economies of scale in spares production (longer runs) ($n = 4$)
   (iii) Pooling and spreading of risks on spares provision ($n = 2$)
   (iv) three-nation training school for Tornado ($n = 3$)

C. Benefits of and costs of joint projects (replies from European and US firms)

1. Major benefits

Europe	USA
10	4
8	No
1	
1	
3	1

(a) Reduces chances of cancellation
(b) More aircraft for given budget
(c) Retains domestic aircraft industry for
   (i) Strategic reasons
   (ii) Employment
   (iii) Balance of payments
   (iv) technology
(d) Prevents US monopoly

Appendix B 217

Europe	USA
7	
6	
3	
8	
6	
5	3
4	
4	
2	
2	
1	

(e) Stimulus of joint work for
    (i) UK industry (and partner industries)
    (ii) UK procurement agency (and partners)
(f) Others (specify)
    (i) Allows projects not possible on a national basis (independence too costly)
    (ii) Creates European industry able to compete with USA
    (iii) Standardisation and inter-operability
    (iv) Pooling of knowledge and competition in ideas
    (v) Reduces national barriers and prejudice
    (vi) Spreading of R & D costs
    (vii) Greater incentives to sell joint projects in world markets
    (viii) Eliminates lunatic fringe

2. Major costs

Europe	USA
7	5
1	
2	2
8	6
5	1
3	
2	
1	
1	2
1	

(a) Compromise in operational requirement
(b) Inferior aircraft
(c) Domestic industry 'loses' technology
(d) More difficult to cancel
(e) Administrative costs of international projects
(f) Others (specify)
    (i) Delays
    (ii) Loss of independence in defence industry
    (iii) Exchange rate problems
    (iv) Duplication
    (v) Adverse effect on industry's competitiveness
    (vi) Costs of learning to work with each other

References

Aaronovitch, S., and Sawyer, M. C. (1975). *Big Business* (London: Macmillan).
Angus, R. (1979). *Collaborative weapons acquisition: the MRCA (Tornado)–Panavia project*. Aberdeen Studies in Defence Economics, University of Aberdeen.
Anon. (1977). F-16 multinational fighter program. *Aviation Week and Space Technology*, 2 May 1977, pp. 44–130.
Ashcroft, G. (1969). *Military logistic systems in NATO: the goal of integration*. Part I. Economic aspects. Adelphi Paper 62, International Institute for Strategic Studies, London.
Balassa, B. (1977). Revealed comparative advantage revisited, 1953–71. *Manchester School* of Economic and Social Studies, vol. XLV, December 1977, pp. 327–44.
Burn, D., and Epstein, B. (1972). *Realities of Free Trade: Two Industry Studies* (London: Allen and Unwin).
Callaghan, T. A. (1975). *US–European economic co-operation in military and civil technology (revised)*. Center for Strategic and International Studies, Georgetown University.
Cavallari, F., and Faustini, G. (1978). Labour costs and employment in Italy and the EEC. *Banca Nazionale del Lavero Quarterly Review*, September 1978.
Chandrasekar, K. (1973). US and French productivity in 19 manufacturing industries. *Journal of Industrial Economics*, vol. XXI, April 1973, pp. 110–20.
Cockerill, A. (1974). *The steel industry: international comparisons of industrial structure and performance*. Occasional Paper 42, Department of Applied Economics, University of Cambridge.
Cmnd 2853 (1965). *Report of the Committee of Inquiry into the Aircraft Industry* (London: HMSO).
Cmnd 5976 (1975). *Defence Statement* (London: HMSO).
Cmnd 7198 (1978). *A Review of Monopolies and Mergers Policy* (London: HMSO).
Cmnd 7826-I (1980). *Defence in the 1980s* (London: HMSO).
Cmnd 8212 (1981). *Statement on the Defence Estimates 1981* (London: HMSO).
Committee of Public Accounts (1974). *Third Report of the Committee of Public Accounts: Minutes of Evidence* (London: HMSO).
Committee of Public Accounts (1978). *Third Report of the Commitee of Public Accounts: Minutes of Evidence* (London: HMSO).
Constantopoulos, M. (1974). Labour protection in Western Europe. *European Economic Review*, vol. 5, pp. 313–28.
Cornell, A. H. (1980). Collaboration in weapons and equipment. *NATO Review*, vol. 28, October 1980, pp. 14–19.
CPRS (1975). *Future of the British Car Industry* (London: HMSO).
CPRS (1976). *Future of the UK Power Plant Manufacturing Industry* (London: HMSO).

Dassault-Breguet (1977). *Avions Marcel Dassault-Breguet Aviation* (Paris: Marcel Dassault-Breguet Aviation).
de Jong, H. W. (ed.) (1981). *The Structure of European Industry* (The Hague: Martinus Nijhoff).
Demsetz, H. (1968). Why regulate utilities? *Journal of Law and Economics*, vol. XI, April 1968, pp. 55–65. Reprinted in C. K. Rowley (ed.) (1972) *Readings in Industrial Economics*, Vol. 2, pp. 173–86 (London: Macmillan).
Dosser, D., Gowland, D., and Hartley, K. (eds) (1982). *The Collaboration of Nations* (Oxford: Martin Robertson).
Downs, A. (1957). *An Economic Theory of Democracy* (New York: Harper).
EEC (1980). *The European Aerospace Industry: Trading Position and Figures* (Brussels: Commission of the European Communities).
EEC (1981). *The European Aerospace Industry: Trading Position and Figures* (Brussels: Commission of the European Communities).
Elstub, St. J. (1969). *Productivity of the National Aircraft Effort* (London: HMSO).
Friedman, M. (1955). The theory and measurement of long-run costs. In *Business Concentration and Price Policy*, pp. 230–7 (Princeton, N. J.: Princeton University Press). Reprinted in G. C. Archibald (ed.) (1971) *The Theory of the Firm* pp. 44–52 (Harmondsworth: Penguin).
Gansler, J. S. (1980). *The Defense Industry* (Cambridge, Mass.: MIT Press).
General Dynamics (1974). *The team-leader's role in 'design-to-cost' preliminary design. Lightweight fighter prototype.* General Dynamics, Fort Worth, Texas.
General Dynamics (1977). *F16 multinational program.* General Dynamics, Fort Worth, Texas.
General Dynamics (1982). Public Affairs Department information sheet. General Dynamics, Fort Worth, Texas.
Glennan, T. K. (1966). *Innovation and product quality under the total package procurement concept.* Rand Corporation RM-5097-PR, Rand Corporation, Santa Monica, California.
Gold, B. (1981). On size, scale and returns: a survey. *Journal of Economic Literature*, vol. XIX, March 1981, pp. 5–33.
Green, W. G. (1981). *The Observer's Book of Aircraft* (London: Fredrick Warne).
Greenwood, A. (1975). Response to research policy article on MRCA. *Research Policy*, vol. 4, pp. 207–10.
Greenwood, D. (1979). The employment and other consequences of reduced defence spending. In *Democratic Socialism and the Cost of Defence*, M. Kaldor, D. Smith and S. Vines (eds), pp. 315–54 (London: Croom Helm).
Gunston, B. (1977). *Modern Military Aircraft* (London: Salamander Books).
Hall, G. R., and Johnson, R. E. (1967). *Aircraft production and procurement strategy.* Rand Corporation R-450-PR, Rand Corporation, Santa Monica, California.
Hall, G. R., and Johnson, R. E. (1968). *Competition in the procurement of military goods.* Rand Corporation P3796-I, Rand Corporation, Santa Monica, California.
Han, S., and Liesner, H. (1971). *Britain and the Common Market.* Occasional

Paper 27, Department of Applied Economics, University of Cambridge.
Harman, A. (1970). *A methodology for cost factor comparison and prediction.* Rand Corporation RM-6269, Rand Corporation, Santa Monica, California.
Hartley, K. (1969). Estimating military aircraft production outlays: the British experience. *Economic Journal*, vol. LXXIX, December 1969, pp. 861–81.
Hartley, K. (1974). *A Market for Aircraft*, Hobart Paper 57 (London: Institute of Economic Affairs).
Hartley, K. (1977). *Problems of Economic Policy* (London: Allen and Unwin).
Hartley, K. (1979). The industrial strategy and manpower policy: some puzzles. In *Labour Economics*, F. Fishwick (ed.), pp. 42–50 (Cranfield: Cranfield Institute Press).
Hartley, K. (1981a). UK defence: a case study of spending cuts. In *Big Government in Hard Times*, C. Hood and M. Wright (eds), pp. 125–51 (Oxford: Martin Robertson).
Hartley, K. (1981b). The aerospace industry: problems and policies. In *The Structure of European Industry*, H. W. de Jong (ed.), pp. 237–55 (The Hague: Martinus Nijhoff).
Hartley, K. (1982). Defence and advanced technology. In *The Collaboration of Nations*, D. Dosser, D. Gowland and K. Hartley (eds), pp. 154–84 (Oxford: Martin Robertson).
Hartley, K., and Corcoran, W. (1978). Time–cost trade-offs for airliners. *Journal of Industrial Economics*, vol. XXVI, March 1978, pp. 209–22.
Hartley, K., and Cubitt, J. (1978). Costs and escalation on UK aerospace projects. *R & D Management*, vol. 8, February 1978, pp. 83–9.
Hartley, K., and McLean, P. (1981). UK defence expenditure. *Public Finance*, vol. 36, no. 2, pp. 171–92.
Hartley, K., and Tisdell, C. (1981). *Micro-economic Policy* (Chichester: John Wiley).
Hartley, K., and Watt, P. (1981). Profits, regulation and the UK aerospace industry. *Journal of Industrial Economics*, vol. XXIX, June 1981, pp. 413–28.
Harvey, R. A. (1980). *International aerospace collaboration.* Paper presented to the Symposium on Life Cycle Costing, Cranfield, June 1980.
Harvey, R. A. (1981). Learning to improve productivity and cut costs. *The Aeronautical Journal*, May 1981, pp. 169–73.
HC155 (1976). *Second Report of the Defence and External Affairs Expenditure Committee: Defence* (London: HMSO).
HC254 (1977). *Defence and External Affairs Sub-Committee: Cumulative Effects of Cuts in Defence Expenditure* (London: HMSO).
HC265 (1981). *Second Report from the Industry and Trade Committee: Concorde* (London: HMSO).
Heath, B. O. (1978). Co-operation: Europe and Tornado. Paper presented at the conference on New Directions for NATO, Brussels; *Aviation Week and Space Technology*, Supplement, June 1978, pp. 38–41.
Heath, B. O. (1979). MRCA Tornado: achievement by international collaboration. *The Aeronautical Journal*, September 1979, pp. 329–43.

Henderson, P. D. (1977). Two British errors: their probable size and some possible lessons. *Oxford Economic Papers*, vol. 29, July 1977, pp. 159–205.

Hirsch, W. (1956). Firm progress ratios. *Econometrica*, vol. 24, April 1956, pp. 136–43.

HM Treasury (1981). Costing unemployment. *Economic Progress Report*. HM Treasury, London.

Howard, R. (1976). *Meeting the requirements for equipment from European sources*. Paper presented to a Royal Aeronautical Society Symposium on Co-operation in Air Transport, London, February 1976 (reference no. 99013 PG430).

Hsich, C. (1973). Measuring the effects of trade expansion on employment: a review of some recent research. *International Labour Review*, vol. 107, January 1973, pp. 1–29.

Jefferson, P. (1981). Productivity comparisons with the USA – where do we differ? *The Aeronautical Journal*, May 1981, pp. 179–84.

Jones-Lee, M. (1976). *The Value of Life: An Economic Analysis* (London: Martin Robertson).

Kaldor, M., Smith, D., and Vines, S. (eds) (1979). *Democratic Socialism and the Cost of Defence* (London: Croom Helm).

Kennedy, C., and Thirlwall, A. (1972). Technical progress: a survey. *Economic Journal*, vol. 82, March 1972, pp. 11–72.

Kennedy, G. (1979). *Burden-sharing in NATO* (London: Duckworth).

Kirby, S. (1980). The Independent European Programme Group: the failure of low profile high politics. *Journal of Common Market Studies*, vol. 18, pp. 175–96.

Knutton, H. (1972). The management of army R & D projects. *R & D Management*, vol. 2, no. 3.

Komer, R. W. (1977). Statement of Hon. R. W. Komer, Adviser to Secretary of Defense on NATO Affairs. In *Western Europe in 1977: Security, Economic and Political Issues. Hearings before the Sub-Committee on Europe and Middle East of the Committee on International Relations*, pp. 202–10 (Washington, D.C.: US Government Printing Office).

Large, J. P., Hoffmayer, K., and Kontrovich, F. (1974). *Production rate and production cost*. Rand Corporation R-1609, Rand Corporation, Santa Monica, California.

Lefebvre, J. (1978). Advancing toward Alliance goals. Paper presented at the conference on New Directions for NATO, Brussels; *Aviation Week and Space Technology*, Supplement, June 1978, pp. 4–6.

Legrand, F. (1976). European prospects in the helicopter field (Part 2). *Aerospatiale*, no. 64, July–August 1976, pp. 4–8.

Leibenstein, H. (1978). X-inefficiency Xists: reply to an Xorcist. *American Economic Review*, vol. 68, March 1978, pp. 203–11.

Macdonald, A. (1973). Exchange rates for national expenditures on R & D. *Economic Journal*, vol. 83, June 1973, pp. 477–94.

Maddison, A. (1979). Long-run dynamics of productivity growth. *Banca Nazionale del Lavoro Quarterly Review*, March 1979.

Maddock, Sir I. (1977). Quoted in C. Tisdell (1981) *Science and Technology Policy* (London: Chapman and Hall).

Marshall, A. W. (1967). NATO defense planning: the political and beaurocra-

tic constraints. In *Defense Management*, S. Enke (ed.), pp. 353–68 (Englewood Cliffs, N. J.: Prentice Hall).
Maxcy, G. (1981). *The Multinational Motor Industry* (London: Croom Helm).
Meeks, G. (1977). *Disappointing marriage: a study of the gains from merger.* Occasional Paper 51, Department of Applied Economics, University of Cambridge.
Metcalf, M., and Edmonds, M. (1981). RSI and the main battle tank. In *International Arms Procurement*, M. Edmonds (ed.), pp. 144–63 (New York: Pergamon Press).
NATO (1976). *Facts and Figures* (Brussels: NATO Information Service).
NATO (1980). *NATO Handbook* (Brussels: NATO Information Service).
Nelson, R. R. (1981). Research on productivity growth and differences. *Journal of Economic Literature*, vol. XIX, September 1981, pp. 1029–64.
NIESR (1971). The Common Market. *Economic Review*, no. 57, August 1971, pp. 35–61.
Nobbs, R. (1979). Air industry policy report. In *The European Alternatives*, G. Ionescu (ed.) pp. 283–309 (The Hague: Sijthoff and Noordhohh).
North Atlantic Assembly (1977). *Twenty-third Meeting of the North Atlantic Assembly: Report of the US Delegation* (Washington, D.C.: US Government Printing Office).
OECD (1970). *Gaps in Technology: Analytical Report* (Paris: OECD).
Olson, M. (1965). *The Logic of Collective Action* (Cambridge, Mass.: Harvard University Press).
Olson, M,, and Zeckhauser, R. (1966). An economic theory of alliances. *Review of Economics and Statistics*, vol. 48, August 1966, pp. 266–279.
Owen, N. (1976). Scale economies in EEC. *European Economic Review*, vol. 7, pp. 143–63.
Pavitt, K. (ed.) (1980). *Technical Innovation and British Economic Performance* (London: Macmillan).
Pavitt, K. (1982). High technology. In *Britain in Europe*, D. Cohen (ed.), in press (London: Butterworth).
Peacock, A. T. (1972). The public finance of inter-Allied defence provision. In *Essays in Honour of Antonio de Viti de Marco*, pp. 371–82 (Bari: Caccuci Editore).
Peck, M., and Scherer, F. (1962). *The Weapons Acquisition Process* (Cambridge, Mass.: Harvard University Press).
Perry, R., Smith, G., Harman, A., and Henrichsen, S. (1971). *System acquisition strategies*. Rand Corporation R-733-PR, Rand Corporation, Santa Monica, California.
Prais, S. (1976). *The Evolution of Giant Firms in Britain* (London: NIESR).
Pratten, C. (1971a). *Economies of scale in manufacturing industries*. Occasional Paper 28, Department of Applied Economics, University of Cambridge.
Pratten, C. (1971b). Economies of scale for machine tool production. *Journal of Industrial Economics*, vol.XIX, April 1971, pp. 148–65.
Pratten, C. (1976). *Labour productivity differentials within international companies*. Occasional Paper 50, Department of Applied Economics, University of Cambridge.
Pratten, C., and Dean, R. M. (1965). *The economies of large-scale production*

in British industry. Occasional Paper 3, Department of Applied Economics, University of Cambridge.
Rees, R. (1973). Optimum plant size in UK industries: some survivor estimates. *Economica*, vol. XL, November 1973, pp. 394–401.
Rhys, D. (1972). Heavy commercial vehicles. *Journal of Industrial Economics*, vol. XX, July 1972, pp. 230–52.
Rogers, B. W. (1981). Increased threats to NATO's security call for sustained response. *NATO Review*, vol. 29, June 1981, pp. 1–6.
Royal Aeronautical Society (1969). *Effectiveness in R & D* (London: Royal Aeronautical Society).
Rupp, R. W. (1981). Assessing Soviet military expenditure: a complex and controversial task. *NATO Review*, vol. 29, October 1981, pp. 23–8.
Sandler, T. (1977). Impurity of defence: an application to the economics of alliances. *Kyklos*, vol. 30, fasc. 3, pp. 443–60.
Sawyer, M. C. (1971). Concentration in British manufacturing industry. *Oxford Economic Papers*, vol. 23, November 1971, pp. 352–83.
Saul, B. (1975). MRCA: comments on the article by W. B. Walker. *Research Policy*, vol. 3, pp. 373–4. (See also reply by Walker on pp. 375–8.)
Scherer, F. (1973). The determinants of international plant sizes in six nations. *Review of Economics and Statistics*, vol. LV, May 1973, pp. 135–45.
Scherer, F. (1975). *The Economics of Multi-plant Operation* (Cambridge, Mass.: Harvard University Press).
Shepherd, W. G. (1967). What does the survivor technique show about economies of scale? *Southern Economic Journal*, vol. XXXIV, July 1967, pp. 113–22.
Silberston, A. Economies of scale in theory and practice. *Economic Journal*, Supplement, March 1972, pp. 369–91.
Smith, A. (1979). Methodology to quantify the potential net economic consequences of increased NATO commonality, standardization and specialization. Department of Defense Study Contract MDA-903-78-C 0166, vol. III, Department of Defense, Washington, D.C.
Smith, C. (1955). A survey of empirical evidence on economies of scale. In *Business Concentration and Price Policy*, pp. 213–30 (Princeton, N.J.: National Bureau for Economic Research).
Smith, D. (1980). *Defence of the Realm in the 1980s* (London: Croom Helm).
Stigler, G. (1958). The economies of scale. *Journal of Law and Economics*, vol. 1, p. 54.
Swann, D. (1970). *The Economics of the Common Market* (Harmondsworth: Penguin).
Taylor, J. W. R. (ed.) (1981). *Jane's All the World's Aircraft* (London: Jane's Publishing).
Tisdell, C. (1981). *Science and Technology Policy* (London: Chapman and Hall).
Tucker, G. (1976). *Towards Rationalising Allied Weapons Production* (Paris: Atlantic Institute).
Udis, B. (1979). Technology transfer in the case of the F16 military aircraft. In *Technology Transfer in Industrialized Countries*, S. Gee (ed.), pp. 245–62 (The Hague: Sijthoff and Noordhoff).
United Nations (1971). *Methodological Problems of International Compari-*

sons of Levels of Labour Productivity in Industry, Conference of European Statisticians no. 21 (New York: United Nations).
USACADA (1978). World Military Expenditures and Arms Transfers, 1967–76 (Washington, D.C.: US Arms Control and Disarmament Agency).
Vandevanter, E. (1964). Co-ordinated weapons production in NATO: a study of alliance processes. Rand Corporation RM-4169-PR, Rand Corporation, Santa Monica, California.
Walker, W. B. (1974). The multi-role combat aircraft (MRCA): a case study in European collaboration. Research Policy, vol. 2, January 1974, pp. 280–305.
Weiss, L. (1976). Optimal plant size and the extent of sub-optimal capacity. In Essays on Industrial Organization in Honor of Joe S. Bain, R. T. Masson and P. D. Qualls (eds), pp. 123–41 (Cambridge, Mass.: Ballinger).
Westland (1982). Information supplied by Publicity Department, Westland Helicopters, Yeovil.
Williamson, J. (1971). Trade and economic growth. In Economics of Europe, J. Pinder (ed.), pp. 19–45 (London: Knight).
Wolf, C. (1978). Trade liberalization as a path to weapons standardization in NATO. International Security, vol. 2, winter 1978, pp. 136–57.

Index

aerospace industry: aircraft research and development and manufacture, economics of 101–3; companies in NATO *108*; competition in 115–16, 186, 190, 191–2; competitive prototyping 118–20, 196; efficiency of US and European industries 110–12, 185–6, 189, 193–5; producer preference 120–2, 197–8, 199–202; licensed manufacture and co-production *see* licensed manufacture; joint projects *see* joint projects; market structure and performance 103–9; questionnaire results on 185–9; scale of output *113*; size of firms 109–10, 186, 196
aircraft manufacture: questionnaire results on 189–97; research and development and economics of 101–3
alliances, military, benefits of 22–4

Belgium: aerospace companies in NATO *108*; aerospace industry *106*; defence burden of *29*; equipment expenditure *33*; labour productivity and costs 65; NATO collaborative ventures *34*

Canada: aerospace companies in NATO *108*; aerospace industry *106*; defence burden of *29*; equipment expenditure *33*; NATO collaborative ventures *34*
collaboration, industrial: cost penalties of 130, *131*; *see also* joint projects
comparative advantage and gains from trade, and model of standardisation 61–7, 68
Concorde; cost control *170*; as example of collaborative organisation *147*, 156
Conference of National Armament Directors (CNAD) 33
costs, weapons, in NATO 30–2

defence: burdens of, in NATO 28–30; choices of, and NATO 5–6, 20–2; nationalism, and case for domestic defence industry 82–7; and political market place 6–8

Denmark: defence burden of *29*; equipment expenditure *33*; labour productivity and costs *65*; NATO collaborative ventures *34*
duplicate organisations, and higher R & D costs on joint projects 149–50

economic policy issues, overview of 3–19; defence choices and NATO 5–6; market failure and lack of standardisation 12–13; and Memoranda of Understanding (MOUs) 13–18; methodology of economic policy 4–5; political market place 6–8; standardisation policy, objectives of 8–11
economics, and politics of NATO 20–40; collaborative ventures, 33, *34*; competition and free trade 37–9; defence burdens 28–30; expenditure on equipment *33*; military alliances, economics of 22–4; NATO as a defence club 20–22; political market of 24–6; Warsaw Pact, threat of 26–8; weapons costs 30–2
economies of scale, and model of standardisation: evidence on 53–61; and gains from trade 43–8; reliability of evidence on 48–53
engineering estimates, and estimates of scale curves 49
Europe: defence burden of *29*; NATO aerospace companies *108*; joint projects, examples of 141–2; *see also* joint projects
European Economic Community (EEC): aerospace industry 103, 104, *106*; labour productivity and costs 64, *65*, 66, 67; within NATO 21
evaluation, of joint projects 158–61, 163–77, 186; alternative criteria 163–4; of costs 158, *159*–61; firms views on benefits and costs 164–6, 216–17; organisation of 173–6; performance indicators 166–73
expenditure, military, and threat from Warsaw Pact 27

Federal Republic of Germany: aerospace companies in NATO *108*; aerospace industry *106*, 107; defence burden of

Federal Republic of Germany – *contd.*
29; equipment expenditure *33*;
labour productivity and costs *65*; and
NATO collaborative ventures *34*
France: aerospace companies in NATO
108; aerospace industry *106*, 107;
defence burden of *29*; labour
productivity and costs *65*; NATO
collaborative ventures *34*
free trade versus nationalism 101–23;
aircraft research and development
and manufacture, economics of
101–3; competition 115–16, 186,
190, 191–2; competitive prototyping
118–20, 196; efficiency of US and
European industries 110–12, 185–6,
189, 193–5; market structure and
performance 103–9, 189; producer
preference 120–2, 197–8, 199–202;
scale of output *113*; size of firms
109–10, 186, 196

Germany *see* Federal Republic of
Germany
Greece, defence burden of *29*

Holland *see* Netherlands

Italy: aerospace companies in NATO
108; aerospace industry *106*; defence
burden of *29*; equipment
expenditure *33*; labour productivity
and costs *65*; NATO collaborative
ventures *34*

Jaguar, as example of collaborative
organisation *147*; cost control *170*
joint projects 140–77, 200–2, 203–5;
alternative assumptions on 146, 148;
case against European collaboration,
154–8; case for joint European
projects 148–53, 186, 214–15;
central hypothesis of 142, *143*; cost
savings on *143*; evaluation of
158–61, *see also* evaluation of joint
projects; examples of, in Europe
141–2, *147*; inefficiencies of 153–4;
methodological problems 143–6;
organisation of 173–6; and political
market 176–7; production, efficiency
of 152–3, 154; questionnaire on
212–17

learning curves: in American and
European aerospace industry
112–15, 128, 207–9; and model of
standardisation 51–2, 67
licensed manufacture and co-production
124–39; cost penalties of 126, *127*,
129–30, 207–9; costs of 126–30;
benefits of 130–8, 209–10;
definitions 124–5; reasons for 126,
205–7; questionnaire results 205–10
long-run average cost (LAC) curves: and
research design for aerospace
projects 93, *94*, *95*; and model of
standardisation 43, *44*, 45–6, 71
Luxembourg: defence burden of *29*;
equipment expenditure *33*

market failure, as lack of standardisation
12–13
Memoranda of Understanding (MOUs):
and economics of politics 15–18; and
standardisation 13–15
military alliances, economics of 22–4
minimum efficient scale (MES): and
model of standardisation 53–61;
questionnaire results 191
model, of weapons standardisation
41–67; assumptions of, and
standardisation policy 69–73;
comparative advantages and gains
from trade 61–7, 68; cost savings,
sources of 42–3, *47*; economics of
scale and gains from trade 43–8;
evidence on 53–61; reliability of
evidence of scale economies 48–53
mutual balanced force reductions
(MBFR) 25

nationalism: and case for domestic
defence industry 82–7; versus free
trade *see* free trade
Netherlands: aerospace companies in
NATO *108*; aerospace industry of
106; defence burden of *29*;
equipment expenditure *33*; labour
productivity and costs *66*; NATO
collaborative ventures *34*
Norway: defence burden of *29*;
equipment expenditure *33*

policy of weapons standardisation,
critical appraisal of 69–88; and
assumptions of model 69–73; ceteris
paribus 72, 78; framework for
weapon choice 77–82; and industrial
policy 74–7; internal efficiency of
firms 70–1; nationalism, and case for

domestic defence industry 82–7; problems of 69; re-allocation of resources 72

politics: economics of, and MOUs 15–18; of NATO *see* economics and policy of

Portugal: defence burden of *29*; equipment expenditure *33*; NATO collaborative ventures *34*

questionnaire studies, on aerospace projects 96–100; 'firms' questionnaire 96–8, 183–211; 'joint projects' questionnaire 98–9, 212–17; problems of 99

research and development, in aerospace industry: cost of, in joint ventures 149–52, 153–4; and manufacture of aircraft, economics of 101–3, 105, 111; and size of firms 109–10, 186, 196

research design, for aerospace projects 91–100; costs of alternative policies 93–5; interview questionnaire studies 96–100, 183–217

standardisation, of weapons: and effect on equipment expenditure 32–7; market failure, as a lack of 12–13; and Memoranda of Understanding (MOUs) 13–15; model of *see* model of weapons standardisation; objectives of policy 8–11; policy of, critical appraisal *see* policy of weapons standardisation

statistical cost analysis, and estimation of scale curves 49

Strategic Arms Limitation Treaty (SALT) 25

survivor technique, and estimation of scale curves 49–50

Tornado, as example of European joint aerospace project 155, 156, 165; cost control *170*; methodological problems 143–6, *147*

Turkey: defence burden of *29*; equipment expenditure *33*; NATO collaborative ventures *34*

United Kingdom: aerospace companies in NATO *108*; aerospace industry of *106*, 107; cost escalation on weapons 75, 76; defence burden of *29*; efficiency of aerospace industry 110–12, 185–6, 189, 193–5; equipment expenditure *33*; estimates of minimum efficient plant scale 53, *54–5*; labour productivity and costs *65*; NATO collaborative ventures *34*; slope of scale curves 53, *56–7*, *58*; weapons costs *31*

United States of America: aerospace companies in NATO *108*; aerospace industry of *106*, 107; comparative advantage of research-intensive industries 63, 75; defence burden of *29*; cost escalation on weapons 75, 76; efficiency of aerospace industry 110–12, 185–6, 193–5; equipment expenditure *33*; labour productivity and costs *65*; monopoly of, fears of 116–18, 187, 197; weapon costs *31*

United States Arms Control and Disarmament Agency (USACADA) 27

Warsaw Pact, 25; threat from 26–8

weapons: and cost to NATO 30–2; framework for choice 77–82; expected life-cycle costs of 81; pricing policy for 70; standardisation of *see* standardisation